mplete Book of

ICAN
KING

OTHER BOOKS BY ELISABETH LAMBERT ORTIZ

The Book of Latin American Cooking

Clearly Delicious: An Illustrated Guide to Preserving, Pickling & Bottling

The Complete Book of Caribbean Cooking

The Complete Book of Japanese Cooking

The Complete Book of Mexican Cooking

Cooking with the Young Chefs of France

The Encyclopedia of Herbs, Spices & Flavorings

The Festive Food of Mexico

The Food of Spain and Portugal: The Complete Iberian Cuisine

From the Tables of Britain: Exploring the Exciting New English Cuisine

Little Brazilian Cookbook

A Taste of Latin America

The New Complete Book of

MEXICAN COOKING

ELISABETH LAMBERT ORTIZ

HarperCollins*Publishers*

For my late husband, César Ortiz Tinoco, who gave me a new career with the key to his great knowledge of Mexico's contribution to the world of food, and also gave me thirty years of happy marriage.

This book was originally published in the United Kingdom in 1998 by Grub Street, Ltd. It is here reprinted by arrangement with Grub Street, Ltd.

HarperCollins books may be purchased for educational, business, or sales promotional use. For information please write: Special Markets Department, HarperCollins Publishers Inc., 10 East 53rd Street, New York, NY 10022.

First HarperCollins edition published 2000.

Designed by Peter Bertolami

Printed on acid-free paper.

ISBN 0-06-0195991

00 01 02 03 04 RRD 10 9 8 7 6 5 4 3 2 1

CONTENTS

MEXICO

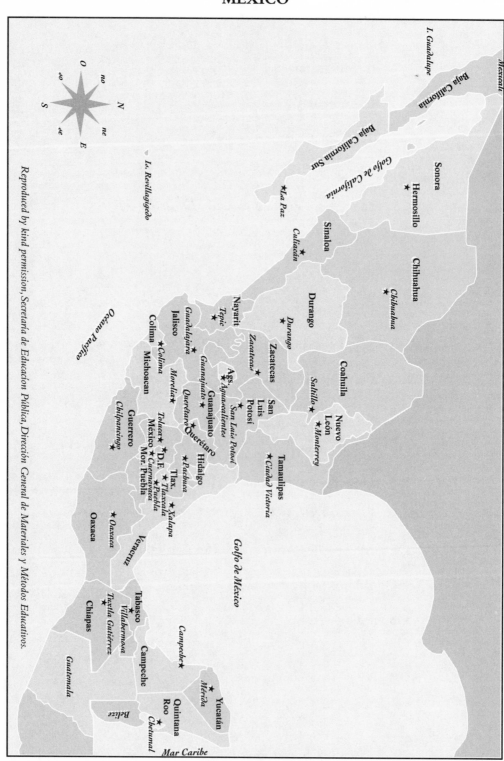

INTRODUCTION

This book really began with the *habañero chile* whose taste haunted me for years though I didn't know then what it was. We were living in the West Indies at the time, as my father had a special job that took him there. At recess at school I was allowed to buy a little meat pie costing a *quatée*, the local name for two cents, from an elderly black lady who brought a cloth-covered wicker basket of them to the school daily. They had a special flavor that captivated me. I was too young to know how to track it down but the memory of it stayed with me.

When I first married and we were still in New York, César told me about Mexico's extraordinary contribution to the world's cultivated food. Chocolate, vanilla, corn (maize), chilies (sweet, pungent and hot), tomatoes, avocados, green beans, the dried beans like kidney beans, pumpkin and the summer squash including *chayotes* (cho-chos), *papayas*, turkeys and others. New dating methods claimed that agriculture first developed in the Fertile Crescent of the Middle East and in the Valley of Mexico at about 7000 B.C. with differing foods and with no contact between the two centers. That contact came when, to quote the schoolroom rhyme, "In fourteen hundred and ninety-two, Columbus sailed the ocean blue" and stumbled on the New World believing he was somewhere else.

The real food contact only developed fully when Hernán Cortés conquered the Aztec Empire, center of the agricultural outburst, in 1521. That encounter doubled the foods in the world's larder, is the most important single event in the history of food, and led me to discover at long last, the evocative taste in *quatée* pie, *Capsicum chinense*, variety *habañero*. The small orange-red lantern-shaped chili is the hottest native to North America, has an exquisite flavor and is known in Jamaica as the Scotch Bonnet, in Guatemala as the *chile caballero* (gentleman chili) and mostly as the *habañero*, which translates as "the chili from Cuba", a debatable point.

My late husband, César Ortiz Tinoco, a Mexican national, was transferred from United Nations Headquarters in New York to the United Nations Information Center in Mexico City and I began the voyage of discovery that ended with the original edition of this book. There was an enormous lot for me to learn and I was handicapped by not knowing Spanish and by stubbornly clinging to some of my cultural habits, like having dinner at night instead of having *comida* at midday followed by a siesta. It was not practical anyway as César could not join me, his work making it impossible. One cannot have a large, leisurely meal alone and then tell your husband when he comes home from work that you've already eaten. I took some Spanish lessons and learned the names for chair, table, wastepaper basket, pen, pencil and India rubber. The maid tried to help but she spoke no English and César said she was picking up my bad grammar as I began to pick up the language. So I took to the markets, San Juan, La Merced, Medellín where the market women put up with my beginning Spanish and taught me how to make some of the things I had eaten in other people's houses and in restaurants. I had a simple technique. I would look around for someone whose stall had some of the things I thought I would need, an older woman preferably as I felt age would confer not only knowledge but kindness. We would begin with the woman seated at her stall (usually in a full skirt and white blouse, and a white apron, round her shoulders a *rebozo*, a colored woolen stole, and her hair in long plaits), selecting the ingredients from the neat little piles of chilies, herbs, tomatoes, onions and garlic in the order in which they were to be cooked. I'd be sent off to buy tortillas from the tortilla-sellers, avocados from the avocado-seller, eggs from one of the little grocery stalls or whatever else my stall didn't carry, as the market women in Mexico all specialize as they have done from time immemorial when they were Mayans and Aztecs and others.

Then the cookery lesson would begin with an amused but pleased stall-owner achieving a miraculous kind of pidgin Spanish so that I would understand what she was talking about, while other market people, men and women, would call out from time to time, "*Qué va a llevar, marchanta?*" (What are you going to buy, customer?), as a way of drawing attention to their own stalls without impoliteness. I would understand from my teacher that I was to chop this and this and this, and fry them together, then add this and this and simmer them all together, grinding this to be added later, and so on. I would make notes identifying strange herbs and chilies and note the unfamiliar cooking methods, and for a modest number of *pesos* carry off the ingredients for the dish to be cooked in my shopping basket, a brightly colored woven one from the same market. The system worked very well and I cooked authentic Mexican dishes to everyone's surprise. I was careful not to annoy the family maid by invading the kitchen when she was still on duty. As she left shortly after *comida* it was easy enough. My Spanish became rapid, fluent and grammatically a terror and in no time I had a working knowledge of Mexican herbs, spices, fruits and vegetables, though even now I am still learning.

We moved into our own apartment and had our own maid and I very foolishly and stubbornly tried to cling to my own way of life, and my own meal hours. My husband's family were just as stubborn and with more justification. I was, after all, in their country. I did give a dinner party, at night, for some visiting American friends and asked my mother-in-law to join us. On sitting down she called my maid and said, "*Francisca, tráigame un pedazo de pan y vaso de leche, nada mas*" ("Bring me a piece of bread and a glass of milk, nothing more"). Then she told my guests not to eat the food I was about to serve as it would make them sick. There was, and still is, a firm belief that if you eat as late as 8 P.M. in the high plateau, the altitude will do you serious harm. None of us got sick, Elenita ate her slice of bread, and I learned to compromise.

On holidays and sometimes for the United Nations we travelled all over the Republic. I made notes, collected recipes and bought strange, small cookbooks and visited pre-Columbian ruins, Colonial churches, museums and markets and I found Mexican food to be strongly regional, more varied and interesting than I had first believed, and that it was even harder to get good recipes than I had thought possible. "How much of that do you put in?" "The right amount, of course." In time you know what the right amount is. The Mexicans call it having a *buen mano*, a good hand.

Through César I discovered Spanish writers of the very early period of the Conquest, Bernal Díaz del Castillo, a captain with Hernán Cortés who wrote *The Conquest of New Spain*, and Fray Bernadhino de Sahagún who wrote *A General History of the Things of New Spain*. Sahagún was a Spanish priest who arrived in Mexico in 1529 before the Conquest was consolidated. Their work is invaluable, as they saw everything before conquest changed it, and makes it possible to understand the Mexican kitchen that arose out of the marriage of old and new worlds. I found descriptions of the markets, the kitchen, the banquet hall, the food of the ordinary people, of soldiers, nobles and the emperor himself. My husband helped with translations so that I properly understood. He insisted, however, on going into the deeper matter of the books. It wasn't a lack of interest in food on his part. It was that he wanted me to have as full an understanding of pre-Columbian Mexico as possible, since the Mexican kitchen of today rests very solidly on its Aztec and Mayan foundations. I was even able to cook a shrimp stew by following Fr. Sahagún's description of one he observed in the main market of Tenochtitlán, the original capital, still operating in his time.

You don't really understand a country's cuisine until you know and understand its history. We began my education with the Maya-Toltec ruins of Chichén Itzá and Uxmal in Yucatán, great stone temples and dwellings with magnificent carvings, breathtaking in their grandeur. To Palenque, in Chiapas, most beautiful of the Maya ruins and the farthest into what is now Mexico the Maya penetrated. Recently a royal tomb was found at Palenque. Dating back to the 8th century the tomb was reached through stairs leading to three chambers one of which contained a sarcophagus with the skeleton of the king. An earlier tomb had the jade-bedecked mask of King Pakal "Lord Shield" who died at the age of 80 after a long reign. I marvelled at carved jade heads and masks, gold objects, full-size figures of priests and gods carved from basalt, at museums and in the collection of a good friend, Dr. Kurt Stavenhagen who bequeathed it to the Archeological Museum after half a lifetime of devoted collecting, as a way of saying thank you to the people of Mexico for giving him and his family safe haven from the Nazis. Palenque, Chichén Itzá and Uxmal were quite long journeys from Mexico City but right on our doorstep we had the ruins of the older city of Teotihuacán, birthplace of the gods and site of the magnificent pyramids of the Sun and the Moon. There were endless riches in the pre-Columbian past and César was a lovingly perceptive guide to it all.

I did not realize how lucky I was in those first few months in Mexico to be staying with the family when they lived in Bolivar *ocho*, number 8 Bolivar Street. It was no distance from the Zócolo, the great plaza that is the heart of the city with the massive Cathedral, the National Palace, the municipal government building and the Palace of Fine Arts. These are great buildings that withstand earthquakes when modern buildings fall down. The murals show off the genius of Mexico's modern painters and in addition the area rejoices in marvellous food. Just across from the apartment block where the family had a flat, two in fact, was the Cafe Tacuba with a history going back to the last century and even more important from my point of view with the best Oaxacan *tamales* steamed in banana leaves not corn husks, outside Oaxaca. I could have lived on them. Then there was the Hostería Santo Domingo, a restaurant serving Mexican food. It was celebrating its hundreth anniversary and they gave me a copy of the menu cover with two brilliantly colored paintings. I had them framed and they are hanging on my kitchen walls still, as they have in country after country where I have lived. Then there was Las Cazuelas, where you walk through the kitchen, with its tiled stove and long row of earthenware casseroles, to get to your table. The casseroles hold *moles* of various kinds and are a link with the huge *ollas* Sahagún investigated in the great market just before the Conquest. Of course they differ but not as much as might be expected after so long a time. I learned a lot just eating at Las Cazuelas. There were lots of other places to be visited; Chapultepec Park with the incomparable Museum of Anthropology which makes the past come alive and that makes the colonial kitchen seem to be a natural extension of yesterday, Xochimilco which is all that remains of the floating gardens on Lake Texcoco which the Spanish filled in, Chapultepec Castle, once the home of poor doomed Emperor Maximilian and Carlota who nevertheless brought a French kitchen influence to Mexico, and everywhere flowers in vast abundance and food that I kept on learning about.

Because Spain had been invaded by the Moors and only regained its freedom after nearly 800 years, at the time it invaded Mexico, the Spanish cuisine was strongly influenced by the Middle East. Rice dishes for one thing and *picadillo* made with chopped beef, *empanadas* (turnovers) to name just a few. It meant more trips to Spain and Portugal, home of César's early ancestors.

Learning was a continuous business, sort of travel with a purpose, and I am still learning as new work has been done on Mexico's Aztec and Maya past, and that throws new light on the evolution of the kitchen. Then the Ortiz side of the family who lived in other parts of the Republic, mostly in the North, were visited. When General Ortiz welcomed me into the family and said there was a slab awaiting me in the family mausoleum in Chihuahua City where the first, and very famous General Ortiz is buried, it seemed odd but I came to realize that I was truly part of the family, and I found that the grandmothers were great sources of information on food habits and customs. I owe a debt to China Ortiz in Quéretero, who without losing her great good looks, was the mother of a large number of Ortizes. She is also a fine cook, and Connie (Consuelo) Ahnert, her husband and children at their silver mine in Zacatecas, who went back to Durango, which was where Doña Carmelita (one of the grandmothers) told me all about the *tamaladas* (tamal parties) she was famous for. They were all generous with information and if I listed all of them there would not be room for anything but thank-yous.

We were in Mexico for a conference long after César's tour of duty at the Information Center had ended, when a friend and colleague José Wilson asked me to write a back of the book selection of Mexican recipes for New York *House and Garden*, in the section she edited. All this time I had been learning about Mexican food I hadn't thought of writing about it as I was writing other things. I wrote the small cookbook for José and then Jim (James Andrews) Beard asked me to go on and do a whole book and since Jim, friend and mentor, was worth listening to, I did. Craig Claiborne of the *New York Times*, a great authority, wrote an article about me and Mexican food, and Marcia Nasatir of Bantam Books telephoned me and told me she had bought the book even though it wasn't quite finished. I remember her asking where I had got to and when I said that I was testing the drinks section she said she didn't think it a good thing to interrupt me when I was so happily engaged. The book came out published by M. Evans and Bantam, and won the R. T. French award and I had the great joy of writing for *Gourmet* magazine. I worked for the Time-Life *Foods of the World* series, and César made it possible for me to write about the whole kitchen of Latin America, and the Caribbean, using our UN holidays.

I owe a considerable debt to scientists kind enough to take my thesis seriously and to clarify controversial points for me. Charles B. Heiser Jr., Distinguised Professor of Botany at Indiana University, gave me the chance to correct some errors, not major ones perhaps but important if the truth is to prevail. Dr. David R. Harris, who was lecturer in the Department of

Geography, University College, London, gave me invaluable information on plant domestication and the origins of agriculture in the tropics. My good friend the late Dr. Alex B. Hawkes chased obscure herbs for me and Dr. Jean Andrews told me, and the rest of the world, just about all there is to know about peppers, the domesticated *capsicums*, giving me confidence in my own humbler researches. Raymond Sokolov, the author of *Why We Eat What We Eat* understood what I had been trying to do about the effects of the collision of food worlds, and if I don't stop I will be accused of name dropping.

Mexico has changed a lot since the time when I wrote my first book but so has everywhere else. More señoras cook than in the past, and the work done by Sra. Josefina Velázquez de León has borne fruit. When we were in Mexico she ran a cookery school for señoras and their maids near where the family lived. She tirelessly collected, tested, recorded and published books on the regional kitchen as well as other aspects of the cuisine. In spite of revolutions, and other disasters she has made sure the colonial kitchen can never be lost. Today there are gifted people recording the modern Mexican cuisine as Mexico becomes more and more industrialized but does not lose its fabulous past.

This book tells how I came to write the original, which was published in New York. It is a memorial to my husband César and tells how I came, with his help, to write it. He was a superb journalist but alas could not be persuaded to write about his years with the United Nations and earlier with Associated Press. I am deeply grateful to Anne Dolamore of Grub Street for wanting this book and for giving me unhurried time in which to write it.

Elisabeth Lambert Ortiz
London 1997

INGREDIENTS

Acitron

is often wrongly translated as citron. It is candied *biznaga* cactus and has a delicate flavor. Citrus peel is too strongly flavored a substitute. It is not usually available so any candied fruit that is not strongly flavored, pineapple for example, can be used. Used in meat dishes such as *picadillo*.

Allspice

(in Mexico *pimienta gorda* or *pimienta dulce*) are the fruits of the bay tree of the myrtle family, which the Spanish found growing all over Jamaica. The berries are slightly larger than black peppercorns which they closely resemble. The flavor is that of nutmeg, cloves and cinnamon combined though there are differing opinions about this. They are available wherever spices are sold and are widely used in pickling.

Annatto

(in Mexico *achiote*) are the seeds of a small evergreen flowering tree, *Bixa orellana* which grows throughout tropical America. The fruit is covered in soft spines and holds about 50 seeds. It is the hard pulp surrounding the seeds that, when ground, gives that bright orange dye that colors and flavors food. In Yucatán the whole seed is ground for use as a flavoring. It has a flowery, lemony taste. It is called by a number of names in other parts of Latin America, *bija*, *bijol*, *roucou* among them.

Avocado

(*aguacate* in Mexico) *Persea americana*, is a Mexican original, first cultivated there as far back as 7000 B.C. The avocado salad-sauce, guacamole, is almost as old as the fruit itself. There are many different varieties available, those like the Fuerte with shiny green skin and the Hass with a purple-black rough skin. The avocado is now available all year-round and is cultivated in many countries around the world including South Africa, the U.S., Israel, Spain and the Caribbean. The Mexican favorite, not exported, is small with a smooth purple-black skin and a delicate flavor of anise. They should be bought hard and unripe. The best way to ripen them is to put them in a bag, preferably brown paper and leave them in a dark place for a few days. They are ripe when they yield to gentle pressure at the stem end.

Avocado Leaves

(*hojas de aguacate*) have an anise-like, herby flavor and are often used in *barbacoa*. They can be fresh or dried, whole or ground and in dishes such as the *moles* and *pipiánes*.

Bacalao

(dried salt cod fish) a Spanish and Portuguese favorite was introduced by them to the New World where it retains popularity. Widely available especially in Spanish and Portuguese specialty shops.

Banana Leaves

(*hojas de plantano*) are used to wrap *tamales* in Oaxaca instead of the corn husks used more generally. They are available in specialty shops and markets and are sometimes sold frozen. Banana leaves are also used to line the *pib*, the Yucatán earth oven. [Defrost the leaves if frozen and soften them before using, steamed briefly over a flame.] They give a distinctive flavor to food cooked in them.

Beans

(*frijoles*) of the legume family are another of Mexico's culinary gifts to the world. The large grouping, *Phaseolus vulgaris*, the common bean, originated at about 5000 B.C. They may be white, red (kidney beans), pink, yellow (*bayos*), or black which is the favorite bean in Yucatán and is always cooked with the herb *epazote*. Probably Mexico's oldest bean is the scarlet runner.

Bitter Orange or Seville Orange

(*naranja agria*) was the orange that was popular in Spain before the sweet orange was introduced from Valencia. It is the *bigarde* of France and the orange of Seville orange marmalade. It has a rough highly aromatic skin though only the juice is used in Mexico, especially in Yucatán. It has a distinctive flavor. When it is not available a substitute can be made using equal amounts of grapefruit, orange and lime juice mixed with 1 teaspoon grated grapefruit zest. Use enough juice to make 1 cup. When Seville oranges are in season I chop them, skin and all, discarding the pips and reduce to a purée in a food processor. I strain them through a sieve and freeze them. They keep indefinitely and can be used whenever Seville orange juice is needed.

Cactus

is the *nopal* cactus, commonly known as prickly pear. It is one of the *Opuntia* species and it is the young paddles that are eaten as a vegetable. In Mexican markets they are sold cleaned of spines and eyes. They exude a little of the same sort of slippery substance as okra and have a slighty crunchy texture and a light flavor like green beans mixed with asparagus. They are sold canned, ready to cook and are used in salads and with eggs as well as other dishes. They have a fruit called tuna or cactus pear. It is prickly on the outside and is usually sold cleaned and is red inside with a refreshing flavor. Eaten raw.

CHEESE

Following the introduction of cattle around 1530 cheese (*queso*) was introduced into Mexico. Nowadays local versions of the best known cheeses are made successfully. There are some cheeses that were developed regionally that are special to Mexican cooking. *Queso de Oaxaca* is a soft, braided cheese that *hace hebras* (strings) when melted, considered a desirable quality. Mozzarella is a good substitute.

Queso de Chihuahua

(Chihuahua cheese) was created by the Mennonites when they arrived in the Northern State. It is a very well flavored creamy cheese used in stuffing chilies in *enchiladas* and grated over dishes. A good farmhouse mild cheddar is an adequate substitute.

Queso Anejo

is best substituted by Parmesan for use in *antojitos* and cooked dishes.

Queso Fresco

(fresh cheese) is a white crumbly cheese. A local white crumbly cheese can be used as a substitute. Cottage cheese can also be used.

Chicharron

are fried pork cracklings, available packaged in ethnic markets.

CHILIES, FRESH AND DRIED

The family of the cultivated *capsicums* are central to Mexican cooking, not just in the original Aztec and Maya cooking of the pre-Columbian civilizations but also in the colonial cuisine that developed after the Spanish Conquest. *Chilli*, the original name in Nahuatl became *chile* in Spanish, they were called peppers by Columbus and after the conquest spread all over the world with astonishing rapidity. They may be sweet, pungent or hot and were first cultivated in Mexico in 7000 B.C. Different peppers, called *aji* were cultivated in Peru but did not spread with the speed of the North American chili. There are believed to be more than 100 species, many of them regional. It is easy to cook with about a dozen chilies available in specialty shops, some supermarkets and by mail order.

FRESH

Anaheim

is the chili also called long green/red chili and was taken to New Mexico from Mexico shortly after the Conquest. It is smooth skinned, its flavor ranging from mild to hot. Medium sized, smooth and tapering, it ripens to red from green and is a useful chili as it can be used in a wide variety of dishes including stuffed peppers. They are becoming increasingly popular.

Bell Pepper

is a fairly large, almost square pepper that is sweet and is often called sweet red or green pepper and is sometimes available in the yellow stage of ripening. It is less used in Mexico than here. It can be used as a substitute for *poblanos* though it lacks this chili's distinctive flavor. Useful as a garnish, in salads and in any stew or rice dish. It can substitute for another sweet pepper, the *pimiento*, a large, sweet, heart-shaped aromatic pepper which is the Spanish favorite. Popular in Mexican cooking whenever a sweet pepper is needed. Often available canned.

Cayenne

are long (up to 12 in), narrow and sharply pointed. This chili, red when ripe, is mostly available ground as cayenne pepper. A yellow cayenne is available by mail order from Kitchen, New York, NY, tel. (212) 243-4433. Is easily grown as a pot plant and is mostly used in hot sauces. A useful substitute for *serranos*, *jalapeños*, and *habañeros*.

Chilaca

is a long, thin (about 6 in x 1 in) reddish-brown, almost chocolate-colored chili that is very hot. Toasted and skinned before using, they are a regional chili in Mexico, used fresh mostly in the central and states parts of the northwest. When dried they are *chile pasilla*.

Chiltecpin, chili pequín and *Tepin*

have the same names in both the fresh and dried forms. Small, red and hot, they are used mostly to make chili powder. In Nahuatl the name means "flea chili" because of its small size and its bite.

Guero

is a pale yellow chili, smooth skinned and varying in size but on average about 5 in x 1 in, pointed at the end and with a distinctive flavor. It can be mildly hot or very hot. Sometimes called *chile largo*, it is the *x-cat-ik* of Yucatán. Used in stews and salads, is often available canned. The best substitute is the yellow cayenne which is hot enough to be used with caution.

Habañero

is a small lantern-shaped orange-red chili, the hottest of the North American, that is, Mexican peppers. It is popular in the Caribbean and is called the Scotch Bonnet in Jamaica.

There is some debate about its origin as it is not a *Capsicum annuum* but a *Capsicum chinense*. It may have originated in Peru and made its way north or originated in the Caribbean. Though mostly used red it can be used green. It is used a great deal in Yucatán and Campeche and has an exquisite flavor.

Jalapeño

is a smooth green chili, larger than a *serrano* and very flavorful as well as hot. They are sold *en escabeche* (pickled) and are immensely popular as a condiment. They are used with all sorts of *antojitos* and in many cooked dishes. When ripe, dried and smoked they become *chipotle chiles*.

Poblano

is a dark green almost black smooth tapering chili, (about 3 in x 5 in) and the one used for stuffing especially for the Independence Day dish *Chiles en Nogada* (Chilies in Walnut Sauce).

They vary from mild to quite hot. They can be soaked in salted water to reduce the heat if liked, about 15 minutes. They have a very special flavor and are used extensively as *rajas* (strips) with steak and other dishes. To prepare the chilies for use, hold them on a fork over a gas flame turning them until the skin is blistered and charred all over. Put them into a brown paper or plastic bag for about 30 minutes when the papery burned skin will rinse off. This process vastly improves the flavor and is worth the small extra effort. They are available here by mail order, fresh. Like many other of the *capsicums* this chili suffers a sea change when ripe. It becomes the dried, wrinkled *ancho*, the most used of the dried chilies.

Serrano

is a small (1½ in x ½ in) smooth green chili sometimes available red when it is ripe, hot and much used in sauces like guacamole, *salsa cruda* and *tomate verde*. They are also used *en escabeche* (pickled). In cooking they are just seeded and chopped and are useful whenever a little heat is needed in a dish. Pickled *serranos* are served as a side dish to be taken according to taste.

DRIED

Ancho

is the ripe, dried *poblano* and the most used of the dried red chilies. It is large, about 5 in x 3 in, wrinkled and dark red. It is one of the three peppers used for the national festive dish, *Mole Poblano de Guajolote* (Turkey in Chili and Chocolate Sauce). The others are *mulato* and *pasilla*. It is toasted, stem and seeds discarded, torn up, soaked and puréed for cooked sauces in a great many dishes. The flavor is rich and the chili is mild. It keeps indefinitely if stored in a plastic bag in a cool dark cupboard.

Cascabel

is a small, round, smooth-skinned chili about 1 inch in diameter. The *cascabel* sounds like a tiny rattle when it is shaken. It is not very hot and has a pleasant flavor when toasted and ground for sauces. It is reddish brown in color.

Chipotle

is the *jalapeño* when ripe, dried and smoked. It is very hot and has a distinctive and exotic flavor. It is sold canned *en escabeche* and also in a red *adobo* sauce. It is hard to believe that it is the *jalapeño*. The *morita* is smaller and darker than the *chipotle* with an almost identical taste.

Guajillo

unlike most of the dried chilies is smooth-skinned, and red in color. It is quite long, about 4 in on average and about 2 in wide. It lends a beautiful color to anything it is cooked with. It can be unexpectedly hot with a fierce bite, and for this reason is known as the mischievous (*travieso*) chili.

Mulato

is brownish black and a type of *poblano*. The *mulato* closely resembles the *ancho*, except that the skin is tougher and it has a sweeter taste. Like the *ancho*, it is toasted, stem and seeds discarded, the pepper torn up, soaked to soften and reduced to a heavy paste-like purée. Used in the national dish and in cooked sauces.

Pasilla

are long and thin, about 6 in x 1 in, wrinkled, almost chocolate brown, and very hot. The *pasilla* is the dried, ripe chili *chilaca*. It is very rich tasting. It is lightly toasted, stem and seeds discarded, torn up, soaked and ground ready to be used in sauces, especially with seafood. It is sometimes called *chile negro* (black chili). Available by mail order.

Cho-cho

is *Sechium edule* of the squash clan, a native of Mexico and very old, perhaps going back to 7000 B.C. Its name in Nahuatl, the language of the Aztecs, was *chayotl* which became *chayote* in modern Mexico, cho-cho in Britain, *christophene* in French speaking countries and a host of other names as well including vegetable pear. Roughly pear shaped it has crisp fine textured flesh and a large, edible seed which should be cooked with the vegetable. There are several types, light green, creamy white and dark green with soft spines, which are the best flavored. They usually weigh from 8 oz to 1 lb. They are simply boiled and eaten as a vegetable, stuffed or as salad.

Chocolate

(*Cacao, Theobroma cacao*), food of the gods was first cultivated by the people of the Olmec civilization which flourished in the humid lowlands and treeless plains south of Veracruz and in Tabasco from about 1500 to 400 B.C. Unfortunately their language has not been deciphered but they left behind them huge heads of their kings carved from basalt, exquisitely carved jades and cultivated chocolate. They may have invented the drink, chocolate or it may have been the Maya who did so and who also gave the world the word *cacao*. We still drink chocolate in basically the same way as the Maya did except that the spices used differ and they had no milk or sugar. They did have honey if they wanted a sweet drink and vanilla. Chocolate in solid form is sold in Mexico flavored with ground almonds, cinnamon and vanilla. The name comes from two Nahuatl words meaning bitter water. It is no longer drunk unsweetened and is no longer used as currency which it once was in the past. It is available by mail order and in specialty markets.

Chorizo

is the Spanish chorizo sausage in its Mexican incarnation. It is a highly spiced pork sausage and varies in its seasonings from place to place. It is widely used. Spanish chorizos can be used instead and are widely available in supermarkets and specialty shops.

Cooking Fat

or the preferred fat of the Mexican kitchen is lard. To get the right type get pork fat from the butcher and render it down. Today many people prefer to use oil. Corn (maize) oil, peanut or safflower oils are all suitable and olive oil for some dishes, see the recipes.

Cilantro

(*Coriandrum sativum*) closely resembles flat parsley but is lighter in color with more feathery leaves. Both seeds and fresh leaves are used in Mexican cooking, especially the leaves in sauces, with fish, in *moles* and stews. It is sometimes called coriander or Chinese parsley and has slightly varying names, *culantro* for example, in the Caribbean. *Eryngium foetidum*, a coarse, strongly flavored type of cilantro, which earned the herb its Greek derivation from *koris*, bed bug, sometimes, though rarely turns up.

Corn

See the chapter The Corn Kitchen (page 23).

Cream

(*Crema Espesa*), Mexican cream is like French crème fraîche. It is easily made from local cream, see recipe (page 314).

Dried Shrimps

are small shrimps, dried and cleaned and sold packaged in Chinese and Japanese markets as well as Latin American markets. They are ready to use and will keep indefinitely. They are best stored in glass screw top jars.

Epazote

(*Chenopodiun ambrosioides*) is one of the Anserinas. The name comes from the Nahuatl *epazotl*. It is known under many names in English, wormseed, goosefoot, lamb's quarters, Jerusalem oak and Mexican tea. It grows wild all over the Americas and much of Europe. It is easy to grow from seed and it is as good dried as fresh. Seeds are available by mail order. It is a favorite herb in Yucatán, especially with black beans, and is more popular in the central and southern States than in the north.

Huitlachoche

(*Ustilago maydis*) is a fungus which grows on corn. Like truffles and other special members of its tribe, the fungus has an exquisite flavor, hard to describe. It is sometimes available canned from specialty markets or shops.

Jícama

(*Pachyrrhizus erosus*) is the underground bulbous tuber of a leguminous plant native to Mexico. It ranges in size from 8 oz to about 5½ lb, has a tan colored skin and white flesh that is crisp and juicy with a rather bland, sweetish flavor. It is sometimes sold outside Mexico as yam bean. It is eaten raw mostly in salads and a favorite way is to peel and slice the *jícama* and season it with salt, hot paprika and lime juice. It is eaten as a snack, often with drinks.

Tomatillos

are not ordinary unripe tomatoes. They are *Physalis ixocarpa*, small, green and with a papery brown covering. They are related to the Cape gooseberry. Though their origin is a little obscure, they are believed to be of Mexican origin and were called *miltomatl* by the Aztecs because of their many tiny seeds. When ripe they turn pale yellow but are always used green and usually lightly cooked. They have an exquisite flavor and are used for that most popular of sauces *salsa verde* (green sauce). They are used in many chicken dishes and sauces. Available canned, they are available fresh by mail order. They keep well if refrigerated.

Pumpkin Seeds

(*pepitas*) have been used in pre-Columbian cooking for thousands of years and are still popular as a thickening and flavoring in many dishes in the colonial kitchen, the most notable being *Papa-dzules*. Buy hulled packaged ones from health food stores and supermarkets as well as from specialty markets. The members of the squash family which includes pumpkins and summer squashes like zucchini are eaten as vegetables and in a few desserts, the seeds as above and the squash blossoms in *antojitos*, soups and stuffed. Gourds made drinking vessels in pre-Columbian times.

Xtabentun

is a honey-based liqueur from Yucatán and is difficut to find here though travelers to Yucatán may seek it out and enjoy it.

THE CORN KITCHEN

•

It is impossible to overestimate the importance of corn in Mexico. It is the major food crop, and more than that, was the focal point of religious and social life. In the Mayan Empire which stretched from Honduras to Yucatán and Chispas, and which predated the Aztecs, everything was based on corn, including the calendar. In the sacred book of the Maya, the *Popol Vuh*, the creation myth tells how the gods decided to create mankind and began with the men of clay but they were washed away, dissolved by water. The next were the men of wood but they abused their kitchen tools who turned on them and burned them out of existence. Then the gods created the men and women of corn and they were a success but wanted to know too much, as much as the gods themselves, so the gods blew dust in their eyes so they could never know the mind of the gods.

On earth the greatest of the corn gods was Quetzalcoatl, the Plumed Serpent, descended from Kukulkan, founder of the city of Chichén Itzá in Yucatán whose ruins can still be visited with those of Uxmal, not far from the modern city of Mérida. Corn was equally important to the Aztecs as a staple food and with a corn god, Cinteotl and a corn goddess, Chicomecoatl.

Corn was cultivated as early as 5000 B.C. but there is still controversy over its earliest beginnings. Was its ancestor wild corn or was it the grass, *teocincle*? Whichever, its cultivation so early in history was a superb achievement. Columbus found it growing on the island called Hispaniola, now the Dominican Republic, when he made landfall there. The local Indians called it *mahis*, corrupted by the Spanish to *maiz* and by the English to maize. It had come from Mexico where it was first cultivated and we should all be grateful Columbus found it in the islands as its name on the mainland, Nahuatl, was taolli. Not only that but these brilliant agriculturists had developed *iztaotlolli* (white corn), and *yautlaolli* (black corn), among others like blue corn and purple corn. They had invented the tortilla. Here we should be grateful for Spanish linguisic simplicity. Faced with *tatonqui tlaxcalli tlacuelpacholli* for a large white tortilla, the kind the nobles usually ate and which was just one of the many kinds made daily, they fell back on their simple word for "small cake" which was what a tortilla looked like to them. It proved to be a good name, now used whenever there are corn tortillas, which is almost everywhere. The fact it is also the Spanish word for "omelette" does not seem to have caused as much confusion as might have been expected.

What the Aztecs and Mayas did with corn was fascinating. One great and early triumph was nixtamalization, which is a complex process but from a practical point of view means soaking and cooking dried corn with lime or wood ashes. This enhances the protein value of the grain, and of course makes it easier to grind into the flour that is made into tortillas. They were a clever lot as we still make *masa harina*, literally dough flour, that way. The tortilla has rightly been called the bread of Mexico though there are very good wheat and other breads available nowadays. No meal is complete without a supply of fresh, hot tortillas. They are still served in the traditional woven basket called a *chiquithuite* which is lined with a cloth that completely covers the tortillas. The top one is never taken, always the second one so they are kept warm both by the cloth and the top one. When the Spanish found how many ways the tortilla is used and how many variations there are on it, they called them *antojitos*, "little whims", "fancies" or "hankerings" which can be interpreted as appetizers, first courses, starters. They can be eaten as street food, market snacks, light lunches, light suppers and something to serve with pre-dinner or lunch drinks. They can be simple like tacos or elegant like *enchiladas*.

The cooks in ancient Mexico were all women and Fray Sahagún makes it clear that they were highly esteemed. A good cook, he wrote, is honest, discreet, likes good food, is an epicure and is clean, bathes and washes her hands but above all likes good food and drink. Achieving good food meant very hard work. After the corn was boiled with lime and the skins rubbed off the kernels, a process which turned it into *nixtamal*, it was ground on a *metate*, a three-legged, flat, oblong stone, with a *metlalpil*, a stone rolling pin, to make the *masa* for tortillas and *tamales*. The dough was patted by hand into circles and briefly baked on a *comal*, a round iron or earthware baking sheet. It was hard work, especially for army cooks who had to turn out vast numbers of tortillas to satisfy the large appetites of the fighting men.

The next Spanish contribution was the invention of the tortilla press. The press is a beautifully simple way of converting the flour, moistened with water to a dough, into perfect circles, ready for brief baking, to make tortillas. The baking is brief as the flour is already cooked when the corn kernels were boiled with lime. Mexican women and girls can pat out perfect thin tortillas by hand but it is a hard act to master. The press was just two hinged circles of wood with a handle on the top one so that it could be brought down on a small ball of dough with enough force to flatten it. The early presses were often very attractive and are now regarded as valuable antiques. Modern presses can be made of cast iron, aluminium and even, not very successfully, of plastic. In Mexico our maid went daily to the market to buy freshly made tortillas but she could have bought the dough by the kilo and brought it back and patted it out by hand and cooked tortillas on a *comal* but she sensibly avoided this chore. All the maids did. Every now and then some cousin or other would announce that the *masa* (or tortillas) in some village market or the other were made from a very superior corn and someone would drive out, usually on a Sunday, to buy the fabled article. Since the same sort of rumor circulated for milk, cream, eggs, fillet steak and cheese, shopping could be very lively.

Corn tortillas are available nowadays packaged from supermarkets, or specialty shops or by mail order. *Masa harina*, the flour for making tortillas, is available packaged and tortilla presses can be bought from department stores selling kitchen equipment. It is almost as easy to have a good tortilla here as it is in Mexico.

TORTILLAS
Tortillas

Using packaged *masa harina* and a tortilla press, tortillas are easy to make, it is a knack easily acquired. I remember when Craig Claiborne was interviewing me for the *New York Times*, where he was the prestigious editor of the cookery section, he asked me to show him how to make a tortilla. He acquired a skill better than mine in less than 10 minutes. Admittedly, he is an exceptionally gifted cook, food writer and journalist and learned fast, even so it is not a lengthy or difficult process for the rest of us.

2 cups *masa harina* (tortilla flour)
½ teaspoon salt (optional)
1¼ cup lukewarm water
Small plastic bag, cut open and halved crosswise

In a bowl combine the *masa harina*, the salt though this is not traditional, and 1 cup of the water to form a soft dough. Line the press with the plastic and test the dough. Put a small ball on the press and press it out using the handle to bring down the top circle onto the dough. If it is too moist it will stick to the plastic, if it is too dry it will crumble. Scrape off and return to the bowl. If too moist add more *masa*, if too dry add the rest of the water (see note below on liquid).

Form the dough into small balls about 1-1½ inches. Do a few at a time or all at once. Put a ball of dough on the bottom circle of the press and flatten with the top circle to the size wanted, 4 inches to 5 inches. Peel off the top piece of plastic and put the tortilla, paper side up on the palm of the left hand, peel off the plastic then flip the tortilla gently onto the moderately heated ungreased *comal* or griddle. Cook over moderate heat until the edges begin to curl, about one minute. With the fingers or a spatula turn the tortilla over and cook for one minute longer. It should be lightly flecked with brown and the first side cooked is the top.

As they are done stack the tortillas in a cloth napkin then wrap in foil, napkin and all, and put into a warm oven where they will stay warm for hours, or eat immediately. To reheat cold tortillas pat them between damp palms then put over very low direct heat turning constantly for about 30 seconds.

MAKES ABOUT 14-16 TORTILLAS.

Note on liquid: It is not possible to be absolutely precise about the amount of water as less will be needed if the masa harina *is very fresh, and in very humid weather it may take moisture from the air. I recall one time in New York when James Beard was coming to dinner and I was making tortillas ahead of time. Jim was flying down from Montreal where he had been on culinary business. He was held up by a violent storm. In New York it was raining cats and dogs, bucketing down, and I was having trouble. I kept having to add more* masa harina *to get a dough that held together and did not act as if it had a secret ambition to turn into soup. I finally won and Jim told me later that the flour is very sensitive to moisture in the air. I had learned my tortilla making in Mexico where the air is usually dry and had been puzzled by the effect of the rain.*

TACOS

Tacos, pronounced *tackos* not *tarkos*, are the most popular of all the *antijitos* and there are even places, *taquerias*, devoted to selling tacos with a formidable array of fillings. There are two types. The soft taco is a fresh tortilla stuffed and with any sauce chosen, loosely rolled and eaten by hand. The hard taco is more tightly rolled, stuffed, secured with a cocktail stick and lightly fried in lard or oil. The cocktail stick is removed halfway through frying so that the taco can be turned. They should not be fried hard and crisp, just lightly golden, about a minute on each side and eaten as soon as possible.

There are a great many traditional fillings for tacos, in addition leftovers from meat or poultry dishes, *picadillo* or *Mole Poblano* for example. Seafood and vegetables can be used with imagination adding sauces, chilies, guacamole or cheese. In fact, almost anything can be used to stuff a taco provided one stays within the framework of the Mexican kitchen.

For a party set out bowls of various sauces (*salsas*), chilies, preferably pickled, chopped fried chorizo sausage, shredded cooked chicken and pork, guacamole, *frijoles refritos*, chopped shredded lettuce, and fingers of cheese. Serve with batches of freshly made warm tortillas to be made into soft tacos and eaten by hand.

One of the family cooks liked to add ground *ancho* or *pasilla* chilies (about 3) to *masa harina*. I was never able to find out if this was her own inspiration, César did not know, and she vanished from our lives. Here are a few traditional fillings:

TACO FILLINGS

HAM TACOS
Tacos de Jamon

> ½ lb boiled ham, finely chopped
>
> 1 tablespoon finely chopped onion
>
> 3 oz cream cheese, softened at room temperature
>
> ½ lb tomatoes, peeled, seeded and chopped
>
> Pickled *serrano* or *jalapeño* chilies, to taste, chopped
>
> Salt
>
> 12 (4 to 5-inch) freshly made warm tortillas
>
> Guacamole (page 74)

In a bowl combine the ham, onion, cheese, tomatoes and chilies and mix thoroughly. Season to taste with salt, if necessary and use to stuff the tortillas. Fold over lightly and eat by hand, or secure with a cocktail stick and fry lightly in oil. **Serve with guacamole.**

MINCED BEEF TACOS
Tacos de Picadillo

> ½ recipe for *Picadillo* (page 221) or *Picadillo de la Costa* (page 222)
>
> *Salsa de Jitomate* (tomato sauce) (page 81) or *Salsa Verde*
>   (green sauce) (page 80) or any *salsa* of your choice
>
> Chopped romaine or iceberg lettuce, shredded (optional)
>
> Guacamole (page 74)
>
> 12 (4 to 5-inch) freshly made warm tortillas

Make the *Picadillo* and use it to stuff the tortillas. Top with *salsa* and lettuce, if liked. **Serve with guacamole or use to top the *salsa*.**

POTATOES AND CHORIZO
Papas y Chorizo

½ lb new potatoes
Salt
1 tablespoon corn or peanut oil
2 chorizo sausages, skinned and chopped
1 onion, finely chopped
1 or 2 pickled *chipotle* chilies
12 (4 to 5-inch) freshly made warm tortillas
Guacamole (page 74)

Boil the potatoes in salted water to cover until just tender, about 10 minutes. Drain, cool slightly and chop, unpeeled into ½ inch dice. In a frying pan heat the oil and add the diced potatoes, sausages and onion and cook, stirring from time to time until the sausage is done and the potatoes and onion are slightly colored. Chop the chilies and add them to the pan and sauté a few minutes longer. Cool and stuff the tortillas which may be served hard or soft. **Serve with guacamole.**

CHEESE TACOS
Taco de Queso

2 *poblano* chilies
¾ lb tomatoes, peeled, seeded and chopped
1 onion, chopped
Salt
2 tablespoons corn or peanut oil
½ cup Cheddar or similar cheese
12 (4-inch) warm tortillas
Sour cream

Hold the *poblanos*, one at a time, over a gas flame until the skin is charred and blistered. Wrap in a damp cloth or put into a small plastic bag and leave for 20-30 minutes. The thin, papery skin will easily peel off and any remaining bits can be rinsed off. Remove the stems and shake out the seeds. Chop coarsely.

In a food processor combine the chopped *poblanos*, tomatoes and onion and process to a purée. Season to taste with salt. Heat the oil in a frying pan and cook the purée, over moderate heat, for 5 minutes, stirring from time to time. Remove from the heat and set aside.

Slice the cheese into 12 strips and put one on each tortilla, top with a spoonful of chili purée and a little sour cream. Fold over and eat immediately by hand. **MAKES 12 TACOS.**

TOSTADAS

Tostadas are tortillas that have been fried in hot oil or lard until golden brown then covered with various combinations of meats, poultry, fish, sauces, chilies, etc. in layers. They are meant to be eaten by hand so should not be fried so crisp that they may break, with very messy results, when bitten into. Like all tortillas that are to be fried they should not be fresh as they will absorb too much oil, day old is ideal. The most useful size for tostadas is a 5-inch tortilla but they can be larger or smaller according to taste. 2-inch tortillas, quite untraditional, make very good appetizers to serve with drinks. I found it hard to stick to the straight and narrow when dealing with Mexican food. It invited experimentation, not the least in the corn kitchen. Aztec and Maya cooks play variations on a theme. Even in the modern world they are endlessly inventive. I think they very much enjoyed cooking. Fried in this context does not mean greasy. Only about ½ inch of oil is needed in the frying pan for the tortilla. The lettuce may be tossed in a vinaigrette dressing. Radishes and pitted green olives are favorite garnishes. Anything can be used as a topping so long as it is in the framework of the Mexican kitchen, but there are traditional toppings from the various regions. Here are some:

BEAN TOSTADAS
Tostadas de Frijol

> **3 cups cooked Mexican black beans (*frijoles de Olla*) (page 158)**
>
> **8 oz cream cheese, cubed**
>
> **12 (5-inch) tortillas, lightly fried**
>
> **1 large onion, very finely chopped**
>
> **1 large avocado, peeled, pitted and cut into strips**
>
> **1 or 2 pickled *chipotle* chilies, cut into strips**

The beans should be cooked until very soft and thick, not watery. Over low heat cook the beans adding the cream cheese. Remove from the heat before the cheese melts. It should remain separate. Spread a layer of the bean mixture on the tostadas followed by layers of the onion, avocado and *chipotle*.

PRAWN TOSTADAS
Tostadas de Camaron

1 tablespoon corn or peanut oil

1 onion, finely chopped

½ lb tomato, peeled, seeded and chopped

1 lb cooked prawns, chopped

Salt, freshly ground pepper

12 (5-inch) tortillas, lightly fried

3 tablespoons freshly grated Parmesan cheese

Shredded lettuce, preferably romaine or iceberg

Vinaigrette dressing (page 184)

Salsa Verde (green sauce) (page 80)
   or strips of pickled *jalapeño* chilies

Heat the oil in a frying pan and sauté the onion until it is soft. Add the tomato and cook over moderate heat until well blended and thick. Add the prawns, stirring to mix, season with salt and pepper and remove from the heat.

    Spread a layer of the mixture onto the tostadas, followed by grated cheese and the lettuce sprinkled with a little vinaigrette. **Serve with the *salsa* or *jalapeño* chilies.**

SARDINE TOSTADAS
Tostadas de Sardinas

1 tablespoon corn or peanut oil

1 onion, finely chopped

½ lb tomatoes, peeled, seeded and chopped

½ lb potatoes, freshly cooked and finely diced

1 can boned sardines, preferably Portuguese, in oil, mashed

Salt, finely ground black pepper

12 (5-inch) tortillas, lightly fried

3 tablespoons freshly grated Parmesan cheese

Shredded lettuce, preferably romaine or iceberg

Vinaigrette dressing (page 184)
Chipotle **(page 78) or tomato sauce (page 81)**

Heat the oil in a frying pan and sauté the onion until it is soft. Add the tomato and cook over moderate heat until well blended and thick. Add the potato and cook for a minute or two, stirring. Add the sardines, season with salt and pepper and remove from the heat. Spread a layer of the mixture on the tostadas, followed by grated cheese and the lettuce lightly sprinkled with vinaigrette. **Serve with** *chipotle* **or tomato sauce.**

MIXED TOSTADAS
Tostadas Compuestas

12 (5-inch) tortillas, lightly fried
1 cup *frijoles refritos* **(page 159)**
Vinaigrette dressing (page 184)
Shredded lettuce, romaine or iceberg
¾ lb freshly cooked potatoes, diced
2 cooked chicken breasts, shredded
1 cup guacamole (page 74)
Freshly grated Parmesan cheese
Pickled *chipotle* **chilies, cut into strips**

Spread the tortillas with a thin layer of beans and top with a layer each of lettuce and potato tossed in the vinaigrette dressing. Follow with a layer of chicken, guacamole and a little cheese. Finish the tostadas with strips of *chipotle* or since the chilies are very hot it may be better to serve them on the side.

GUADALAJARA-STYLE TOSTADAS
Tostadas Tapatias

3 chorizo sausages
2 cups *frijoles refritos* **(page 159)**
Corn or peanut oil
12 (5-inch) tortillas
Shredded lettuce, preferably romaine or iceberg

1 onion, finely chopped

2 cups guacamole (page 74)

3 tablespoons freshly grated Parmesan cheese

Skin, finely chop the chorizos and cook in a frying pan over low heat in their own fat. Lift out and set aside in a bowl. Discard most of the fat leaving just enough to film the pan. Add the beans to warm through. Pour ½ inch of oil into a frying pan and lightly fry the tortillas on both sides, adding more oil as needed. Spread the tortillas with a layer of beans, then a layer of sausage, then a layer of lettuce, onion, guacamole and some Parmesan cheese. Serve immediately.

TURNOVERS
Quesadillas

Having once tasted *quesadillas* I had to learn how to make them, so one morning I set off for La Merced market stopping at the lady who gave me a kindly smile. She was early middle age, with the traditional long hair in plaits, white embroidered blouse, full skirt, and *rebozo*, the universally worn stole. She was sitting on the ground with her merchandise which included squash blossom flowers. Just what I needed as it had been *Flor de Calabaza* (Squash or Pumpkin or Courgette Blossom) filling that had seduced me. Quite how I managed to convey in my hardly existent Spanish what I needed but the market seller must have been a born teacher gifted with second sight. Anyway she sent me to another seller who had tortillas and I paid for them and came for more instructions. I trotted off and came back after a number of small journeys, with *chile poblano*, *epazote*, onion and garlic. Her teaching method was simple. She mimed chopping onion, garlic, blossoms, chilies and *epazote* and then because *freir* is just like fry retreated into speech indicating that I fried this lot in a little oil seasoning it with a little *xsal*, same word as salt. She took a tortilla in the palm of her hand, put some of the imaginary filling on it just off center, folded it over, pressed the edges together and voila, a *quesadilla*. I do not know how I grasped the fact that the tortillas must be uncooked ones, but I did and went home and made *quesadillas de flor* right first time off. As we were still staying with my mother-in-law this was quite a triumph but was not totally approved of. The family cook did not like me messing in her kitchen. Later she relented and gave me recipes for *quesadilla* doughs and I acquired recipes for fillings and learned that the turnovers could be baked on a *comal* though fried they taste better.

QUESADILLA DOUGH

2 cups *masa harina*

2 tablespoons all-purpose flour

½ teaspoon baking powder

½ teaspoon salt

3 tablespoons melted butter or corn oil

1 large egg, lightly beaten

½ cup milk, about

Oil for frying

In a bowl mix the dry ingredients together thoroughly. Stir in the butter or oil, egg and enough milk to make a fairly stiff dough. Form into 12 balls, press out into tortillas, stuff and fold over. Seal the edges, pressing them together, dampened if necessary. Pour enough oil into a frying pan to about ½ inch depth and fry the *quesadillas* over moderate heat until golden brown on both sides, about 2 minutes a side. The *quesadilla* may be cooked on a *comal* or griddle. Very lightly oil the *comal* and place it over a moderate heat, put the *quesadilla* on the preheated *comal* and bake for about three minutes a side. Makes 12 (5-inch) turnovers. Serve immediately. If necessary keep warm in a very low oven, covered, until they are all cooked. Eat by hand, any time as a snack or as part of a lunch or supper.

DOUGH WITH *ANCHO* CHILIES
Masa de Quesadilla con Chile Ancho

2 *ancho* chilies

2 cups *masa harina*

½ teaspoon salt

Toast the chilies lightly in a dry frying pan. Do not overcook. Remove from the pan, pull off the stems and shake out the seeds. Tear into pieces and put into a bowl with warm water just to cover. Soak for 30 minutes, drain and purée in a food processor. Reserve the soaking water.

In a bowl mix the salt and *masa harina*, add the chili purée and just enough of the soaking water to make a fairly stiff dough.

USE TO MAKE 12 *QUESADILLAS*.

DOUGH WITH CHEESE
Masa de Quesadilla con Queso

In Mexico *queso anejo* (aged cheese) would be used for this. Freshly grated Parmesan makes an admirable substitute.

2 cups *masa harina*

¼ cup freshly grated Parmesan

2 tablespoons all-purpose flour

½ teaspoon salt

1 tablespoon melted butter or corn oil

½ cup light cream

In a bowl mix all the dry ingredients thoroughly. Add the butter or oil, cream and enough warm water to make a fairly stiff dough.
USE TO MAKE 12 *QUESADILLAS*.

DOUGH WITH BEEF MARROW
Masa de Quesadilla con Tuetano

This was very popular in Mexico when I was first there. Today with beef under suspicion marrow is not available. But as time passes the situation may alter so I am including the recipe.

1 lb. beef marrow bones

1½ cups *masa harina*

½ teaspoon baking powder

¼ cup all-purpose flour

½ teaspoon salt

1 large egg, lightly beaten

½ -¾ cup milk

Heat the oven to 350°F and bake the marrow bones for 15 minutes. Remove from the oven and scrape the marrow with a spoon into a bowl. In a large bowl mix together all the dry ingredients. Mix in the marrow, the egg and enough milk to make a fairly stiff dough.
USE TO MAKE 12 *QUESADILLAS*.

STUFFED MINIATURE TORTILLAS
Sambutes o Salbutos

We first came across these on a trip to Yucatán where they are a specialty. I tried to find the correct spelling and came to the conclusion that either will do. It is the end result that matters. They make a wonderful accompaniment to drinks and are not hard to make. Leftover meat can be used for the filling. They can be served with or without a topping of sauce, or pickled onion and are just another example why we admired the Yucatán cuisine so much. Relished it too.

For the filling:

2 tablespoons corn oil

½ lb ground pork pork

1 onion, chopped

½ lb tomatoes, peeled and chopped

Salt

In a frying pan heat the oil and sauté the pork until it has lost all its color and is lightly browned. In a food processor purée the onion and the tomato and pour them over the pork. Season with salt and cook stirring, over moderate heat until the mixture is thick and well blended. Set aside.

For the *salsa*:

1½ lb tomatoes, peeled, seeded and chopped

1 *habañero* chili, seeded and chopped or
    2 *serranos*, seeded and chopped

Salt

In a food processor combine the ingredients and reduce to a purée. Transfer to a small bowl and set aside. The amount of hot chili is a matter of taste. The *habañero* is very hot.

For the pickled onion: Use the recipe for Pickled Onion (page 83)

For the tortillas:

2 cups *masa harina*

1 teaspoon salt

4 tablespoons all-purpose flour

Corn oil for deep frying

In a bowl mix together the *masa harina*, salt, and all-purpose flour. Add enough cold water to make a fairly stiff dough. Pinch off pieces about the size of a walnut and flatten them on the tortillas, press to miniature tortillas, no more than 2 inches across. Do not bake them. Hold a tortilla in the palm of the left hand and put 1 tablespoon of the filling on it. Cover it with another tortilla, pinching the edges together. Continue until all the tortillas and the filling are used up. In a frying pan heat enough oil to reach a depth of about 2 inches and fry the tortillas, a few at a time, turning once, until they are golden brown, about 3 minutes. Drain on paper towels and eat immediately or garnish with a little chopped lettuce, sauce, pickled onion, and grated cheese, or just sauce and onion. Eat hot. **MAKES ABOUT 18.**

CHILAQUILES

Tortillas in Mexico are never wasted; in fact Mexicans have the same attitude to the tortilla as Chinese and Japanese do towards rice. Day-old tortillas can be used in a number of ways but perhaps the most popular is for making *chilaquiles*, whose name comes from the Nahuatl for "herbs in chili broth." There is also a slang meaning "broken up old sombrero." It seems unfair to call such a good dish such an ugly name but come to think of it the Spanish of that time called their good beef dish *Roipa Vieja*, "Old Clothes." César loved *chilaquiles*. He could eat them at any time of day—for lunch, dinner, supper. He told me he became attached to them during his student days at Monterrey University when, as he graphically put it, his family tried to starve him to death. Translated that means that he couldn't often get home for *comida* and when he did get home for supper there wasn't anything he thought of as food available. A friendly family cook knowing how hungry a hungry student can be would sometimes cook some *chilaquiles* for him and even let him know there would be a robust casserole of them enough for four, one student and three student friends, all of them rescued from starvation. As well as the rich *chilaquiles de estudiante*, César also relished simpler versions of the dish, so did I, but we parted company over ones with chicken breasts and the lightly sour *Crema Espesa* which is used in the Mexican kitchen. César didn't like cream, any cream, even ice cream, preferring sorbets. He used to insist it was because he was from an anti-lactic culture, which would have been true if he had been pure Aztec or Maya, but though grand sounding, this wasn't true of a post-Conquest *mestizo*. I've included a recipe for *Crema Espesa* (page 314) and for recipes using it.

STUDENT *CHILAQUILES*
Chilaquiles de Estudiante

Originally from Oaxaca these *chilaquiles* are to be found whenever there are hungry students which means just about everywhere in the Republic. This is a hearty dish which needs only a green salad and a little dessert for a satisfying meal whether there are students around or not.

Corn oil or lard

1 recipe tortillas made into 18 (4-inch) tortillas, cut into ½ inch strips (page 26)

4 *ancho* chilies

½ lb tomatoes, peeled and chopped

1 onion, chopped

2 cloves garlic, chopped

1 lb cooked boneless pork or chicken, shredded

16 *pimiento*-stuffed green olives, halved

3 tablespoons seedless raisins

1 tablespoon red wine vinegar

½ teaspoon sugar

Salt to taste

For the sauce:

1 onion, chopped

1 clove garlic, chopped

1 teaspoon sugar

¼ teaspoon cinnamon, ground

¼ teaspoon ground clove

½ lb tomatoes, peeled and chopped

Chicken stock if needed

In a frying pan heat 2 tablespoons oil or lard and fry the tortilla strips in batches until lightly golden, do not let them brown. Drain on paper towels and set aside.

Toast the *anchos* lightly on both sides in a dry pan. Remove the pan, pull off the stems and shake out the seeds. Tear into pieces and put into a bowl of warm water and leave to stand for 30 minutes, turning from time to time. Set aside.

In a food processor combine the tomatoes, onion and garlic and purée. Add enough oil or lard to the frying pan to bring the quantity up to 2

Enchilada Torta

e, the shredded meat or chicken and simmer for
olives, raisins, vinegar, sugar and salt to taste and
minutes or until it is well blended and very thick.
strips in a greased ovenproof dish, spread the
top with the rest of the tortilla strips.

food processor combine the *anchos* and the liquid in
aked, the onion, garlic, sugar, cinnamon, clove and the
to a purée. In the rinsed out and dried frying
il or lard and cook the mixture, stirring for 5 minutes.
e. Add enough chicken stock to make up the quantity
heat and when it is hot, pour it over the tortilla and
chilaquiles in a preheated 350°F oven for 20 minutes or
immediately. Garnish if liked with crumbled cheese,
fresh cheese.

ING TO APPETITE.

or lard
ade into 18 (4-inch) tortillas cut into
(page 26)
tomatoes (*tomatillos*), chopped
n, finely chopped
ies, seeded and chopped
eded and chopped

h coriander, chopped

eddar cheese
hicken stock

eat 3 tablespoons oil or lard and fry the tortilla strips, a few
on both sides. They should not be fried long enough to
paper towels. Add more oil or lard to the pan if needed dur-
aside.

ocessor combine the *tomatillos*, onion, chilies, *epazote* and
ce to a purée. Cook the purée in the fat in the frying pan,
necessary, for about 3 minutes, stirring constantly. Add salt to

---

RANCH BEANS

ckwagon cooks used to simmer beans for
s, and the cowboys always thought they
ed best on the third day. This version,
ed frijoles de olla in Spanish, is even bet-
reheated. The beans cook in flavorful
es that are also served with them.

6 SERVINGS

cups (or more) water
pound dried pinto beans, picked
over, rinsed
12-ounce bottle of dark beer
cup chopped onion
bacon slices, cut into ½-inch pieces
garlic cloves, finely chopped
jalapeño chili, seeded, finely
chopped
teaspoon minced canned chipotle
chilies*

cup crumbled cotija cheese*
cup chopped seeded tomato
cup chopped fresh cilantro

nbine 5 cups water and next 7 ingre-
ts in heavy large pot. Gently simmer
overed over medium-low heat until
ns are tender and liquid is reduced
ugh to cover beans by 1 inch, adding
re water if necessary and stirring occa-
ally, about 2½ hours. Season to taste
salt and pepper. *(Can be made 1 day*
d. *Cool slightly. Cover and refrigerate.*
arm before serving.)
Garnish beans with cotija cheese,
pped tomato and cilantro.

Tacos, Burritos & Enchiladas **33**

Grease an ovenproof casserole and make a layer of sauce, followed by one of the tortilla strips, and some of the cheese. Repeat using up all the ingredients except some of the cheese and sauce. Mix the stock into the remaining sauce and pour it over the casserole, then top with the remaining cheese. Bake in a preheated 350°F oven for about 30 minutes or until the cheese is melted and the casserole heated through. **SERVES 6.**

GREEN *CHILAQUILES* WITH CHICKEN BREASTS
Chilaquiles Verdes con Pechuga de Pollo

Corn or peanut oil or lard

1 recipe tortillas made into 18 (4-inch) tortillas cut into ¼-½ inch strips (page 26)

¾ lb Mexican green tomatoes (*tomatillos*), chopped

1 small white onion, finely chopped

1 tablespoon fresh coriander, chopped

3 or 4 fresh *serrano* chilies or to taste, seeded and chopped

Salt

1 cup thick cream (*Crema Espesa*) (page 314)

3 cooked chicken breasts, skinned, boned and shredded

½ cup freshly grated Parmesan cheese

In a frying pan heat 3 tablespoons oil or lard and fry the tortilla strips, a few at a time, lightly on both sides. Do not let them brown. Drain on paper towels. Add more oil or lard to the pan if needed during cooking. Set aside.

In a food processor combine the tomatoes, onion, coriander and chilies and reduce to a purée. Add a little oil to the skillet (there should be about 2 tablespoons) and cook the purée for 2-3 minutes over moderate heat, stirring constantly. Taste for seasoning and add salt as necessary.

Grease an ovenproof casserole and make a layer of sauce, a layer of tortillas, some of the cream, and a layer of chicken. Repeat the layers until all the ingredients are used, finishing with a layer of tortillas topped by cream. Sprinkle with all of the cheese and bake in a preheated 350°F oven for 30 minutes and the cheese has melted and the dish is heated through. **SERVES 6.**

Chilaquiles

This cheesy tortilla casserole can be served for brunch with eggs and refried beans.

Vegetable oil
12 (6-inch) corn tortillas, cut into 1-inch strips*
1 cup (1 small) chopped onion
1¾ cups (16-ounce jar) ORTEGA Thick & Chunky Salsa, mild
1¼ cups (10-ounce can) ORTEGA Enchilada Sauce
1½ cups (6 ounces) shredded Monterey Jack or cheddar cheese
¼ cup ORTEGA Pickled Jalapeño Slices
Sour cream (optional)
Sliced avocado (optional)

ADD oil to 1-inch depth in medium skillet; heat over high heat for 3 to 4 minutes. Place tortilla strips in oil; fry, turning frequently with tongs, until light golden brown. Remove from skillet; place on paper towels to soak.

REMOVE all but 1 tablespoon oil from skillet. Add onion; cook, stirring occasionally, for 1 to 2 minutes or until tender. Stir in salsa and enchilada sauce. Bring to a boil. Reduce heat to low; cook, stirring frequently, for 3 to 4 minutes.

LAYER *half* of tortilla strips in ungreased 13 x 9-inch baking dish. Top with *half* of salsa mixture and *half* of cheese; repeat layers. Bake in preheated 350°F. oven for 10 to 15 minutes or until cheese is melted. Top with jalapeños, sour cream and avocado just before serving. Makes 8 servings.

*NOTE: The frying step may be eliminated by breaking ORTEGA Taco Shells or ORTEGA Tostada Shells into small pieces and using them in place of tortilla strips.

Comfort Food

Chilaquiles was created by thrifty cooks looking for a creative way to use leftovers. For that reason, its ingredients and method may vary from region to region, as well as from cupboard to cupboard. Although chilaquiles was once referred to as a "poor man's dish," today it is eagerly enjoyed by everyone.

One-Dish

Shrimp Enchiladas (front) (recipe page 85)
Enchilada Casserole (back left) (recipe page 84)

RED *CHILAQUILES* WITH CHICKEN BREASTS
Chilaquiles Rojos con Pechuga de Pollo

4 *ancho* chilies

Corn or peanut oil or lard

**1 recipe tortillas made into 18 (4-inch) tortillas cut into
¼-½ inch strips (page 26)**

1 onion, chopped

1 sprig *epazote*

1 lb tomatoes, peeled, seeded and chopped

Salt, pinch sugar

1 cup thick cream (*Crema Espesa*) (page 314)

3 cooked chicken breasts, skinned, boned and shredded

½ cup grated Cheddar cheese

Toast the chilies lightly on both sides in a dry frying pan. Pull off the stems and shake out the seeds. Tear in pieces and put into a bowl with water barely to cover. Soak for 30 minutes. Drain reserving soaking water.

In a frying pan heat 3 tablespoons oil or lard and fry the tortilla strips, a few at a time, lightly on both sides. Do not let them brown. Drain on paper towels. Add more oil or lard to the pan during cooking if needed. Set aside.

In a food processor combine the chilies, onion, *epazote* and tomatoes with a little soaking water if needed, and reduce to a purée. Add enough oil or lard to the frying pan to make the quantity up to 2 tablespoons and cook the purée over moderate heat for 5 minutes, stirring. Season with salt and pinch of sugar.

Grease an ovenproof casserole and pour in a layer of the sauce, a layer of tortilla strips, some cream and a layer of shredded chicken breast. Repeat until all the ingredients are used finishing with a layer of tortilla strips and cream. Sprinkle on the cheese and bake in a preheated 350°F oven for 30 minutes and until the cheese is bubbly and the dish heated through. **SERVES 6.**

TOTOPOS DE MICHOACÁN

2 *ancho* **or** *pasilla* **chilies**
1½ cups *masa harina*
½ cup cooked and mashed red kidney or pinto beans
½ teaspoon salt
Corn or peanut oil or lard for frying
Guacamole (page 74)
Freshly grated Parmesan cheese

Toast the chilies lightly in a dry frying pan, remove the stems and shake out the seeds. Tear them into pieces and put into a bowl with warm water to cover. Soak them for 30 minutes, turning them from time to time. Drain, reserve the soaking liquid and reduce the chilies to a purée in a food processor. In a bowl mix together the puréed chilies, the *masa harina*, mashed beans and salt to a fairly stiff dough, using a little of the reserved soaking liquid if necessary. Using pieces of dough about the size of a walnut, make 12 (2-inch) *totopos* with the tortilla press. They should be a little thicker than tortillas. Bake on the *comal* then fry in hot oil or lard in a frying pan until lightly golden on both sides. Drain on paper towels, spread with guacamole then with a sprinkling of cheese. **MAKES 12.**

SOPES

It was very perceptive of the Spanish in Mexico to call the *antojitos* "little whims" or "fancies." It gives us a single name to cover a large and complicated group of appetizers which can be something to have with drinks, or make a lunch or supper. All through Mexico this group of enticing whims are called different names in different regions, but everyone knows them as *sopes* so there is not reason to anyone to get into the tangle I did when trying to sort them out. César's maternal family were resolutely northern and persisted in thinking I was difficult for wanting to know how to cook Mexican. All except the grandmother of course who loved food and cooking and liked to work with her cook. The others thought I should leave the cook unmolested and eat what she provided. The Ortizes, his father's side were much more helpful but the best cook of them all wanted me to teach her my sort of cooking, especially curry. She had no English and I had little Spanish, so progress was cheerful but slow and I sometimes had too many Margaritas for my own good. Only once actually, and the ranch, well away from Mexico City, was a good place to sleep it off, as if it were just a routine everyday siesta.

I think these regional names are correct but allow room for error. Yucatán has *garnachas*, Puebla calls them *chalupas* (little boats), Veracruz has *pickadas* and Sonora *gorditas* (little fat ones) to list just a few. They are all slightly different in filling because Mexican cooks are endlessly inventive.

Make a batch of dough for 12 (4-inch) tortillas but instead roll the dough into 12 balls about 1½ inch in diameter and press them out into tortillas about 3½ inches across. They will be a bit thicker than the usual tortilla. Pour enough oil to reach a depth of about 1 inch and fry the tortilla until it is lightly golden, just a minute or two. Turn it over and while the second side is cooking pinch up the edges to form a little ridge—take out and drain on paper towels. They can be baked on a *comal* in the usual way if preferred. Fill them and serve immediately. **MAKES 12.**

Use any of the following fillings. For *chalupas* pinch the tortilla into an oval shape, like a boat.

THE CLASSIC FILLING FOR GUADALAJARA'S *SOPES TAPATIOS*

1 cup *frijoles refritos* (page 159)
½ lb chorizo sausages, skinned, chopped and fried
1 recipe *Salsa Verde* (green sauce) (page 80)
½ cup grated *queso anejo* or Parmesan cheese
For garnish, shredded lettuce and sliced radishes

When ready to fill the *sopes*, have the beans and sausages warm, and make a layer of beans, sausage, sauce, and cheese with a garnish of lettuce and sliced radish. Serve immediately.

THE CLASSIC FILLING FOR *GARNACHAS* FROM YUCATÁN

1 cup warm *picadillo* (page 221)
1 cup warm *frijoles refritos* (page 159)
½ cup warm Yucatán-style tomato sauce (page 56)
½ cup freshly grated Parmesan cheese

Make a layer of beans, then one of *picadillo*, and top wth tomato sauce and garnish with cheese.

Everyday fillings for *sopes* are usually *frijoles refritos*, chorizos or a little shredded meat or poultry, a little sauce like *salsa verde* or *salsa cruda*, chopped onion, crumbled or grated cheese, shredded lettuce, and sliced radishes. Sometimes chilies, like *chipotles* or *jalapeños*, pickled and chopped are used. These are not formal and the general rules are quite clear; choose from the ingredients listed above and use about 3 layers such as chicken, sauce, onion, cheese. It is a great way to use any leftover meat, poultry, beans or sauce. Remember these are little whims and you can indulge your fancies.

PANUCHOS

These are another of the triumphs of the cooking of Yucatán. They are great fun to make as the tortilla must be made to puff up into an *inflado*. This is quite easy to do. Just press the cooked side of the tortilla with a spoon, or even your fingers, gently all over and it will puff up as the other side cooks. It can then be lifted up for stuffing. Another Maya refinement is the *Cebolla Escabechada* (Pickled Onion) that is used as a garnish (page 83). Whenever they were around I found them irresistible and frequently made them myself when I could not easily go out and get them. It is no wonder that many lovers of Mexican food never get beyond the *antojitos*, one could live on them. Almost.

12 (4-inch) tortillas

1 cup mashed black beans

2 large hard-boiled eggs, each cut into 6 slices

Corn oil for frying

2 cooked chicken breast halves, boned and shredded

1 recipe *Cebolla Escabechada* (page 83)

Using the tip of a small sharp knife lift up the puffed layer of each tortilla for about halfway round it. Carefully spread a layer of the mashed beans inside the pocket and top it with a slice of egg. Press down the lifted layer. In a frying pan heat oil to reach a depth of about ½ inch and fry the *panuchos* bottom side down. Drain on paper towels, top with shredded chicken and garnish with the pickled onion. Eat immediately. **SERVES 4-6 ACCORDING TO APPETITE.**

ENCHILADAS

As far as I am concerned *enchiladas* are the aristocrats of the *antojito* family and make perfect luncheon dishes, though in Mexico they would not, I think, be regarded as suitable for *comida* though they certainly would be for *almuerzo* and for supper too. My favorite is *Enchiladas Suizas* which have *Crema Espesa*. I guess they are called *Suizas* because of the traditional excellence of dairy products in Switzerland. There are a number of *enchiladas* without any cream and it was one of these César would choose, though usually he would prefer *chilaquiles* if he could get them. *Enchiladas* are not difficult to make, but properly done they can be a little messy as the tortilla is first dipped in sauce then quickly fried with the inevitable splutter. To avoid this some cooks reverse the process, first frying the tortilla, then dipping it in sauce before stuffing it. There is a quite discernable loss of flavor that isn't worth it to avoid a small splutter or two.

There are other *enchilada*-type dishes that can't be called variations, they are relatives. Two of the simplest are *enfrijoladas* and *entomatados*. In the first, tortillas are dipped in bean purée as a preliminary and in the second in tomato sauce, sometimes in a tomato-chili sauce. I'm never sure if *Pan de Cazon* (tortillas layered with shark and black beans) belongs with the *enchilada* family but I'm including them as I have a belated confession to go with the recipe. And *Papa-dzules*, a sublime tortilla dish from Yucatán certainly does. They played a disproportionately large part in my Mexican-food education.

GREEN *ENCHILADAS*
Enchiladas Verdes

Poblano chilies have an incomparable taste and it is worth going to considerable trouble to find them, even canned ones are useful. Rather than lose this dish altogether when no *poblanos* can be had, use fresh sweet green peppers. They are not at all a bad substitute.

6 *poblano* chilies, fresh or canned, or 6 fresh sweet green peppers

¾ lb *tomatillos* (Mexican green tomatoes)

2 tablespoons chopped fresh coriander

1 cup *Crema Espesa* (page 314)

1 large egg, lightly beaten

Salt

3 tablespoons corn or peanut oil

24 (4-inch) tortillas

6 cooked chicken breast halves, skinned, boned and shredded

½ cup cream or cottage cheese

1 onion, finely chopped

¼ cup freshly grated Parmesan cheese

Spear the chilies with a fork and toast them over direct heat turning them so that the skin chars and blisters all over. Put them into a plastic bag and leave for about 20 minutes. Rinse them in cold water when the skin will come off easily. They can be charred under a grill. Slit the chilies and remove the seeds and cut off the stems. Chop them roughly.

In a food processor combine the chilies, *tomatillos*, and coriander and reduce to a thick purée. Turn the mixture out into a bowl and stir in the cream and egg. Season with salt.

Heat the oil in a frying pan. Dip the tortillas, one at a time in the sauce, then fry quickly, a matter only of seconds in the hot oil. Stuff with the chopped chicken mixed with the cream or cottage cheese, roll up loosely and arrange in a greased ovenproof dish. When all the tortillas are filled and in the dish, warm the sauce and pour over them and sprinkle with the Parmesan cheese. Warm them through in a preheated 350°F oven and serve immediately. They should not be hot, just warm. Garnish if liked with shredded lettuce, sliced radishes and chopped onion. **SERVES 6.**

For *Enchiladas Suizas* make as for *Enchiladas Verdes* but do not add beaten egg and cream to the sauce. Dip the tortilla in the all-purpose sauce, fry quickly in the hot oil so that they are limp, stuff them and roll loosely. Arrange in a greased ovenproof dish, warm the remaining sauce and pour over them. Finally pour 1 cup *Crema Espesa* or sour cream over the dish. Heat through in a preheated 350°F oven for 15 to 20 minutes. Serve immediately. **SERVES 6.**

RED *ENCHILADAS*
Enchilada Rojas

6 *ancho* or *mulato* chilies

1 lb tomatoes, peeled, seeded and chopped

2 onions, finely chopped

2 cloves garlic, chopped

Sprig *epazote*

Corn or peanut oil

Salt, pinch of sugar

1 cup *Crema Espesa* (page 314)

2 large eggs, lightly beaten

6 chorizo sausages, skinned and chopped

½ cup freshly grated Parmesan cheese

24 (4-inch) tortillas

Toast the chilies lightly on both sides in a dry frying pan, pull off the stems and shake out the seeds. Tear into pieces and put into a bowl with warm water to cover for 30 minutes, turning the pieces from time to time. Drain and reserve the soaking water. In a food processor combine the chilies, 1 onion, garlic and *epazote* and reduce to a purée. Heat 2 tablespoons of oil in a frying pan and cook over moderate heat, stirring constantly for 5 minutes. Season to taste with salt and sugar, stir in the eggs and the cream and remove from the heat. Set aside.

Wipe out the frying pan and add 1 tablespoon of oil and sauté the sausages until browned. Drain and mix with a little of the sauce and ⅓ of the cheese.

Add the 2 tablespoons oil to the frying pan and set over moderate heat. One by one dip each tortilla in the sauce then quickly fry on both sides in the hot oil, only a matter of seconds. Stuff the tortillas with the sausage, roll them up and put into a lightly greased ovenproof dish. When they are all rolled and in the dish, cover with the remaining cheese and the other onion. Heat the sauce and pour over the tortillas. Heat them through in a preheated 350°F oven. Serve warm, four to a person. **SERVES 6.**

ENCHILADAS DE MOLE

This does not mean just *Mole Poblano* even though this is the festival dish and the best known. It means a sauce made with any of the *capsicums*, sweet, pungent or hot and comes from the Nahuatl word *molli*. Oaxaca is famous for its seven *moles*, some with chilies that are hard to find outside Oaxaca. A favorite for *enchiladas* is *Mole Coloradito* which I have found, used in *enchiladas* with slightly altered ingredients and under different names, sometimes with *ancho* chilies, sometimes with *guajillos*. This is surely the genius of the Mexican kitchen, that it can make so many variations on a theme and still manage, somehow, to come up with authentic versions of dishes.

ENCHILADAS DE MOLE POBLANO

Leftover *Mole Poblano* sauce
Shredded cooked chicken or turkey
24 (4-inch) tortillas
Sesame seeds
For garnish:
Shredded lettuce and finely chopped onion
Guacamole (page 74)

Warm the sauce. Dip the tortillas one by one in the sauce, fill with chicken or turkey and roll them loosely. Arrange in a greased ovenproof dish. When all the tortillas are filled and in the dish, pour the remaining sauce over them and sprinkle them with sesame seeds. If necessary warm through in a preheated 350°F oven. Serve 4 to a portion, garnished with lettuce and onion. Serve guacamole on the side. **SERVES 6.**

ENCHILADAS DE MOLE COLORADITO

Leftover *mole* sauce, warmed
Shredded cooked chicken
24 (4-inch) tortillas
3 tablespoons corn oil
Chopped onion

Heat the oil in a frying pan and fry the tortillas for a few seconds. Spread a layer of the sauce on the tortillas, stuff with the chicken and roll loosely. Place in an ovenproof baking dish, pour over the rest of the warm *mole* sauce and garnish with chopped onion. Serve immediately. **SERVES 6.**

TORTILLAS LAYERED WITH DOGFISH
Pan de Cazon

I have guilt feelings about this recipe. If only someone had called it dogfish instead of shark so that the recipe would no longer translate into "Bread of Shark." Of course dogfish is a shark and we call another shark, rock salmon and other members of the shark family have aliases, as I am not the only person who thinks of sharks in an unfriendly way. It is a traditional dish in Yucatán and Campeche, and Graciela Iduarta, who is from Campeche wanted to cook it for me. She was the wife of a close friend of my husband, Andres Iduarte, a Mexican Government Minister and later a professor at Columbia University in New York. Our paths crossed from time to time in various countries. I am not often so stupid and I regret it. I should have taken up her offer with enthusiasm, but her tolerance and kindness were such that she sent me her own two recipes for two versions of *Pan de Cazon*. When I did taste the dish I had her excellent recipes, one of which I've given here, as a reference point. I think Graciela knew I would someday see the light. There is a small shark called *jaqueton* much used in Campeche and if the dish had been called *Pan de Jaqueton*, which is a pretty name, I should not have had an image of a vicious man-eater. Though it is one of the *antojitos*, it is hearty enough to make a good lunch or supper. Most fishmongers sell a suitable type of cartilaginous sea creature as rock salmon or simply rock. I recommend it. César very kindly never said I was being silly over this, and his favorite English dish was "Toad in the Hole." There is not much to choose in awfulness between the two as far as names go.

**1 lb dogfish (or rock salmon), skinned and boned and cut about
   1 inch thick**

Salt

6 sprigs *epazote*

**1 cup cooked and mashed black beans cooked
   with 1** *habañero* **chili**

2 recipes Tomato Sauce, Yucatán-style (*Salsa de Tomate Yucateca***)
   (page 56)**

12 (5-inch) tortillas

Put the fish into a saucepan with 3 sprigs *epazote* and salt water to cover, bring
to a simmer and cook for 10 minutes. Drain and lift out the fish and shred.
Chop the remaining *epazote* and mix with the fish. Set aside in a warm place.
Preheat the oven to 350°F and have an ovenproof dish large enough to hold
two tortillas side by side. Warm the beans and the tomato sauce and assemble the dish. Dip two tortillas in the tomato sauce and lay in the ovenproof
dish, spread a layer of beans, then one of fish on them. Top with a tortilla
dipped in sauce and pour 1 cup tomato sauce over them. Continue with the
rest of the tortillas, beans, fish and sauce. Return the dish to the oven and
cook just long enough to heat it through, about 10 minutes. Serve cut into
wedges like a cake. **SERVES 6.**

FLUTES
Flautas

I had an awful time sorting out *flautas*. Fierce authorities said they must be
made with corn tortillas, that they were only crisp fried tacos, that they
should be made with flour tortillas, should be stuffed with chicken, should
be stuffed with beef and so on. What had happened with the *flauta* is that it
had become popular sometime in the 1980s in the Southwest of the United
States and then everywhere. So now you can make *flautas* with either corn
or flour tortillas, stuff them with chicken or beef, roll them tightly or loosely
and fry them in plenty of oil making sure it is at the right temperature so that
they do not absorb too much of it.

24 corn or flour tortillas

Corn oil for frying

For the chicken filling:

½ lb tomatoes, peeled, seeded and chopped

1 small onion, chopped

1 clove garlic, chopped

2-3 tablespoons corn oil

Salt

2 freshly cooked chicken breasts, skinned and shredded

For the garnish:

Romaine lettuce leaves, sliced radishes and stuffed green olives

Set the tortillas aside and cook the filling. In a food processor combine the tomatoes, onion and garlic and reduce to a purée. In a frying pan heat the oil and cook, stirring, until the mixture is thick and well-blended. Season with salt, add the chicken and remove from heat. Set aside.

To finish the dish: If the tortillas need softening so that they can be rolled, heat a little oil in a frying pan and fry the tortillas quickly, about 2 seconds a side. Lift out onto kitchen towels. Do the tortillas in pairs and put onto the work surface with one tortilla overlapping its partner by 2 inches. Spread about 2 tablespoons of the filling down the length of the tortillas then roll them up tightly. Secure with a cocktail stick. Continue with the rest of the tortillas.

Heat ½ cup oil in a large frying pan and when it is quite hot fry the *flautas*, as many as the pan will take at one time, turning to brown them all over, about 3-4 minutes. Take out and drain on paper towels and continue with the rest of the prepared *flautas*. To serve line a platter with romaine lettuce, arrange the flautas on the dish, and garnish with sliced radish and green olives. **MAKES 12 *FLAUTAS*.**

ENFRIJOLADAS AND *ENTOMATADAS*

These *antojitos* from Oaxaca can best be described as relatives of *enchiladas*. I first ate them at a *Guelaguetza*, a festival held each July to honor the god of corn, *Centeotl*, and to ask for good harvests. It was in Oaxaca City, capital of this wondrous state of Oaxaca. The Zapotec, an ancient people, were the first settlers and they called the city Huaxyacac, which time and the invading Spanish changed to the slightly easier Oaxaca, though I have heard of it causing trouble with visitors who wanted to call it Oh-Axe-Ah-Ka, instead of, correctly, Wha-Ha-Kah. They were descended from the Olmec, a people about whom very little is known. They left the great mysterious stone heads in the jungles of Veracruz and Tabasco and also played a key role in the development of chocolate as a drink. Later arrivals in Oaxaca were the Mixtec. Their descendants are two of the 15 major tribes in the region, each of which has a special costume. The Valle women wear full, embroidered skirts

and blouses, the Mixtec wear short, white embroidered *huipils* (tunics) over full skirts, and wear *rebozos*, the people of the Sierra wear full white skirts and sashed and colored tops and white *rebozos*. The Yalalog wear heavy white cotton *huipils* with tasseled embroidery down front and back over long skirts. Their most striking feature is the way they do their hair braided into elaborate headdresses with black wool. The Tehuana from the Isthmus wear heavily embroidered *huipils* over long, finely pleated, lace-trimmed white skirts and lots of necklaces, gold where possible. But it is their headdress that is most notable. It is a sixteenth-century Spanish baby's baptismal dress, the pleated skirt falling to the shoulders and the lace-trimmed sleeves hanging decoratively on each side. After all that glory and color, the men's simple costume of white cotton trousers tied at the ankles and white cotton shirts made an effective contrast. All these brilliant costumes and many others were at the festivities. César was there on business for United Nations connected with his job. Though the festival has become Christianized it is still very much a pre-Columbian affair and the Indians stage dances and present gifts of their produce and wares to officials. They honored me with a carved round wooden tray with a brilliantly painted pattern of flowers. I still have it, infinitely cherished but I don't have the sandals that were the other gift. Someone had lovingly drawn an outline of my foot on a piece of paper and someone else set off to make the sandals for me. They were a disaster. They would have fit a giant. Somehow I managed to give them away and settled down to enjoy the day's events. You think of Oaxaca, and you think of antiquity, the colonial past and the lively present and the food. We kept coming back on visits to experience more of it. Which reminds me of our first trip with César as information chief. He was giving a lecture at the local university and the students were eager to welcome us. They brought us a bottle of *mescal*, the regional tipple, like tequila but made from a different *agave* and with a maguey grub in the bottle. In their enthusiasm they knocked it over in our car, having failed to make sure the cork was secure. A quantity escaped, mostly into the upholstery and the smell of *mescal* remained with us for a long time. It is a very powerful sort of aroma as any tequila lover will tell you. Still what could one say, they were nice young men and they meant well and what remained of our *mescal* tasted very good.

ENFRIJOLADAS

1 cup cooked pinto or red kidney beans
12 (4-inch) tortillas
Water or chicken stock

1 cup *Salsa Verde* (green sauce) (page 80)

6 chorizo sausages, skinned, chopped and fried

1 onion, finely chopped

2 oz crumbly white cheese such as goat cheese

3 tablespoons finely chopped coriander

Corn oil for frying

Put the cooked beans and any liquid into a food processor and reduce to a purée adding enough water or chicken stock to bring the quantity to 3 cups. In a frying pan heat enough oil to reach a depth of about ½ inch and very quickly fry the tortillas on both sides. Lift out, drain on paper towels and keep warm. Have the bean purée warm and dip the tortillas in it then stuff them, one by one, with chorizo and the *salsa verde*. Traditionally they are folded into fours but it is much easier to roll them loosely and arrange them in a shallow warmed ovenproof dish. Pour the rest of the bean purée over the tortillas and serve, garnished with the onion, cheese and coriander. Note when making the *salsa verde*, canned *tomatillos* just need draining, but fresh ones should be cooked in salted water for about 5 minutes until tender. Be careful not to pierce the skin. **SERVES 4.**

ENTOMATADAS

This is another Oaxacan original and though it is simple there is an even simpler version claimed by the north. César who was from Chihuahua, disclaimed all knowledge of this northern branch of the *enchilada* family but acknowledged that no lifetime is long enough to know the entire Mexican kitchen.

1½ lbs tomatoes, peeled, seeded and chopped

1 onion, chopped

Corn oil for frying

12 (4-inch) tortillas

2 chicken breast halves, cooked, skinned, boned and shredded

For garnish: finely chopped parsley, grated cheese, chopped onion

In a food processor combine the tomatoes and onion and process to a purée. Heat 2 tablespoons corn oil in a frying pan, add the purée and cook, stirring, until it has thickened to sauce consistency. Season with salt. Dip the tortillas in the sauce to coat them lightly then fry them quickly in the frying pan, adding more oil as necessary. Fill each tortilla with chicken breast and arrange in an ovenproof dish. Warm the remaining tomato sauce and pour it over the tortillas. Heat them through in a preheated 350°F oven and serve immediately garnished with the parsley, cheese and chopped onion. They should not be too hot, just warm. **SERVES 4 TO 6.**

PAPA-DZULES

After our first visit to Yucatán which was principally to see the ruins at Uxmal and Chichén Itzá, both of which César had visited when he was studying at Mexico City's university and during his early days as a journalist, we were both homesick for Yucatán. A sort of cure was to go to the Circulo del Sureste for lunch and it was there that I became forever hooked on *Papa-dzules*, so that when my book on Mexican cooking was being published some time later, it was natural this was the dish I cooked for Craig Claiborne when he interviewed me for the cookery section of *The Times*. I think Craig became hooked on this subtle Mayan dish as I had done. At any rate when he interviewed Diana Kennedy when, some years later, her book on Mexican cooking was being published, it was *Papa-dzules* he wrote about and still later when he interviewed Zarela Martinez, who has a wonderful Mexican restaurant in New York and has written about Mexico, it was once again *Papa-dzules* that he wrote about. Has ever a dish been so honored? I am sure the Circulo del Sureste had a number of beguiling dishes to offer and I wish now I had tried more of them but I never got beyond the tortillas, dipped in a pumpkin (*pepitas*) seed sauce, stuffed with chopped hardboiled eggs, garnished with more of the sauce and finally topped with tomato sauce and decorated with green pumpkin seed oil. I had fun with the *pepitas* and the oil yield. I had not been very successful the first time I tried it and that night I dreamed I was visited by some Maya chieftans, very fine in their feathered costumes, who addressed me in better Spanish than I had at the time, and told me how to go about things. I remember one phrase of the instructions to this day: "*Mire señora vd savez bien que es necessario nuele sus pepitas en seco.*" The end result of this cooking lesson was that the next day I got lovely green oil from my *pepitas*.

Pumpkin seed sauce (*Salsa de Pepitas*) (page 55)
Tomato Sauce, Yucatán-style (*Salsa de Tomate Yucateca*) (page 56)
24 (4-inch) tortillas
12 hard-boiled eggs, very finely chopped

Dip the tortillas one by one into pumpkin seed sauce then stuff with the chopped egg. Roll lightly and put into a greased ovenproof dish. Mask the tortillas with the remaining pumpkin seed sauce, then pour on the tomato sauce which should be warm. Top with the green pumpkin seed oil. Warm the dish through in a warm oven. Serve immediately, warm not hot.
SERVES 6.

PUMPKIN SEED SAUCE
Salsa de Pepitas

One of the secrets of *Papa-dzules* is the green oil that is squeezed from the *pepitas* and used to garnish the finished dish. I don't think the flavor of the dish is altered much whether the oil remains in the *pepitas* or is squeezed but it does add to the pretty look.

1 lb Mexican pumpkin seeds, hulled (*pepitas*)
3 *serrano* chilies, chopped
2 sprigs *epazote*
4 cups hot water
Salt

Heat an ungreased frying pan, ideally cast iron, and toast the pumpkin seeds over low heat, stirring constantly, until they begin to color slightly. They should be toasted very lightly. Put the seeds into a nut grinder or food processor and grind as finely as possible with the *serranos*. Transfer to a bowl and sprinkle with enough hot water, about ½ cup to make a paste. Knead and squeeze the paste which will exude a bright green oil. Collect the oil in a little dish. 4 tablespoons is about enough. Put the *epazote* sprigs into the remaining water and simmer for about 5 minutes. Remove and discard the herb. Put the *pepita* paste into a small saucepan and, over low heat, gradually stir in the hot *epazote* water and cook stirring until the sauce is the consistency of heavy cream. Do not let it boil as it will separate. Use to complete the dish of *Papa-dzules*.

TOMATO SAUCE, YUCATÁN-STYLE
Salsa de Tomate Yucateca

This tomato sauce from Yucatán is always served with *Papa-dzules* (tortillas in pumpkin sauce), a specialty of the region. Two ingredients make this sauce distinctive: the use of the herb *epazote*, popular in this kitchen, and the *habañero* chili, which is the hottest pepper in North America. It is also very aromatic so that it imparts a magnificent flavor along with heat. Sometimes a tablespoon of Seville (bitter) orange juice is added. For a less *picante* sauce, leave the *habañero* whole and just steep it in the sauce.

1 onion, chopped

1 sprig *epazote*, chopped

4 tablespoons corn or peanut oil or lard

2 lbs tomatoes, peeled, seeded and mashed

1 *habeñero* chili, seeded and chopped or left whole

Salt

Combine the onion and *epazote* in a food processor and reduce to a purée. Heat the oil or lard in a frying pan and cook, stirring from time to time, for 5 minutes. Add the tomatoes and the chopped chili if using in this form, and salt and simmer for about 10 minutes, stirring from time to time, until the sauce is thick and well blended. If using the whole *habañero* add it with the tomatoes and remove and discard when the sauce is cooked.
MAKES ABOUT 2 CUPS.

FLOUR TORTILLAS

There was no wheat grown in Mexico until after the arrival of Hernán Cortés, the conqueror. Cattle, goats and lamb were introduced with wheat and quite soon the flour tortilla using wheat flour instead of *masa harina* was invented, useful in parts of the country where wheat grew well and corn didn't. It is especially popular in the northern states and seems to have a special affinity for roast kid (baby goat) *cabrito* in Spanish, roast beef ribs (*agujas*) and green sauce (*salsa verde*). There was one restaurant in Mexico City, Los Norteños, where we would go when César was homesick for the food of the north, and I was hungry for roast *cabrito* or *agujas*. It is sublimely simple food and all you should drink with it is a good beer, a drink at which Mexico excels. I still think of the one called Bohemia, my favorite, with affection.

The tortillas are easy to make as all that is needed is all-purpose flour, lard or vegetable shortening, baking powder, a rolling pin and a griddle. Nowadays flour tortillas are widely available in supermarkets, and mail order and can be used to make such dishes as *burritos* and *chivichangas*.

2 cups all-purpose flour

1 teaspoon salt

1 teaspoon baking powder

1½ tablespoons lard or vegetable shortening

½ cup warm water

In a large bowl sift the flour, salt and baking powder together and rub in the lard or vegetable shortening with the fingertips until it resembles a coarse meal. Stir in the water to make a fairly stiff dough, cover the bowl with a cloth and let the dough rest for 20 minutes. Divide the dough into 12 balls. On a lightly floured surface roll out the dough to a 6-inch circle and bake on a hot griddle for about 30 to 45 seconds a side, flipping it over as the first side is done. Take care not to overbake as the tortilla will not be flexible. As each tortilla is done wrap it in a cloth, it is important to keep the tortillas warm. These tortillas are best fresh but they can be reheated, stacked and wrapped in foil, in a preheated 325°F oven for about 20 minutes.

MAKES 12 TORTILLAS.

BURRITOS AND CHIVICHANGAS

Flour tortillas filled and rolled are the *burritos* that have become popular all over Mexico, immigrants from the north, and in the United States and just about everywhere else. When they are fried they become *chivichangas*. One or two make an adequate light lunch or a more than adequate lunch if they are served with guacamole and refried beans. They should always be accompanied by northern-style tomato sauce (*salsa verde*, page 80). Any taco filling can be used and there are some fillings special to them. What started life as *charqui*, became jerky and I knew it in Mexico as *cecina*. It is strips of beef, seasoned with lime juice and salt, and dried in the sun. It was a good way to preserve in the cattle states of the north in the days before refrigeration. Names abound. In the *burrito* filling of jerky with scrambled eggs, the jerky is called *machacado* which means "crushed" and there is even a special large flat stone used by cooks to pound the meat into submission. Dried beef is the best substitute and will taste much better if it is flavored with a little lime juice. A mortar and pestle can be used to pound the jerky, or a food processor can be used with care.

JERKY WITH SCRAMBLED EGGS
Machacado con Huevo

½ lb beef jerky (strips dried salted beef), shredded

6 large eggs

6 tablespoons lard or corn oil

1 onion, finely chopped

4 *serrano* chilies, seeded and finely chopped or
  2 *poblanos* peeled, seeded and finely chopped

1 large tomato, peeled and diced

Salt, if necessary

12 flour tortillas

If necessary pound the beef in a mortar with a pestle until it is almost fluffy. Heat the oil in a frying pan and fry the onion, chilies, and tomato over moderate heat until they are well blended, about 5 minutes. Stir in the beef and cook, stirring, for about 5 minutes longer. Break the eggs into a bowl and stir just to combine the whites and yolks. Do not beat them. Stir into the beef mixture and cook, stirring, just until the eggs are lightly set. Season with salt if necessary. Have 12 flour tortillas ready and stuff with the mixture.
MAKES 12 *BURRITOS*.

CHILORIO

This is a favorite filling for *burritos* in the north. The pork is cooked in the same way as *carnitas* on which I doted and I would make *chilorio* when we were no longer living in Mexico as I could get the ingredients, especially very good pork, in New York. I would pinch the pork at the *carnita* stage of its cooking for a small private feast in the kitchen. Those filched pieces of pork were what the distinguished elder stateslady of the cooking world, Helen McCully, used to call "cook's perks."

2 lbs boneless pork shoulder cut into 1½-inch cubes

4 *ancho* chilies

3 cloves garlic, chopped

1¼ teaspoon ground cumin

½ teaspoon dried oregano

1 teaspoon black peppercorns, crushed

½ cup mild vinegar

Salt

Put the pork cubes into a heavy casserole and pour in enough water barely to cover. Over low heat bring to a simmer, uncovered, stirring from time to time until the water has evaporated and the meat is tender, 1-1½ hours. The meat should not have browned but all the fat will have rendered out. Lift the pork pieces from the casserole and reserve the fat. Shred the pork and set it aside.

In a dry frying pan toast the *anchos* lightly on both sides. Tear off the stems and shake out and discard the seeds. Tear into pieces and put into a bowl with warm water to cover. Soak for 30 minutes, turning from time to time. Drain and transfer to a food processor with the garlic, cumin, oregano, peppercorns and vinegar and reduce to a purée. Transfer to the casserole with the fat and shredded pork and cook, stirring occasionally for 15-20 minutes. Season to taste with salt and use to stuff 12 flour tortillas for *burritos*.

FAJITAS

When we were living in New York I was introduced to skirt steak by James Beard and to flank steak, very inexpensive cuts of well flavored tender beef. It is grilled and cut into thin slices on the diagonal. Skirt is a thin narrow piece just above the tenderloin and because every country cuts its beef carcass differently and names them differently, skirt and flank steak led me a merry dance in Mexico. I kept hearing about *Fajitas* and since *faja* is Spanish for "sash" or "belt" deduced that they were thin slices of steak. The north is cattle country so when they seemed to be mixed up with flour tortillas I thought it thoroughly proper. Were they a filling for a taco? Or what? I did learn that the skirt and flank steaks were grilled over mesquite in Texas. The family had connections in Texas, some of them having gone to El Paso when there was too much revolution going on in Mexico for their liking, even though they had a revolutionary general, Eulogio Ortiz Reyes in the family. It wasn't a pleasant time especially for César whose happy childhood was destroyed when his father died in Mexico City and his mother carted him off to join the El Paso contingent. However he was sent to school in Houston and had the great privilege in those early days of his high school education of having the late president of the U.S., Lyndon B. Johnson, as his teacher. Lyndon befriended him and César said the lifelong friendship did much to make up for his early unhappiness. Not that that got me much nearer to unravelling the mystery of *fajitas* except that César remembered that later, back in Monterrey they had tacos made from grilled *arrachera* (skirt steak). He said the steak itself was often marinated in lime juice and served with flour tortillas, guacamole and refried beans and *salsa verde*.

Years later reading Zarela Martinez' delightful book *Food From My Heart* I found the answer. Zarela is from Chihuahua, like my husband, and at one time she had a catering business in El Paso. She remembers that in the late 1970s a big food distributor had Saturday cookouts for his truckers and they would make *fajitas* and like so many foods, they became fashionable in the U.S. Rick Bayless has an admirable description of skirt steak in his book *Authentic Mexican Regional Cooking*. Though I agree the ideal way to cook the steak is grilled over mesquite for 2-3 minutes a side, then cut into ¼ inch diagonal slices, I have had great success cooking the steak on top of the stove in a cast iron frying pan lightly filmed with oil. Somehow they taste of the north and remind me of the fun I had when we visited Monterrey and the press described me as "*exquisita poeta y jounalista Inglesa.*" I think we were buying them drinks, or something. The description was a generous exaggeration, which should happen once in everyone's lifetime.

2 lbs skirt or flank steak, trimmed of all fat
[handwritten: add a little oil + fajita seasoning]
½ cup fresh lime juice, if unavailable use lemon juice
Salt, freshly ground black pepper

Put the steak into a flat dish and pour the lime or lemon juice over it. Season with salt and freshly ground pepper and marinate for 1 hour, turning once or twice. Drain and pat dry and grill for 2-3 minutes a side. *[handwritten: until done all through – no red]* Cut the steak into ¼ inch diagonal slices, then into convenient lengths, 4 inches for example. Serve with flour tortillas, refried beans, guacamole and *salsa verde*, or any *salsa* to your taste. Assemble your own tacos. **SERVES 4-6.**

[handwritten: finely grated cheese / sour cream / lettuce / pico de gallo / sliced avocado]

THE
TAMALES

•

Tamales

Tamales are fiesta food. They are also very ancient, going back if not quite to the early cultivation of corn in about 5000 B.C., then not long after that time. Fray Bernadhino de Sahagún in his great history of Mexico, written in the early 16th century, told of the many types of *tamal* he found in the markets. He tells of dried corn husk stuffed with dough that was light and fluffy, so perhaps the modern *tamal* is not wholly different from the Aztec-Maya original. Today just about every region has its own special style of *tamal* from the small ones from the north, Coahuila, Chihuahua and Nuevo León, like very fat fingers, only about 2½ inches long, stuffed with pork with chili *ancho* and cumin, to the *sacahuil* from Pánuco in Veracruz, 3 to 4 feet long, stuffed with pork and spices and *anchos*, wrapped in banana leaves and baked in a wood-heated oven. Oaxaca has wonderful *tamales* stuffed with chicken in *Mole Poblano* sauce and wrapped in banana leaves which I first had at the Cafe Tacuba just across the street from Bolivar 8, where César's mother, aunt and uncle were living in Mexico City. Also the *uchepos* of Michoacán. I have treasured for years a recipe given me by a friend of the *uchepos* of Patzcuaro. These are sweet and not stuffed though some of the sweet *tamales* are stuffed with raisins and candied fruit. My most treasured *tamal* recipe is one from my mother-in-law which I think was from the grandmother, Doña Carmelita. These are called *Tamales de Cambray* wrapped in banana leaves instead of the more usual dried corn husks. Just right for a beginner I thought when I glanced at it—for 300 *tamales* and using 40 eggs. I have never got round to making them but from what César has told me about the grandmother's *tamaladas* she wouldn't even have thought it a challenge.

Tamales make a party and are an excuse for a party. It may be just Sunday night fare in a restaurant. A *tamalada*, a *tamal* party is more usually a family affair, a family reunion, a birthday, an engagement. César told me of his grandmother's *tamaladas* when she was living in Durango. I wish I had been there as his description was vivid enough to make one's mouth water. It was a three-day cooking effort with friends and neighbors and their maids all coming in to help. I somehow got the impression that Carmelita's *tamales* were so good that excuses were invented to have a party. First of all there was buying to be done, the meats and poultry for fillings and ingredients for sauces and the drinks organized. The party, César told me, would be held in the garden which was large, and the weather was reliable. Chairs and tables would be set out for the guests, and long trestle tables to bear the happy weight of *tamales*, *salsas*, fruit and candies, soft drinks, and tequila, with bowls of halved and quartered limes, beer and wine. To finish there were sometimes sweet *tamales* and coffee. As soon as one platter of *tamales* was finished, another would appear. They were the result of a lot of hard work when the *tamal* was prepared, corn husks softened, *tamales* made and got ready for steaming having been stuffed with meats and poultry shredded and sauced. I can see the maids in their full long skirts, and embroidered blouses, their dark hair in plaits, and everyone in bright, summery clothes, with colored *rebozos* (stoles) ready against evening chill. There would be lanterns and perhaps music with *mariaches* and much eating, drinking, laughter and lively talk. If anyone had the heart to eat *merienda* that night it would be something very, very light.

Years later on a snowy day in New York I had a mini-*tamalada*, a sort of indoor picnic with two types of *tamal*, one with *mole*, the other with *adobo* stuffing. There were eight of us, not a gardenful, but even with the snow falling, the *tamal* somehow exerted its happy magic, turning the occasion into a fiesta.

Tamal Making

It may be difficult to get *masa para tamales* but I have found that Quaker *masa harina* which I use for tortillas gives a very good result. It is important to have good lard. If this is hard to find the butcher may supply leaf lard (pork fat) which is easy to render providing care is taken not to let it color in the process. Just chop the fat, cover with water and cook, over very low heat on top of the stove, pouring off the lard from time to time as it renders out, and taking care not to let the fat color.

If using dried corn husks, soak them in hot water until softened, about 15 minutes. If using banana leaves, cut them into 10 inch squares and put them into a bowl with hot water to cover and soak until softened, about 15 minutes, though the time may vary.

Tamales freeze well. To reheat, thaw thoroughly then steam for 20 minutes.

TAMALES AND FILLINGS

24 or more dried corn husks

⅓ cup lard

2 cups Quaker™ *masa harina* or *masa para tamales*

1 teaspoon salt

1 teaspoon baking powder

1½ cups lukewarm chicken stock

Fillings, see below

Put the corn husks to soak in hot water. If some in the package are very small it may be necessary to use two overlapping. In a bowl cream the lard until it is very light and fluffy. In another bowl mix the *masa harina* with the salt and baking powder then beat in the creamed lard. Gradually beat in enough of the chicken stock to make a rather mushy dough. To test if the dough is ready to use carefully slide a small piece of dough into a cup of cold water. If it sinks to the bottom, beat the dough some more. If it floats, make the *tamales*.

Shake the excess water from the corn husks and pat them lightly dry. Spread 1 tablespoon of dough in the center of each corn husk leaving enough room at top and bottom for folding over. Place a 1 tablespoon of filling in the center of the dough then fold the corn husk over, one side over the other, so that the dough completely covers the filling and the corn husk covers the dough. Fold the ends of the husks over at top and bottom. If liked tie them loosely round at both ends with strips from the corn husks though this is not usually necessary. When all are ready pour boiling water into the bottom of a steamer that has a trivet or rack and stack the *tamales*, standing up, with the bottom end of the husks down and steam for 1 to 1½ hours until the dough comes away from the husks. Serve on a plate and eat out of the corn husk, unwrapping it.

If corn husks are not available substitute sheets of kitchen parchment, measuring 8 inches by 4 inches.

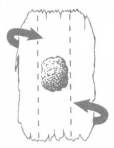  

For the fillings: use 1 cup cooked shredded chicken breast, turkey, pork or chopped prawns to ½ cup sauce

Pollo Verde (**Green Chicken**) (**page 257**)

Pollo en Mole Verde (**Chicken in Green Chili Sauce**) (**page 272**)

Mole Poblano de Guajolote (**Turkey in** *Mole* **Sauce**) (**page 268**)

Tinga Poblano de Cerdo (**Pork Stew**) (**page 261**)

Camarones Adobados (**Prawns in** *Adobo* **Sauce**) (**page 202**)

There are also sweet *tamales* one of which, stuffed with strawberries, was said to be the Emperor Moctezuma's favorite. (See Dessert section.)

BLIND OR ALL-PURPOSE *TAMALES*

These unfilled *tamales* are always served with *Mole Poblano de Guajolote* as an accompanying bread. They are also sometimes served at *merienda* when chocolate or *champurrado* is served as a drink. The only difference when making them is to have twice as much dough (about ¼ inch) spread on the corn husk. They are steamed in the same way as filled *tamales*.

24 dried corn husks, softened in hot water

⅓ cup lard

2 cups *masa para tamales* or *masa harina*

1 teaspoon salt

1 teaspoon baking powder

1½ cups lukewarm chicken stock

Shake the water from the softened corn husks and put ready to use. In a bowl cream the lard until it is very light and fluffy. In a bowl mix the *masa* with the salt and baking powder, then beat in the creamed lard. Gradually beat in enough of the warm stock to make a rather mushy dough. To test if the dough is ready carefully put a small piece of dough into a cup of cold water. If it floats the dough is ready, if it sinks beat the dough some more and test again. Spread about 2 tablespoons of dough in the center of the corn husk, fold the husk over the dough and fold the ends over at top and bottom. Cook in the usual way in a steamer that has a trivet or rack on the bottom and steam over moderate heat for an hour or longer. To test if the *tamal* is ready open one and see if the dough comes away from the husk. Steam longer if necessary. Make sure the water in the steamer does not boil away. Add boiling water if necessary. **MAKES 24 *TAMALES*.**

FRESH CORN *TAMALES*
Uchepos

When we were in Patzcuaro in Michoacán I did not realize how privileged I was to see and experience all that I did. Apart from César's United Nations position, there were old family friends, I think with UNESCO, so that few places were closed to us. I ate the white fish and we visited nearby villages, the spelling of whose names defeats me and we met, and made a lasting friendship with an American poet, Lysander Kemp, who returned to New England and did valuable work translating poetry including Octavio Paz. It was an exciting time for me caught up in a new marriage, and a land of brilliant color, and customs very different from my own. Even the meal hours which I had thought were eternal, fixed from above, 8 for breakfast, 1 for lunch and 8 for dinner. Seems a silly detail but later I researched the evolution of eating times in England and found how the world changes while remaining the same. It was the right time for *uchepos*, August I think, when the new corn is harvested and *uchepos*, made from ground fresh corn kernels are seasoned, usually sweetened and steamed in fresh corn leaves. My recipe, which is a slightly modified one, using less sugar, was given me by a friend who lived in Michoacán. I thought the *uchepos* were delicious, but then so was everything I ate.

4 cups corn kernels, if frozen, thoroughly defrosted, or if available, fresh corn cut off the cob

1 cup *masa harina*

½ cup lard, creamed

½ cup chicken broth, about

1 teaspoon granulated sugar

½ teaspoon salt

½ teaspoon baking powder

Put the corn kernels into a food processor and reduce to a smooth purée. Put the creamed lard into a large bowl and beat in the *masa harina* alternately with the chicken broth. Add the sugar, salt and baking powder. Gradually stir in the corn purée. Make *tamales* the usual way using 1½ tablespoons corn mixture to fill each corn husk. Set them in a steamer and cook for 1½-2 hours. Eat by themselves or with cheese or sour cream.
MAKES ABOUT 24 *TAMALES*.

TAMALES OAXACAN-STYLE
Tamal de Oaxaca

It is worth going to some trouble to find banana leaves as they lend a special flavor to the *tamales* steamed in them. I am told that aluminum foil lined with greaseproof paper makes a good substitute for banana leaves and I expect it is better than no *tamales* at all. I expect kitchen parchment would also serve. Just thinking of Oaxaca makes me long for a flat package of banana leaf with a Oaxacan *tamal* on it.

Make dough as for *Tamales* and Fillings (page 64)

Have ready 12 (10-inch) squares of banana leaves, softened in hot water (page 14)

1 whole chicken breast poached, boned, skinned and shredded, about 1½ cups

1½ cups *Mole Poblano* sauce

(In Oaxaca *Mole Negro Oaxaqueno* [Oaxacan Black *Mole*] would be used but the chilies for this are very hard to get so *Mole Poblano* substitutes very happily.)

Spread 2 tablespoons of dough in the center of each leaf, top with 2 tablespoons chicken and 2 tablespoons sauce, overlap the sides so that the dough covers the filling then fold down the top and bottom to form a square parcel. Tie, as for a parcel with strips of banana leaf, or with kitchen string. Stack the tamales on the rack in the steamer, top with a banana leaf, cover and steam for 1½ hours, until the dough comes away from the banana leaf. **MAKES 12 *TAMALES*.**

CHICKEN *TAMAL* PIE
Tamal de Cazuela con Pollo

For the filling:
6 *ancho* chilies
3½ lbs chicken, cut into serving pieces
1 onion, chopped
2 cloves garlic, chopped
1½ lbs tomatoes, peeled and chopped
2 oz chopped, blanched almonds
3 oz seedless raisins
2 tablespoons lard or corn oil
Salt

Toast the *anchos*, lightly on both sides in a dry pan, pull off the stems, shake out the seeds and tear in pieces. Put into a bowl with warm water to cover and soak for 30 minutes, turning from time to time. When ready to use, drain, reserving the soaking water for use if necessary.

Put the chicken pieces into a large saucepan with the breasts on top, pour in enough water barely to cover, bring to a simmer and cook until tender, about 45 minutes to 1 hour. Lift out and when cool enough to handle remove and discard skin and bones and cut the meat into medium-sized pieces. Set aside.

For the sauce: In a food processor combine the onion, garlic, tomatoes, almonds, raisins and prepared *anchos* and process to a fairly smooth purée. It should have some texture. In a frying pan heat the lard or oil and cook the purée, stirring, over moderate heat for 5 minutes. Season with salt. If it is necessary to thin the sauce a little, use the reserved soaking liquid from the *anchos*. Sauce should have the consistency of a medium white sauce.

For the dough:
½ cup lard
3 cups *masa harina*
1 teaspoon baking powder
½ teaspoon salt
½ cup light cream
½ cup chicken broth from cooking chicken

In a bowl cream the lard until it is very light and fluffy. Mix the dry ingredients together and beat into the lard. Gradually stir in the cream and chicken broth and beat until it is so light a small piece will float on top of a glass of water. Grease a 3½ pint casserole and line the sides and bottom with a layer of the dough. Arrange the chicken pieces in the center, add half the sauce, cover with the remaining dough. Bake in a preheated 350°F oven for 1 hour. Heat the remaining sauce and serve on the side.

VARIATION:

For Tamal de Cazuela con Puerco *(Pork Tamal Pie). Instead of chicken have 2½ lb boneless pork, simmered until tender and shredded. Make the sauce the same way but replace the almonds and raisins with ½ teaspoon ground coriander seeds, 1 teaspoon dried oregano, and 1 bay leaf, crumbled. Use stock from the pork instead of chicken stock.*

TAMAL PIE YUCATÁN-STYLE
Tamal de Cazuela, Estilo Yucateco

3½ lbs chicken, cut into serving pieces

2 onions, finely chopped

2 cloves garlic, chopped

1 lb tomatoes, peeled, seeded and chopped

6 *pequín* chilies, crumbled or any small dried red chili

1 tablespoon annatto, ground

½ teaspoon oregano

½ teaspoon ground cumin

Sprig *epazote*

Chicken stock

Tomato juice

Salt

Put all the ingredients into a large saucepan or casserole and pour in enough liquid (half chicken stock, half tomato juice) barely to cover, bring to a simmer, cover and simmer until the chicken is tender, 45 minutes to 1 hour. Lift out the chicken pieces and when cool enough to handle remove the skin and bones and cut the meat into fairly large pieces. Skim the fat from the broth then pour it through a sieve set over a large bowl or saucepan, pressing down to release all the juices from the vegetables. Measure, and if necessary add a mixture of chicken stock and tomato juice to bring the quantity up to 3 cups. Taste for seasoning and set aside.

Make the dough as for the other *Tamal de Cazuelas* (page 68). Line a casserole with the dough, arrange the chicken pieces in the center and moisten the chicken with the broth, cover with the remaining dough and bake in a preheated 350°F oven for 1 hour. Serve with the remaining sauce heated and if too thin thickened with a little *masa harina*. **SERVES 6.**

SAUCES
AND PICKLES

•

Salsas y Encurtidos

The Mexican kitchen is one of sauces. Meats, poultry and seafood are cooked in mixtures of stock, herbs and vegetables which cook down into a sauce, others like *Mole Poblano de Guajolote* are first cooked then steeped in the sauce, then there are the ubiquitous on-the-table sauces like *salsa cruda* (Fresh Tomato Sauce) and *salsa verde* (green sauce), and the store-bought bottled sauces like *Esta sí Pica* whose name tells that it is *picante*, it stings, and finally there is guacamole used to fill tortillas that are eaten as bread. It accompanies just about everything. Though *salsa* is simply the Spanish for "sauce" it early became attached to one particular Mexican sauce in the early days of U.S. settlement in California. It was just tomatoes, onion, sweet and hot peppers (chilies), salt, pepper, vinegar or lemon juice. Nowadays there are lots of *salsas* which are not Mexican but have a Mexican flavor using the characteristic ingredients of that country's sauces. They have a fascinating variety of flavors ranging from mild through pungent to hot and very hot. Even now so long after the Conquest little use is made of European foods such as flour, cream, butter and eggs for sauce making. Every region has its own sauces many of them inseparable from a special dish, many of them just variations of a standard sauce common throughout the Republic. Then there is *Adobo* which is not just a marinade but that is the nearest category to put it in.

The Mayan kitchen of Yucatán has its own sauces and seasonings, the *recados*. Whenever we managed to get to Mérida the capital of Yucatán to quench our insatiable desire to enlarge our knowledge of the Toltec-Maya ruins of Chichén Itzá and Uxmal we would also visit the Mérida market to buy *recados*, a combination of different spices in paste form not available in the markets in Mexico City. My favorite was *Recado Rojo*, sometimes called *Adobo de Achiote*. Another I liked was *Recado de Bistec*, mixed spices to go with meats, and *Recado Negro*, which I didn't buy. Its black color comes from toasting chilies until they are blackened. When we were no longer in Mexico kind friends brought us *Recado Rojo* and I found it would keep very well frozen. I tend to hoard it as I do with hard-to-get special foods and here the freezer is an encouragement not always for the best. Fortunately more and more things are available. I can remember when annatto (*achiote*) was not available in the shops even though it was imported in liquid form to color cheeses such as Cheddar, among other things. The recipes here are as near as I can get them to the taste of the *recados* that so captivated my palate in the early days of my marriage, as not content with falling in love with my husband I fell in love with Yucatán and all things Maya. To this day I have *huipils*, the loose blouse-like garment that is part of the Mayan native dress and still widely worn. Hoarded to be sure.

Once we were told about a *caracol*, the ruin of a Maya observatory outside Cuernavaca, and went there. A young man told us he was the guardian and he guarded the site with enthusiasm and a rifle. He also assumed the role of tourist guide and pointing to the *caracol* announced "now you can see the way the Maya built their ruins." We agreed that they built ruins very well indeed. They certainly were great astronomers and once walking at night down a road flanking the ruins of Chichén Itzá I could understand why. We could not stop staring upward as the stars blazed out of the blackness of the sky. I saw stars like that once in Egypt but today sadly the sky above most big cities is starless since there is too much light to let us see them.

Demi-Glace
Jugo de Carne

One of the great mysteries in my early days learning about Mexican food was my mother-in-law's reference to *Jugo de Carne*. Knowing no Spanish when I arrived and having a mother-in-law whose English was as sparse as my Spanish, posed problems, but I could and did work out that *Jugo de Carne* was Meat Juice. Beyond that I advanced no further. My husband, even with his encyclopaedic knowledge of Mexican food, didn't know. Friends didn't know, and neither did that other great fund of knowledge, the maids. I tried that terror of the trans-oceanic liner, beef tea, once experienced never forgotten, but it was not that. Years passed and so, eventually did Elena, my mother-in-law. And then, out of the blue, came the answer. A remote cousin of my husband, one of those third cousins twice removed sort of cousins, knowing how this had been nagging at me, not surprisingly since I nagged at everyone in ear- or pen-shot, found the answer in an old colonial cookbook and sent it to me. *Jugo de Carne* is nothing more than a colonial kitchen demi-glace. At least that is what it seems to me. *Sauce Espagnole*, brown sauce, is reduced to a thick, almost syrupy consistency and is then used as an enrichment in a variety of dishes. My *jugo* differs from demi-glace in detail and method though not in spirit. I just wish Elena was here so that I could tell her that I know what she means when she speaks of *Jugo de Carne*. I know that my husband's uncle, General Eulogio Ortiz, a fine soldier and a considerable gourmet, had a French chef. Did he fire Elena's imagination with *glace de viande*? Or is this an inheritance from the brief reign of Maximilian and Carlota when so much that was French in the kitchen was brought to Mexico, including the excellent bread? In Mexico lard would have been used but I prefer to use butter or oil.

2 tablespoons unsalted butter

1 onion, finely chopped

1 leek, cleaned and chopped

2 carrots, peeled and chopped

1½ lbs lean, chopped beefsteak (best very lean mince)

¾ lb tomatoes, peeled and chopped

Salt, freshly ground black pepper

Heat the butter in a heavy frying pan and sauté the onion, leek, carrots until the onion is soft. Add the beef and cook, stirring from time to time to break up any lumps until the beef is well browned. Add the tomatoes and continue to cook until the mixture is well blended. Season very lightly with salt and to taste with pepper. Put through a fine sieve, pressing down to extract all the juice and flavor. Use to enrich other dishes, and sauces. **MAKES ABOUT 1 CUP.**

NOTE

It would be a good idea to reduce the sauce to a purée in a food processor and then push it through a sieve, that way more of the juice will be retained.

GUACAMOLE

My first and abiding interest in Mexico's universal sauce, guacamole, came in a roundabout sort of way. I met the avocado in Jamaica where I was at school for a while. Avocados were an exciting and exotic fruit to us young English children. They were green-skinned, quite large and buttery, in fact they were known to the 16th century English navy in the islands as "Midshipman's Butter." Later in Mexico I had to defend them against my husband's Aunt Tere who insisted they were male avocados, *pawas*, which she held in huge contempt. They were to be avoided at all cost if encountered in the market, large, with smooth green skins and watery, tasteless flesh. Indeed I did find such avocados in the market but they were not like our Jamaican ones. But the desirable local ones were small with purple skins and creamy flesh with a hint of anise.

It is believed that the avocado (*Persea americana*) was cultivated as far back as 7000 B.C. and that guacamole came into existence not long after that. The first version may have been simply mashed avocado, perhaps with a little coriander, *Eryngium foetidum* now happily replaced by *Coriandrum sativum* a gentler, milder relative of the herb. At some point the tomato was introduced, clearly a latecomer. The first tomato used may have been the little husk tomato, *tomatillo* (*Physalis ixocarpa*). It is conjectural but with a dish that has endured as long as guacamole, who knows? People still rate a good guacamole by the amount of avocado to tomato, as avocados are more expensive than the abundant tomato. It is the equivalent of the other economy or emergency measure to deal with unexpected guests, watering the beans. I don't know when onion and garlic became part of the recipe as there were wild versions around before Columbus, and chilies were cultivated at the same date as the avocado, so presumably they were used as they are integral to the cuisine. As for lime juice, I have frowned on its use, though many highly respected authorities use it. I think when I could not get the right fresh chili I used *chile en escabeche*, and the amount of vinegar in the pickled chili was just enough to make lime juice unecessary. I still think lime juice is too strongly flavored, though it may hinder darkening. I prefer to make guacamole at the last minute so this is not important. There is a superstition that putting an avocado pit into a bowl of guacamole will keep it from darkening. It won't. Covering the bowl with cling film helps a little, so does refrigerating the sauce.

Avocados are marketed unripe and hard. The best way to ripen them is to put them in a brown paper bag in a dark warm place. They are ripe when they yield to gentle pressure at the stem end. This may take up to five days.

I remember when shopping in Medellín market, and seeking out our usual supplier, my husband and I had a lesson in the economics of the fruit. She was sitting on the floor of the covered market in her traditional blouse, full skirt and *rebozo*, her hair in plaits, her merchandise, four small pyramids of avocados in front of her. The price had jumped 12½% overnight. She said the price increase was because the peso had been devalued by that amount. I said that regarding her goods nothing had changed, they weren't imported, and so on, the usual arguments devaluation spawned. The logic of her answer was impeccable. "Señora," she told me, "that is not relevant. If I wish to buy a Rolls Royce it will cost me at least 12½% more in this poor devalued currency, so I must put up the price of what I sell if I am to be able to buy imported goods." I asked if she was planning to buy a Rolls Royce in the near future and she said probably not, but it was wise to be prepared. I paid up with no more quibbling. At that time the blender had arrived and relieved domestic cooks of a great deal of kitchen drudgery, as it is no fun grinding chilies, seeds and nuts on a *metate*, a sloping piece of volcanic rock on three legs, with a *mano*, a grinding stone. But when it came to making guacamole I rejected the use of the blender and later of the food processor. I worked out my own way of mashing avocados though many households and restaurants use the traditional *molcajete* and *tejolote*, the Aztec mortar and pestle of volcanic stone. I cut the avocado in half lengthways and discard the pit unless I am planning to grow it into a plant. I hold a half avocado in my left hand and mash the flesh with a fork then scoop it into a bowl. Same with the other half. This way I get a smooth purée with some texture not a featureless pap. A few errant bits of avocado may evade the fork but they are easy enough to capture in the bowl where the halved avocado would slither and slide about and be a big nuisance to mash. Even the name of this sauce/salad/dip is ancient coming from the Nahuatl words *ahuacatl* (avocado) and *molli* (sauce).

2 large avocados

1 tomato, peeled, seeded and chopped

½ small white onion, finely chopped

2 or more canned *serrano* chilies, chopped

1 tablespoon chopped coriander leaves

Salt

Mash the avocados into a bowl and mix with the other ingredients. Season to taste with salt and serve immediately.

MAKES ABOUT 3 CUPS.

VARIATION:

Guacamole del Norte *(Guacamole, Northern-style). Make as above but substitute 4 oz canned* tomatillos, *drained and mashed for the tomato. Many of our northern family and friends liked this version of guacamole for a change of pace.*

PICKLE SAUCE
Adobo

The literal translation of *adobo* into "pickle sauce" hardly does justice to the myriad of flavors *adobo* encompasses. It seemed to me that every cook I met in Mexico had an *adobo* that was the best and only one, until I finally worked out my own version but I would never claim it to be either unique or best. I was helped and guided by the family cook, my own cook, and the cooks of friends. I grasped the essentials, that it must have chilies, garlic, vinegar, salt and herbs and spices. Though this is not just a marinade, recipes that are *en Adobo* means that a meat or fish is cooked in the sauce with added liquid, usually stock, while *Adobado* means that meat or fish is coated with the *adobo* then grilled, fried or baked.

8 *guajillo* chilies

6 cloves garlic, chopped

⅛ teaspoon ground cloves

1 teaspoon annatto (*achiote*), ground

½ teaspoon ground cinnamon

½ teaspoon black peppercorns, ground

½ teaspoon ground cumin

1 teaspoon salt

½ cup mild white vinegar

3 tablespoons corn or peanut oil

Toast the chilies in a dry frying pan, preferably cast iron, turning to toast both sides. Do not let them burn. When cool enough to handle, pull off the stems and shake out the seeds. Tear into pieces and put into a bowl with hot water just to cover, soak for 15 minutes then transfer to a food processor. Add the garlic, cloves, *achiote*, cinnamon, peppercorns, cumin, salt and vinegar and process to a paste. If necessary add up to 2 tablespoons of the water in which the chilies were soaked.

In a frying pan heat the oil and sauté the paste over low heat, stirring, for 3-4 minutes. Transfer to a jar or non-metal container until ready to use. It will keep indefinitely, refrigerated. **MAKES ABOUT 1 CUP.**

VARIATION:

If liked substitute ½ teaspoon each oregano and thyme for the achiote.

COUNTRY-STYLE SAUCE
Salsa Ranchera

This sauce is always used for *Huevos Rancheros* (Country-style Eggs) (page 136), a dish that is almost as evocative of Mexico as *Mole Poblano de Guajolote* (Turkey *Mole* Puebla-style). It need not be confined to its traditional role. It is good with taco fillings and anywhere a rich, smooth tomato sauce is needed.

2 tablespoons corn or peanut oil

1 lb tomatoes, peeled, seeded and finely chopped

1-2 *jalapeño* or 2-3 *serrano* chilies, seeded and finely chopped

Salt, freshly ground black pepper, pinch sugar

Heat the oil in a frying pan and add the tomatoes and chilies and cook over low heat, stirring from time to time, until the tomatoes are reduced to a thick purée with the tomato juices evaporated. Season to taste with salt, pepper and the pinch of sugar, stir to mix.

MAKES ABOUT 1½ CUPS.

CHIPOTLE CHILI SAUCE
Salsa de Chile Chipotle

The *chipotle* is the ripe *jalapeño*, smoked, and gets its name from the Nahuatl for "smoked chili." It is very hot with a quite extraordinary taste, impossible to describe but which grows on one. I am still amazed that the *jalapeño*, always a favorite chili, can change its character so totally when ripe and smoked.

2 tablespoons corn or peanut oil

1 onion, finely chopped

1 clove garlic, chopped

1 lb tomatoes, peeled and chopped

½ teaspoon oregano, crumbled

4-6 canned *chipotle* chilies, seeded and chopped

Salt

Heat the oil in a frying pan and sauté the onion and garlic until the onion is soft. Lift out into a food processor, add the rest of the ingredients and process to a purée. Return the mixture to the frying pan and cook in the remaining oil, stirring from time to time until the mixture is thick and well blended. Taste for seasoning and transfer to a bowl. Serve with any all-purposely cooked meat, especially grilled meats.
MAKES ABOUT 2 CUPS.

YUCATÁN HOT CHILI SAUCE
Ixni-Pec

Pronounced roughly *schnee-peck*, this is the hottest of the chili sauces made in Mexico. It is Mayan and is much hotter than anything the Aztecs have, as it uses the pretty lantern-shaped *habañero* which combines heat with an exquisite flavor. It appears on dining tables through the peninsula in small bowls to be added to food with discretion. The chilies, often available in Caribbean markets, are sometimes called Scotch Bonnets.

1 onion, very finely chopped

½ large tomato, peeled and chopped

2 oz yellow *habañero* chilies, finely chopped

½ cup Seville (bitter) orange juice

Salt

Mix together the onion, tomato, and chilies in a bowl and pour in the Seville (bitter) orange juice. Season to taste with salt.

This is best eaten fresh but will keep for a day to two refrigerated.

MAKES ABOUT 2 CUPS.

VARIATION:

Salsa Picante *(Hot Sauce) is even hotter than* Ixni-Pec. *Choose green* habañeros *and toast and peel them. Seed the chilies and chop them very fine, season with a little salt and mix with enough Seville (bitter) orange juice to make a rather soupy mixture which should not be too runny. There is no substitute for Seville orange juice capturing its unique flavor. Possible substitutes are two-thirds orange juice to one-third lime juice, or orange and grapefruit juice in equal amounts mixed together.*

FRESH TOMATO SAUCE
Salsa Cruda

A bowl of this fresh, crunchy sauce is always on the Mexican table. It is appropriate to every meal from breakfast to supper. It is good with eggs, meats, poultry, fish, beans and in tacos and on *tostadas*. Some cooks leave the tomatoes unpeeled, some leave the seeds in the *serrano* chilies making the sauce quite hot. The family peeled, but never seeded the tomatoes, and always seeded the chilies. I follow their rules.

2 large tomatoes, peeled and chopped fine

2-3 *serrano* chilies, seeded and finely chopped

1 small onion, finely chopped

1 tablespoon fresh coriander, chopped

Salt

Mix all the ingredients together in a bowl, taste for seasoning and serve cold. This is best made at the last minute but can be made two or three hours ahead of time.

MAKES ABOUT 2½ CUPS.

GREEN SAUCE
Salsa Verde

I think this is the most enticing of all the sauces, its flavor unique. I miss it when I cannot get the little green husk tomatoes, *tomatillos,* fresh or canned. It is as often on the table as *salsa cruda.*

1 10-oz can Mexican green tomatoes (*tomatillos*), drained

1 small white onion, finely chopped

1 clove garlic, chopped

2 or more *serrano* chilies, if pickled, rinsed and chopped

1 tablespoon fresh coriander, chopped

Salt, pinch of sugar

Combine all the ingredients in a food processor and process for a second or two. Be careful not to over process. If preferred, mix and mash thoroughly. The sauce is best freshly made. **MAKES ABOUT 1½ CUPS.**
VARIATION:
Make the sauce above but omit the onion and garlic. Double the coriander to 2 tablespoons. Makes about 1 cup.

COOKED GREEN TOMATO SAUCE
Salsa Verde Cocida

This is a popular on-the-table sauce all over Mexico though *salsa verde cruda* is often preferred. It is hard to choose as both are delicious. It can be added to almost anything in the corn kitchen and may be added to any all-purposely cooked meat, poultry or fish. *Tomatillos* are seldom available fresh but the canned ones are very good. They should be drained and then measured.

2 cups Mexican green tomatoes (*tomatillos*)

1 small onion, chopped

1 clove garlic, chopped

2-3 *serrano* chilies, or 2 *jalapeño* chilies, seeded and chopped

2 tablespoons fresh coriander, chopped

1 tablespoon corn or peanut oil

Salt

In a food processor combine the *tomatillos*, onion, garlic, chilies and coriander and process to a purée. It should not be too smooth but retain some texture. Season to taste with salt. Heat the oil in a frying pan and cook the purée, over low heat, stirring from time to time, for about 5 minutes until it is slightly thickened. Cool and use.

MAKES ABOUT 2 CUPS.

TOMATO SAUCE
Salsa de Jitomate

This is a most useful sauce and reminds me all over again of the value of Mexico's food gifts to the world, though there is some controversy as to whether Mexico or Peru is the true birthplace of the fruit. I'm firmly in the Mexican camp on this one, though it is the sauce that matters. It takes little time to make and has a fresh flavor. It goes with eggs, steak, tortilla dishes from *Chilaquiles* to tacos, and fish and shellfish. Every region of Mexico has its own version using different chilies and herbs but all share the basic characteristic, a simplicity of cooking method and a delicious taste.

2 tablespoons corn or peanut oil

1 onion, finely chopped

1 clove garlic, chopped

1 lb tomatoes, peeled and chopped

¼ teaspoon granulated sugar

2 or more fresh *serrano* chilies, chopped

Salt

1 tablespoon fresh coriander, chopped

In a frying pan heat the oil and sauté the onion and garlic until the onion is soft. Add the tomatoes, sugar, chilies and salt and simmer over low heat, stirring from time to time, until the sauce is well blended and thickened. Stir in the coriander and cook for a minute or two longer. Use hot or cold.

MAKES ABOUT 2 CUPS.

STRIPS OF *POBLANO* CHILI
Rajas de Chile Poblano

One of the first restaurant meals I had in Mexico was a dish called *Carne Asada con Rajas* (Grilled Beef with Chili Strips). I fell in love with it and ate it with beans and guacamole so persistently it began to irritate my husband's family, one of whom asserted that so much beef, so much chili would "*me hace daño*" do me harm. It didn't but I did set off to find what was the taste on which I had become so totally hooked. It was the *chile poblano*, the dark, almost black green tapering pepper that is quite large, about 3 x 5 inches, that when ripe and dried turns into the *chile ancho*. They are the chilies used for stuffing and though usually mild can be quite *picante*. Their name gives their origin, *poblano* from the State of Puebla but they are widely grown in north and central Mexico. I can't describe the flavor except to say it is rich and subtle. I also found out the origin of the dish. It should have been called *Carne Asada a la Tampiqueña* (Grilled Beef in the Tampico Style) and was invented in the 1930's by José Laredo, a restaurateur from Tampico who introduced it to Mexico City. I hope one day *poblanos* will be available more widely than they are now.

6 fresh *poblano* chilies, roasted and peeled (page 18)

3 tablespoons corn or peanut oil

1 onion, thinly sliced

2 cloves garlic, chopped

½ teaspoon salt, or to taste

Remove the seeds and stems from the chilies and cut them into strips about 1½ inch long and ½ inch wide. In a frying pan heat the oil and sauté the onion until it is tender. Add the garlic and the chili strips, cover the pan and cook over low heat for about 6 minutes. Season with salt and serve.
SERVES 6.

PICKLED ONION RINGS
Cebolla Escabechada

Traditionally used in Yucatán to garnish *panuchos* or *Cochinita Pibil* (Yucatecan Barbecued Pig), they turn up with many other dishes in Yucatán. And as with many other dishes there are a number of versions, all basically the same but all slightly different. This is my favorite. The variations are almost as delicious.

1 onion, sliced very thin (⅛ inch)

Salt

3 fresh *serrano* chilies, seeded and sliced fine

⅛ teaspoon oregano, crumbled

1 bay leaf

⅛ teaspoon ground cumin

1 clove garlic, chopped

Soak the sliced onion in salted water for 5 minutes. Drain and transfer to a saucepan with the remaining ingredients and ½ cup water. Bring to the boil over moderate heat, remove from the heat immediately and leave to cool. The pickled onion is then ready to eat.

MAKES ABOUT 1 CUP.

VARIATION:
Red onions are often preferred to white ones and a chili habañero *to serrano. Some cooks leave out the chilies and season the pickle with ground black peppercorns instead.*

PICKLED CHILIES WITH VEGETABLES
Chiles en Escabeche

These are always on the table in Mexico to be eaten as a relish with whatever takes one's fancy. They enliven all-purposely cooked meat or poultry and as usual in this cuisine the recipe is not static. Any vegetable such as green beans, broccoli or zucchini can be used, following the method. One day, when we were living in New York, my husband brought home a jar of pickled vegetables given him by a Haitian colleague. It was called *Picklises* and was made of carrot, green beans, and so on pickled with some hot red chili peppers, almost certainly *habañeros*. Clearly good ideas travel.

2 tablespoons olive oil

½ onion, thickly sliced

1 carrot, peeled and sliced

6 cloves garlic

¼ lb *serrano* or *jalapeño* chilies, whole

½ cup mild white vinegar

½ teaspoon salt

1 bay leaf, halved

1 teaspoon mixed dried thyme and oregano

In a frying pan heat the oil and add the onion, carrot, garlic and chilies and sauté over moderate heat, turning from time to time until the onion and carrot are tender, about 10 minutes. Add ¼ cup water, the vinegar, salt, bay leaf and herbs and bring to a simmer. Cover and cook for 5 minutes longer. Cool and pack into a sterilized jar and refrigerate for a day or 2 before using. **MAKES ABOUT 2 CUPS.**

DRUNKEN SAUCE
Salsa Borracha

This sauce is always served with *barbacoa* (page 245) in which the *pencas* of *agave* are used to line the earth oven giving a tequila flavor. The drunken part of the sauce is *pulque*, also made from the maguey (*agave*). *Pulque* is not available outside Mexico but either beer or tequila are adequate substitutes. The traditional chili to use is the *pasilla* which is dried, wrinkled, dark brown, *picante* and slender, about 6 inches long and not much more than 1½ inches wide.

8 *pasilla* chilies

¼ cup white tequila

2 cloves garlic, chopped

2 tablespoons onion, chopped

Salt

1 cup orange juice

1 tablespoon corn oil

Toast the chilies in a dry cast iron frying pan over low heat, turning from time to time, until they are softened. Do not let them burn. As soon as they are

cool enough to handle remove the stems, shake out the seeds, and tear in pieces. Put them into a bowl and pour the tequila over them. Let them soak for 30 minutes then transfer them to a food processor with the tequila, garlic, onion and orange juice and process to a fairly smooth sauce. Season with salt. Heat the oil in a frying pan, add the sauce and cook for about 5 minutes. Cool to room temperature and serve. If liked add a dash more tequila.
MAKES ABOUT 1¼ CUPS.

GUAJILLO CHILI SAUCE
Salsa de Chile Guajillo

This sauce comes from the north central states of Durango, Aguascalientes and San Luis Potosí where the chili is mostly cultivated but it is used in cooking all over the Republic in soups and stews. It is a deceptive chili as it can be mild or hot. The taste is distinctive but most of all it adds a bright red color to foods it is cooked with.

4 *guajillo* chilies
1 large tomato, peeled and chopped
½ onion, finely chopped
1 clove garlic, chopped
1½ cups chicken stock
Salt

Toast the chilies lightly in a dry frying pan, ideally a cast iron one. Remove from the pan, cool, remove the stems, shake out the seeds and tear into pieces. Put into a bowl with hot water to cover and soak for 15 minutes. Put into a food processor with the tomato, onion and garlic and process to a purée. Transfer to a saucepan with the chicken stock, stir and simmer over low heat for 5 minutes. Season to taste with salt and serve with all-purposely cooked meats or with *antojitos*. **MAKES ABOUT 2 CUPS.**

GREEN ALMOND SAUCE
Salsa de Almendra Verde

The Mexican green tomatoes, *tomatillos*, and fresh coriander combine with the *serrano* chilies to give this sauce an exquisite flavor unlike anything in other cuisines. Use it with delicate meats, veal and chicken, not anything strongly flavored.

3 tablespoons olive oil

1 slice firm white bread

¼ cup blanched almonds

10-oz can *tomatillos*, **drained**

2 tablespoons fresh coriander, chopped

1-2 canned *serrano* **chilies, seeded and chopped**

1½ cups chicken stock

Salt

Heat the oil in a frying pan and fry the bread over moderate heat until it is golden on both sides. Lift out, drain on kitchen towels and chop coarsely. In the oil remaining in the pan sauté the almonds until they are golden. Drain and chop coarsely. In a food processor combine the bread, almonds, *tomatillos*, coriander, and chilies and process until smooth. Pour into a saucepan, add the chicken stock, season to taste with salt, bring to a simmer and cook over low heat for 5 minutes, stirring from time to time.

MAKES ABOUT 2 CUPS.

The sauce will keep, refrigerated, for about 1 week.

RED ALMOND SAUCE
Salsa de Almendra Roja

This is rather more robust than its green counterpart. It is excellent over hot, drained green vegetables and over most plainly cooked fish and meat except beef which is too strongly flavored for the sauce.

3 tablespoons olive oil

1 slice firm white bread

1 onion, finely chopped

1 clove garlic, chopped

¼ cup blanched almonds

½ teaspoon chili *pequín*, **or other dried red chili**

¼ teaspoon oregano, crumbled

1 tomato, peeled and chopped

1½ cups chicken stock

Salt, pinch sugar

Heat the oil in a frying pan and fry the bread over moderate heat until it is golden on both sides. Lift out, drain on kitchen towels and chop coarsely. In the oil remaining in the pan sauté the onion, garlic, almonds and chilies until the onion is soft. Transfer to a food processor with the bread, oregano and tomato and process to a smooth purée. Pour into a saucepan, stir in the chicken stock, season with salt and sugar, bring to a simmer and cook over low heat, stirring from time to time, for about 10 minutes.

MAKES ABOUT 2 CUPS.

The sauce will keep, refrigerated, for about 1 week.

SEASONING FOR BEEF
Recado de Bistec

I don't know why this is called beef steak seasoning as it is much more widely used than that. I've used it in *Pollo en Escabeche* (Pickled Chicken) and whenever else it seemed appropriate. It is useful in the way I find *Aliño Preparado* (Prepared Seasoning) from Venezuela is. That has cumin, annatto, paprika and oregano in its ingredients.

8 cloves garlic, crushed

½ teaspoon ground cinnamon

¼ teaspoon ground cloves

½ teaspoon ground cumin

½ teaspoon ground allspice

1 teaspoon ground black peppercorns

1 teaspoon dried oregano, crumbled

1 tablespoon mild white vinegar

½ teaspoon salt

Combine all the ingredients in a small bowl, mixing well. Transfer to a glass jar or other covered container and refrigerate until ready to use.

MAKES ABOUT ¼ CUP.

Keeps indefinitely refrigerated.

ANNATTO SEASONING PASTE
Recado Rojo

Annatto, *achiote* in Spanish-speaking countries, are the seeds of a small flowering tree of tropical America, *Bixa orellana*. The hard orange pulp surrounding the seeds colors food an orange red, while the seeds give added flavor. The best way to grind the seeds is with a spice or coffee grinder.

1 tablespoon annatto (*achiote*), finely ground

1 teaspoon ground black peppercorns

½ teaspoon dried oregano, crumbled

½ teaspoon ground cumin

4 cloves garlic, crushed

½ teaspoon salt

1 tablespoon mild white vinegar

In a bowl combine all the ingredients, mixing thoroughly. Transfer to a jar or container, cover and store in the refrigerator until ready to use according to recipe instructions. It will keep indefinitely.

MAKES ABOUT ¼ CUP.

SOUPS

•

Sopas

Soup is important in the Mexican kitchen. I learned early that a Mexican cookbook begins the soup chapter with *manera de hacer a buen caldo*, how to make a good stock, and I never met anyone of whatever age or experience who did not have a stockpot with a simmering bird or beast creating a delicious base for a dinnertime soup. It is a must for the main meal, *comida*, at the middle of the day, that is at about three in the afternoon or perhaps even later, no matter if the weather is hot. Chicken stock was easily transformed into a delicious light soup with the addition of rice or chick peas, shredded chicken, a slice or two of avocado, perhaps strips of chili and some coriander sprigs. No two cooks will improvise a chicken soup in exactly the same way, but it will always be flavorful and attractive. Restaurants serving the *comida corrida*, the set menu, always begin with soup, soup can even be served to liven up the light supper meal, *merienda*. I began to learn about the regional specialties like *Sopa de Lima* from Yucatán using the special little lime of the region, *Caldo Miche* the fish soup made with the *pescado blanco* from Lake Patzcuaro in Michoacán, involving exciting travels to learn about my husband's country. And I found out that I had a great deal to learn.

I did puzzle over the deep and universal popularity of soup. I knew from earlier travels in Spain and Portugal that soup is esteemed in these countries as indeed it is everywhere, but not with the fervor that it evokes in Mexico. The Franciscan friar Bernadhino de Sahagún tells us in his monumental work, *Historia General de las Cosas de Nueva Espana* (*A General History of the Things of New Spain*) of the cooked foods he found in the central market in Tenochtitlán, the capital of Mexico before the Spanish destroyed it. Great earthenware pots full of poultry or seafood simmered with a mixture of herbs, vegetables, tomatoes and chilies, an admirable method suited to the high plateau where water boils at a much lower temperature than at sea level. At almost 8,000 feet nothing overcooks. These are really pot-au-feu dishes, soup-stews. I came to the conclusion that soup was integral to the Mexican eating pattern. These were the Aztecs, but what of the other great civilization, the Mayan Empire? The answer took longer to find but I finally found it in Sophie D. Coe's book, *America's First Cuisines*. The Maya included soup in their main meal of the day!

Today's kitchen has evolved from the soups of 16th century Spain and Portugal, and Aztec and Mayan Mexico, with introduced and local ingredients, and influenced eventually by modern kitchen tools like the blender and food processor. Spanish classics like *Sopa de Ajo* (garlic soup) have persisted. *Yucatán Sopa de Lima* is still the classic soup of the peninsula. Today's cooks have a rich and varied choice. These are known as the *Sopas Aguadas* (the liquid soups) and are followed in the *comida* by the oddly named *Sopas Secas* (the dry soups).

CHICKEN STOCK
Caldo de Pollo

In Mexico we always used a boiling fowl that my *criada*, maid, got from the market. It always had the feet which went into the stock pot to improve the texture. Now that boiling fowl are not readily available I have found substitutes. First it was necks and backs when I was in New York but now I use chicken carcasses which give a well flavored delicate stock, especially if there is a good deal of meat left on the bones.

2 lbs chicken carcasses

16 cups cold water

1 onion, thinly sliced

1 small carrot, peeled and sliced

1 celery rib, chopped

1 clove garlic

8 whole peppercorns

1 leek, trimmed and halved lengthwise

Few sprigs parsley

Salt

Put all the ingredients, except the salt, into a soup kettle and bring to a simmer over moderate to low heat. Cover and simmer over low heat for 3 hours. Cool then refrigerate and remove the fat. Strain through a fine sieve and discard the solids, season with salt. Use as the base for any soup or sauce calling for chicken stock, or serve as a light soup with the addition of a little rice, chick peas, or sliced avocado, and herbs like coriander or *epazote*. The stock freezes well. **MAKES ABOUT 5½ PINTS.**

BEEF STOCK
Caldo Sencillo

The family cook Herlinda set great store by a good *caldo sencillo*, using a mix of beef and bones and always including a big marrow bone and time, allowing 4 hours simmering. She used the stock for soups, stews and sauces. My mother-in-law talked of something she called *jugo de carne*—meat juice—but we never found out what it was and the cook didn't know. It could not have been better tasting than Herlinda's *caldo*.

2 lbs beef shank

2 lbs meaty beef bones

1 large marrow bone

16 cups cold water

1 medium carrot, peeled and sliced

1 small turnip, peeled and sliced

1 onion, thinly sliced

2 cloves garlic

1 leek, trimmed and halved lengthwise

1 celery rib, chopped

Few sprigs parsley

Bay leaf

6 whole peppercorns

Salt

Have the beef and bones cut into 3 inch pieces. Leave the marrow bone whole. Combine them in a soup kettle with the water, cover and simmer for an hour. Skim if necessary. For a browner stock, sear the meat in hot oil before adding it to the kettle. Add all the remaining ingredients except the salt, cover and simmer over low heat for another 3 hours. Season to taste with salt, cool, refrigerate, and remove the fat. Strain through a fine sieve and discard the solids. Refrigerate or freeze until ready to use.
MAKES ABOUT 5½ PINTS.

To Clarify Stock:
6 cups stock skimmed of all fat
2 large egg whites, beaten

Whisk the egg whites into the cold stock in a saucepan and place over very low heat. Beat constantly with a wire whisk until the stock comes to a simmer. Remove from the heat and let it stand for 15 minutes. Line a colander with 2 or 3 layers of damp cheesecloth and stand it over a large bowl. Pour the stock very gently into the colander and let the clarified stock drain into the bowl. **MAKES ABOUT 4 CUPS.**

The stock freezes well but takes a considerable time to thaw. I freeze it in 2½ cup containers for convenience.

AVOCADO SOUP

A beautiful pale green color and a butter richness makes this very special. It can be served either hot or cold and it takes little time to make. There are just two rules to observe, don't let it boil and don't make it ahead of time as it will discolor. If it does, just stir in the dark portion, it will not affect the flavor. If it must stand, cover it closely to minimize the discoloring.

2 large ripe avocados
6 cups rich chicken stock, skimmed of all fat
For garnish:
1 tablespoon fresh coriander, finely chopped
6 tortillas, quartered and fried crisp in oil

Halve the avocados, discard the pits and mash and scoop out the flesh. Transfer to a food processor and reduce to a smooth purée. If serving hot transfer to a warmed soup tureen. Meantime heat the chicken stock to boiling and whisk into the avocado. Stir to mix, garnish with the coriander and serve with the tortillas. If serving the soup cold, stir chilled stock into the avocado purée and garnish. **SERVES 6.**

VARIATION:
If liked reduce the stock by 1 cup and add the same amount of heavy or sour cream. If serving soup hot, heat with the stock.

CORN SOUP WITH SWEET RED PEPPERS
Sopa de Elote con Pimientos

The peppers used in this soup are not red bell peppers but a slightly sweeter more delicately flavored Mexican one, the *pimiento*. Grown and used extensively in Spain they are often available ready prepared, that is peeled and seeded, in jars or cans. Though peeling the peppers is a little tedious (see note on *poblano*, page 18) it is worth the trouble as the flavor of the finished soup is immeasurably improved. The soup came to me from my Oaxacan cook, Francisca, who was infinitely creative in the kitchen.

3 *pimientos*, peeled, seeded and chopped

1 onion, chopped

1 lb corn kernels, if frozen, thawed

3 tablespoons butter or corn oil

4 cups chicken stock

Salt

½ cup heavy cream

Sweet paprika for garnish

In a food processor combine the *pimientos*, onion and corn and process to a purée. Heat the butter or oil in a saucepan, add the purée and cook, stirring from time to time over low heat for 5 minutes. Add the chicken stock, season with salt if necessary, and simmer over low heat for 10-15 minutes to blend the flavors. Remove from the heat, whisk in the cream and return to the heat just long enough to heat the soup through. Serve in soup bowls and sprinkle with sweet paprika, if liked. **SERVES 6.**

FRESH CORN SOUP
Sopa de Elote

I once cooked this soup for a dinner party and it was as well I had made a lot of it as, for the first time ever at this sort of meal my guests, British, American and one French, all asked for more. It is a delightful soup, subtly flavored, smooth and rich, dotted with little flecks of chili. *Poblanos* give the best results but the green chilies which are also called California green chilies are also good, and are usually mild.

4 cups corn kernels, if frozen, defrosted

1 onion, chopped

3 tablespoons butter

Salt

4 cups chicken stock

1 cup sour cream

6 tablespoons chopped cottage or cream cheese

2 *poblano* chilies, peeled, seeded and diced, or canned California green chilies, chopped

Combine the corn kernels and the onion in a food processor and process to a purée. Heat the butter in a saucepan, add the purée and cook over moderate heat, stirring, for 5 minutes. Stir in the chicken stock and season with salt if necessary. Simmer, over low heat, for 10 minutes longer. Stir in the sour cream and simmer for a few minutes longer. When ready to serve, strain the soup. Have ready 6 soup bowls, each with a tablespoon of cheese and about 2 teaspoons chili, and pour in the soup which sould be the consistency of heavy cream. **SERVES 4.**

NORTHERN-STYLE CORN SOUP
Sopa de Elote del Norte

My husband's family came from the north and though I first met them in Mexico City this was the version of corn soup they preferred, following the recipe from their cook in Monterrey. They would sometimes have it with *jalapeño* chili, sometimes without and then my husband's uncle, Miguel Tinoco, would stir in a little *salsa cruda* or *salsa verde* from the always available bowl on the table saying he could not go without his good *vitamina ch* pronounced *chay* as he characterized chili. I have never been able to make up my mind which of the corn soups I prefer as I enjoy them all.

1 onion, finely chopped

1½ lbs tomatoes, peeled, seeded and chopped

1½ lbs corn kernels, if frozen, defrosted

½ *jalapeño* chili, seeded and chopped, or more to taste (optional)

2 tablespoons butter

3 cups chicken stock

½ cup heavy cream

Salt

Combine the onion, tomatoes, corn and chili, if using, in a food processor and reduce to a smooth purée. Heat the butter in a frying pan and cook the purée over low heat, stirring from time to time, for 5 minutes. Cool slightly and put through a sieve into a saucepan and stir in the stock. Season with salt if necessary and cook over low heat for 5 minutes to blend the flavors. Off the heat whisk in the cream then cook just long enough to heat the soup through. Garnish, if liked, with some whole, cooked corn kernels. **SERVES 6.**

SOUP TLALPAN-STYLE
Caldo Tlalpeño

A community on the outskirts of Mexico City, Tlalpan, gives its name to this soup, no one knows exactly why. You can get very good *barbacoa* there, and I remember enjoying some one Sunday when we were staying in Cuernavaca and had picked up some in Tlalpan on our way to enjoy lunch in our garden. The best guess for the soup's name is that it derives from the vegetable broth, *Consomme de Barbacoa* that is part of the cooking process when the meat, usually a whole lamb, is cooked in the earth oven with vegetables. There are many versions with small variations in the ingredients, all good, all hearty.

½ lb green beans, cut into 1-inch pieces

2 carrots, peeled and sliced crosswise

1 onion, chopped

1 clove garlic, chopped

6 cups chicken stock

1 cup cooked chick peas

Sprig *epazote* if available, or oregano

Salt

2 canned *chipotle* chilies, rinsed and seeded

1 avocado, peeled, pitted and sliced

1 cooked chicken breast, shredded

6 lime wedges

Put the beans, carrots, onion and garlic into a large saucepan with the stock, bring to a simmer and cook until the carrot is tender, about 15 minutes. Add the chick peas, *epazote* or oregano, salt to taste, and the chilies. Simmer just long enough to heat through and to flavor the stock, about 5 minutes. Remove the chilies, cut them into strips and reserve.

To serve pour the broth into 6 soup bowls, distributing the vegetables more or less equally. Add the chicken and garnish with the *chipotle* and avocado. Serve the lime wedges on the side. **SERVES 6.**

VARIATION:

This rather elegant version of the soup is from my maid Enriqueta. She used a whole canned chile largo *in hers, but I've found this hard to get and on her advice substituted a whole fresh* jalapeño *stem on.*

6 cups chicken stock

2 chicken breasts, cooked and cut into strips

1 fresh *jalapeño* chili, stem on

1 avocado, peeled, pitted and sliced

In a large saucepan combine the chicken stock, chicken breasts and *jalapeño* chili and simmer over very low heat, covered, for 5 minutes to heat the chicken through and release the flavor of the chili. Remove and discard the chili or keep for another use. Pour the soup into bowls, distributing the chicken strips equally. Garnish with the avocado. **SERVES 6.**

SWEET RED PEPPER SOUP
Sopa de Pimientos Morrones

The first soup I learned to make in Mexico and one of the best, came from Francisca, my first cook/maid who came to us from my mother-in-law, the best present she ever gave us. Francisca, a Zapotecan Indian from Oaxaca, was a tiny woman with long grey plaits framing a tranquil high cheekboned face. I now make the soup so that it tastes as it did when Francisca cooked. At first I tried short cuts, like using bell peppers that I did not peel. The flavor was good but not up to Francisca's standard. Now I make sure I get *pimientos morrones* which are Spain's favorite Mexican sweet red pepper. *Pimiento* is just the Spanish for pepper but the term is widely used for this deep red, tapering pepper. Toasting and peeling them is a vital step but they are often available in jars or cans ready peeled and seeded. The soup has a deep rich red color and a subtle flavor.

3 tablespoons corn or peanut oil

1 onion, finely chopped

4 sweet red peppers (*pimientos morrones*)

6 cups chicken stock

1 tablespoon tomato purée

Salt, freshly ground black pepper

Heat the oil in a small frying pan and sauté the onion until it is soft. Transfer to a bowl and set aside. Toast and peel the peppers according to the instructions on page 18, as for *poblano*. Seed and chop coarsely and combine in a food processor with the onion and process to a smooth purée. For a very smooth soup, rub through a sieve. Combine the mixture with the chicken stock and tomato purée in a large saucepan, season to taste with salt and pepper, bring to a simmer, and cook, covered, for 15-20 minutes. **SERVES 6.**

HAZELNUT AND ASPARAGUS SOUP
Sopa de Avellanas y Esparragos

This is an elegant soup perfect for a dinner party to celebrate an anniversary or entertain friends or visitors. Though *comida* is the main meal, *cena*, dinner, is served at a fashionably late hour (though not as late as in Spain) on special occasions. Nuts are used to thicken a rich stock graced with Mexico's delicate skinny little green asparagus.

¾ lb asparagus

¼ cup hazelnuts

1 tablespoon unsalted butter

1 onion, chopped

6 cups chicken stock

Salt, freshly ground black pepper

½ cup heavy cream (optional)

¼ cup dry sherry (optional)

Trim the asparagus and peel away the rough part. Tie the asparagus into a loose bundle. Have ready a saucepan large enough to hold the asparagus filled with briskly boiling salted water. Lower in the asparagus. Bring the water back to the boil, reduce the heat and cook the asparagus at a simmer, uncovered, until it is tender when pierced with the point of a small sharp knife, about 10 minutes for the thin green type. Lift out, drain and remove the string. Cool and cut out the tips, the tender part, into 1 inch pieces. Set aside.

Cover the hazelnuts with boiling water and let stand for 10 minutes. Drain and rub off the skins. Dry with kitchen towels. Heat the butter in a frying pan and sauté the nuts and onion until the nuts are golden and the onion is soft. Transfer to a food processor and process to a purée. Pour the stock into a saucepan, add the purée and simmer for 10 minutes to blend the flavors. Season to taste with salt and pepper. Whisk in the cream if using, add the asparagus tips and heat the soup through gently. If liked add the sherry.
SERVES 6.
NOTE:
Hazelnuts are notoriously hard to skin. I have found this alternative method a good one. Put nuts on a baking tin in a 350°F oven for 10 minutes or until the skins blister. Remove from the oven and wrap in a tea towel and leave for 3-4 minutes. Rub vigorously in the towel to remove the skins. Not all of it will come off but most will.

SONORA-STYLE TRIPE SOUP
Menudo Estilo Soñora

Traditionally this is a northern dish popular at any time but a must on the morning of New Year's Day as a cure for, or preventer of, hangover. My version is a family one credited to the northern state of Sonora, but it might as well have come from next door Chihuahua or Durango and I think it could be found in marketplace *fondas* almost anywhere in the Republic at this festive time. It is often hard to get a calf's foot from the butcher; pig's feet (trotters) are recommended as the best substitute. Received wisdom is to add generous amounts of *chile pequín*, a small, dried, hot red chili that can be crumbled. Traditionally hominy is used but if this is not available use an equal amount of frozen corn kernels.

1 lb honeycomb tripe

1 calf's foot, quartered or 2 pig's feet, split in halves

10 cups water

Salt, freshly ground black pepper

1 lb hominy or 1 lb frozen corn kernels, thawed

6 spring onions, trimmed and chopped, using white and green parts

2 cloves garlic, chopped

4 tablespoons fresh coriander, chopped

For the side dishes:

2 limes, quartered

1 large onion, finely chopped

**Dried *pequín* chilies, or other hot red dried chili,
    seeded and crumbled**

Dried oregano, crumbled

In a large soup pot or kettle combine the tripe, calf's foot or pig's feet, salt and pepper and water. Bring to the simmer, and cook, covered, until the meats are tender, about 3 hours. Cool in the stock. Lift out the meats and cut the tripe into squares or strips, remove the bones from the calf's foot or pig's feet and cut the meat into pieces. Set aside.

Add the spring onions, garlic, coriander and hominy to the reserved stock, bring to a simmer and cook covered for 1 hour, or until the hominy is tender. If using corn kernels cook only for 15 minutes or until the corn is tender. Return the meats to the stock and simmer for 5 minutes to heat through. Ladle the soup and solids into large deep soup bowls. Put the side dish ingredients into 4 small bowls on the table for diners to add according to individual taste. Serve with warm tortillas and guacamole to fill them. **SERVES 6-8.**

PORK AND HOMINY SOUP, JALISCO-STYLE
Pozole Estilo Jalisco

A soup that puzzled me when we were living in Mexico was *pozole*. Was it a soup, a stew or better classified as pot-au-feu? I looked it up in a Spanish dictionary which said it was Aztec for a dish of beans and barley boiled. Not very enlightening. Another dictionary gave it as a Mexican stew of young corn, meat, chilies and a lot of stock. I first enjoyed it in Jalisco where my husband's United Nations work, friends, and my desire to get to know the country took us. It was splendidly hearty with pork, corn and vegetables and I was given a recipe which I still love. My husband's family on his mother's side, the Tinocos and Sarabias, were rather formal but the ranch owning Ortizes were very good trenchermen and women. They appreciated my passionate desire to know about *La Cocina Mexica*, the Mexican kitchen and they helped me in my quest for *pozole*. I felt that *pozole* didn't fit into the daily family meal pattern and I was right. *Pozole* is on its own. A soup yes, but not one for everyday.

It comes most fully into its own when served in small market squares or villages at makeshift restaurants, in big earthenware bowls after a party. Very nourishing, very reviving. There was one small market square in Mexico City devoted to *pozole*. There were *mariachi* bands in colorful *charro* costumes with classic big sombreros as well as street vendors of all kinds. They served the Jalisco-style dish. There was a very good rather different *pozole*, *Pozole Verde* to be enjoyed round the silver town Taxco up the mountains from Acapulco which we ate, not to recover from a party but the rigors of buying silver jewelry and even more debilitating, the effects of not buying more than we should. We had driven from Acapulco with a party on a cultural mission who were transported in two buses. I think the *pozole* fortified them for I have never seen more terrified men than they were after a trip down perilous mountain roads in vehicles whose drivers played tag on dangerous bends with sheer drops whenever they could find them. The *pozole* was the famous *Pozole Verde* made with *pepitas*, Mexican pumpkin seeds (see page 102). The soup makes a fine finish to an outdoor summer party sending everyone home contented.

3 pig's feet
1 whole head garlic, separated and peeled
Salt
3½ lbs chicken, cut into serving pieces
1 lb boneless pork loin or shoulder cut into 2½-inch pieces

101

¾ lb canned hominy, drained or frozen corn kernels, thawed

6 cups chicken stock, or more if needed

For the garnish:

2 tablespoons *pequín* (small, hot, dried) chilies crumbled, or more to taste

2 limes, cut into wedges

1 bunch radishes, sliced

1 head lettuce, finely shredded

1 onion, finely chopped

Put the pig's feet and garlic into a large saucepan or soup kettle, cover with salted water and simmer, covered, for 3 hours until almost tender. Add the chicken and pork and enough stock to cover and continue over low heat for about 45 minutes, add the canned hominy, or corn kernels and simmer for 15 minutes longer or until the chicken and meats are tender. Check the seasoning, and since this is a soup, add more stock if much has boiled away in the cooking. Serve the soup and solids in large deep soup bowls. Have the garnishes in small bowls to be added according to individual taste.
SERVES 6-8.

PORK AND HOMINY SOUP WITH PUMPKIN SEEDS
Pozole Verde

The only practical course when cooking this is to use canned hominy, failing that rely on frozen corn kernels, not as good but certainly better than nothing. Two of the herbs are not available but an important one, *epazote* is. Use it fresh or dried. *Tomatillos*, Mexican green husk tomatoes, are worth searching for. The finished soup is worth the effort.

8 cups chicken stock or water

½ pig's head, weighing about 3 lbs

½ lb pork neck bones

2 lbs chicken, left whole

1 lb canned hominy, rinsed and drained, or frozen corn kernels, thawed

¾ cup Mexican pumpkin seeds (*pepitas*), finely ground

1 16-oz can *tomatillos*, drained

2 fresh *jalapeño* chilies, seeded and chopped

1 onion, chopped

2 cloves garlic, chopped

½ teaspoon dried *epazote* **or 1 sprig fresh**

1 tablespoon corn oil or lard

Salt

For the garnishes:

1 medium onion, finely chopped

4 tablespoons dried oregano

1 large avocado, peeled, pitted and cut into ½-inch pieces

6 tortillas fried crisp

2 limes, cut into quarters

Pour the stock or water into a large soup pot or soup kettle and add the pig's head, pork bones, chicken and canned hominy. If using corn kernels add them only in the last 15 minutes of cooking. Simmer the meats and corn, covered, for 1 hour or until tender. Lift out all the solids and when cool enough to handle remove and discard the pork bones. Remove the bones from the halved pig's head and cut the meat into bite-size pieces. Set the meat aside in a large bowl. Skin and bone the chicken and cut the meat into strips. Set aside with the pig's head pieces and the hominy. Cover loosely.

In a food processor combine the ground *pepitas*, *tomatillos*, chilies, onion and garlic and process to a smooth purée. Heat the corn oil or lard in a frying pan and cook, stirring, over moderate heat for about 5 minutes until the mixture is well blended and slightly thickened. Stir in the stock. Add the *epazote*. Simmer the stock for 15 minutes, season with salt if necessary and add more stock if it has evaporated in cooking. There should be plenty. Add the pork, chicken and hominy, or if using corn kernels instead of hominy, add them now. Simmer for 15 minutes. Discard the *epazote* sprigs.

Serve the *pozole* in large, deep soup bowls dividing the meat and chicken among the bowls. Serve the garnishes in 5 small bowls on the table for each diner to take according to taste. **SERVES 6-8.**

BLUE CRAB SOUP
Chilpachole de Jaibas

This magnificent soup from Veracruz is best when made with the little blue crabs bought at the local market. The crabs, it is emphasized, should be lively, a chilling prospect to anyone not liking to deal with eight lively little crabs keen to get back to their ocean home. However, for the faint-hearted, help is at hand. Substitute fresh, canned or frozen crab meat. It won't be quite as rich but spares the anguish.

2 lbs live blue crabs (about 8) or 1 lb crab meat, fresh, canned or frozen, picked over to remove any shell or cartilage

1 onion, chopped

2 cloves garlic

1 lb tomatoes, peeled, seeded and chopped

1 or 2 canned *chipotle* chilies, seeded and chopped
   or 1 or 2 fresh *jalapeño* chilies, seeded and chopped

2 tablespoons olive oil

2 sprigs *epazote*, or ½ teaspoon dried

2 limes, cut into wedges

If using live crabs bring 8 cups water to a brisk boil in a soup pot or large saucepan. Drop in the crabs and put on the lid quickly lest the crabs try to escape. Reduce the heat to moderate and cook at a simmer for five minutes when the crab will be bright red. Lift them out and reserve the broth. Discard the spongy gills. Pick the meat from the shells and claws and reserve any orange roe. Set both aside. Return the shells and any debris to the broth and simmer, covered, over low heat for 30 minutes. Cool and strain through a fine sieve. If using canned or frozen crab meat, substitute fish stock for the broth.

In a food processor combine the onion, garlic, tomatoes and chilies and process to a purée. Heat the oil in a small frying pan and add the purée. Cook, stirring, over moderate heat for 5 minutes then add it to the reserved broth. Add the *epazote*. Simmer for 15 minutes longer then add the crab meat and cook just long enough to heat it through. Serve in soup bowls with the lime wedges separately for the juice to be squeezed in to taste. **SERVES 6.**

LIME SOUP
Sopa de Lima

Yucatán, which is Mayan, boasts a cuisine subtly different from those of Aztec Mexico. The Spanish Conquest and the creation of the colonial kitchen changed both of them. This is Yucatán's most famous soup, greatly esteemed. The lime used is not generally available. It is small, round and a light green when ripe called *lima agria*, and may be the lime I have met in the Caribbean and South America. It is fragrant and tart with a delicious flavor both in the juice and the peel. I have wondered if it is the same as the Key lime from Florida whose trees were destroyed in a hurricane. Our limes can be used without an overwhelming loss of the authentic flavor but lemon cannot be used as a substitute. Whenever we've been in Mérida, Yucatán's capital, we've sought a restaurant or cafeteria serving the soup after a morning spent wandering round the market trying to learn more about the region's special seasonings, and to have a local specialty *Papa-dzules*, another Mayan favorite.

Lard or vegetable oil

1 onion, finely chopped

2 cloves garlic, chopped

½ lb tomato, peeled, seeded and chopped

½ green pepper, seeded and finely chopped

2 or 3 canned *serrano* chilies, chopped

6 cups chicken stock

Juice ½ lime and the rind

Salt, freshly ground pepper

3 chicken gizzards

6 raw chicken livers, chopped

1 chicken breast

6 stale tortillas, cut into thin strips

1 lime, thinly sliced

Heat 2 tablespoons of lard or oil in a saucepan and sauté the onion until it is soft. Add the garlic, tomato and pepper and sauté for 2-3 minutes longer. Add the chilies, chicken stock, lime juice and lime rind. Add the chicken breast and cook for 10 minutes, remove from the stock, cool, shred and set aside.

Put the gizzards into a small saucepan with water to cover, bring to a simmer and cook, covered. Drain, remove the gristle from the gizzards, chop them and add them to the soup with the chicken livers. Simmer 5 minutes longer until the chicken livers are done. Season to taste with salt and pepper.

In a frying pan heat lard or oil and fry the tortilla strips until they are crisp. Drain on paper towels and keep hot. Pour the soup into soup bowls. Distribute the gizzards and liver among them, drop in the hot tortilla strips and garnish with the lime slices, and chicken. **SERVES 6.**

FISH SOUP
Caldo Miche

Lake Patzcuaro in the state of Michoacán is famous for its little *pescado blanco* (white fish) used to make *Caldo Miche*. *Miche* is the word for fish in the language of the Tarascan Indians of the region. As *pescado blanco* is unique, only available there or in Lake Chapala in the nearby state of Jalisco, it is likely neither of these is available here so use any whole fish (such as catfish or carp) with head and tail on weighing about 2 lbs. We were lucky enough to have resident friends when on our visits and Sra. Carolina Escudero, whose family had ties with my husband's family, made sure there were cooks to help me with recipes. The chili to use is pickled *jalapeño*, and fresh coriander is important. It is a beautiful region and this is a very special soup.

6 cups chicken stock or water

1 onion, finely chopped

1 lb tomatoes, peeled, seeded and chopped

2-3 pickled *jalapeño* chilies, rinsed and chopped

2 cloves garlic, crushed

Bay leaf

½ teaspoon oregano

**2 lbs non-oily white fleshed fish,
    whole with head and tail left on**

Salt, freshly ground black pepper

2 tablespoons chopped coriander leaves

In a large saucepan combine the stock, onion, tomatoes, chilies, garlic, bay leaf and oregano. Bring to a simmer, cover and cook until the tomatoes have disintegrated and the onion is soft, about 25-30 minutes. Add the fish and cook for 15 minutes longer. Lift the fish out carefully and remove and discard the head, tail, skin and bones. Cut into 1 inch pieces. Season the soup to taste with salt and pepper and return the fish to it. Simmer just to heat through. Serve in soup bowls sprinkled with fresh coriander. **SERVES 6.**

HALF-HOUR SOUP
Sopa de Media Hora

Given fresh young vegetables this soup really does take only half an hour and is wonderfully useful for those wanting good homemade soup in a hurry. I can think of many times when it would perfectly fit the occasion, mostly being tired out from work. Though it is for 6 servings the amount can easily be altered, and anyway it could be refrigerated as it would keep for a day or two. A lone diner might like more than one serving.

6 medium-size zucchini

1 large onion, chopped

6 baby carrots, peeled and thinly sliced

1 lb tomatoes, peeled, seeded and chopped

1 bay leaf

6 cups chicken stock

Salt, freshly ground pepper

1 large avocado, peeled, pitted and cut into strips

Pickled *jalapeño* chili, seeded and chopped (optional)

Slice the zucchini lengthwise then cut into ½-inch slices. Add with the other vegetables and the bay leaf to the stock in a saucepan, taste for seasoning and add salt and pepper if needed. Bring to a simmer, cover and cook until the vegetables are tender and the tomatoes have disintegrated into the soup. Remove and discard the bay leaf and serve the soup with the vegetables divided among the soup bowls. Garnish with the avocado and serve the chili separately. **SERVES 6.**

Chili lovers can always spike the soup with one of the hot sauces or perhaps toasted crumbled *pasilla*.

TORTILLA BALL SOUP
Sopa de Bolitas de Tortilla

Tortillas are never wasted. Here leftover tortillas are used to make one of the most popular Mexican soups. As always there are many versions of the soup. Hermila, a family cook who gave me this recipe, preferred to make tortilla balls saying they were *muy sabrosa*, very tasty. I think she was from the north and claimed that cooks from central Mexico just fried stale tortillas cut in strips—a friendly rivalry.

12 small (5-inch) stale tortillas

1 cup milk

1 onion, chopped

1 clove garlic, chopped

¼ cup grated Parmesan cheese

Sprig *epazote*, chopped

2 egg yolks

1 whole egg, lightly beaten

Salt, freshly ground black pepper

Lard or oil

6 cups meat stock

½ cup tomato purée

Put the tortillas into a bowl and pour the milk over them. Leave them to soak until they are soft. Combine the softened tortillas with the onion, garlic, cheese, *epazote*, egg yolks, egg and salt and pepper and process to a smooth purée. It should hold its shape. Form into small balls, about 1½ inch. Sauté the balls in a frying pan in lard or oil until lightly browned all over. Set aside and keep warm.

In a large saucepan combine the stock and tomato purée, stirring to mix, and bring to a simmer. Add the tortilla balls and serve. Divide the tortilla balls among the soup bowls and pour the soup over. If preferred do not sauté the balls but poach them in the hot soup for about 10 minutes. **SERVES 6.**

VARIATION:

Remove the stems and shake the seeds out of 2 or 3 dried pasilla *chilies and tear or cut them into pieces. Heat 2 tablespoons lard or oil in a small frying pan and sauté the chilies until they are crisp, about half a minute, lift out, drain on paper towels and when they are cool enough to handle crumble them into a small bowl.*

In a food processor purée 12 oz tomatoes, peeled and seeded, 1 onion, chopped and 2 cloves garlic, chopped.

Heat 2 tablespoons lard or oil (use fat left from sautéing the chilies) in a frying pan, add the tomato purée and cook for 5 minutes. Pour 6 cups chicken stock into a large saucepan and stir in the purée. Simmer for 5 minutes. To serve have 1½ cups grated Cheddar cheese in a bowl with the tortilla strips and chilies in 2 other bowls. Divide the cheese among 6 soup bowls, top with the tortilla strips, add the hot soup and serve the chilies separately. **SERVES 6.**

CHICKEN AND ALMOND SOUP
Sopa de Pollo y Almendras

My husband's grandmother, Doña Carmelita, who looked like an eagle with her special elegance, approved of me wanting to learn about the Mexican kitchen. She approved of having maids to help her but was always near the stove to cook and to direct operations. She taught me a lot and I loved her a great deal. This was one of the soups she felt was suitable for a great occasion, perhaps a family gathering, a wedding or a christening party.

½ cup blanched almonds

2 tablespoons butter

1 onion, chopped

2 boneless cooked chicken breasts, 1 chopped, 1 cut into slivers

6 cups chicken stock

Pinch nutmeg

Salt

¼ cup dry sherry

1 tablespoon chopped coriander, or flat parsley

Heat the butter in a frying pan and sauté the almonds over moderate heat until golden. Combine the almonds, onion and the chopped chicken breast in a food processor and process to a purée. In a large saucepan put the purée, the chicken stock and the nutmeg, stir to mix and cook over low heat to blend the flavors for 5 minutes. Add the chicken breast cut into slivers and continue cooking just to heat through. Taste for seasoning and add salt if necessary. Stir in the sherry. Pour into 6 soup bowls with some chicken in each one, and garnish with coriander or parsley. **SERVES 6.**

CUSTARD SOUP
Sopa de Jericalla

A colonial soup, this was another of Doña Carmelita's choices for elegant dining.

For the custard (*Jericalla*):
4 eggs, lightly beaten
1 cup chicken stock
Pinch nutmeg
Salt, freshly ground white pepper
For the soup:
6 cups rich chicken stock
½ cup dry sherry

To make the custard put the eggs into the top of a double boiler over hot water, on low heat. Gradually beat in the chicken stock and season with the nutmeg, salt and white pepper. Cover and cook until the custard has set, about 20 minutes. Remove from the heat and cool. Cut the custard into small cubes and set aside.

In a large saucepan heat the chicken stock. Off the heat stir in the sherry and the custard cubes, and warm through if necessary. Serve in soup bowls.
SERVES 6.

MEAT BALL SOUP
Sopa de Albondigas

Meat balls came to Mexico by a circuitous route. The Spanish conquerors brought them having acquired them from the Moors when they were invaded from Africa. The invasions and occupations may not have been popular but the meat balls were, and still are. The ones here are half-size, Little Meat Balls, *Albonguidas*.

For the meat balls:
½ lb lean ground beef
½ lb ground pork
1 onion, finely chopped
½ cup fresh breadcrumbs
¼ teaspoon oregano

Salt, freshly ground black pepper

2 eggs, lightly beaten

For the soup:

4 cups meat stock

2 cups tomato juice

1 canned *chipotle* chili, rinsed and chopped

To make the meat balls, combine in a bowl the beef, pork, onion, bread-crumbs, oregano, salt, pepper and eggs and mix thoroughly. Form into 18 balls, about 1½ inches in diameter. Pour the stock and tomato juice into a large saucepan, add the chili and bring to a simmer. Add the meat balls, a few at a time, cover and simmer gently until the meat balls are done, about 30 minutes. Serve, putting 3 meat balls into each soup bowl. **SERVES 6.**

VARIATION:

The soup can be varied and this was a favorite. Sauté a small onion, finely chopped in 2 tablespoons corn or similar oil until tender but not brown. Add it to the meat stock with a clove of chopped garlic and 1¼ cups tomato purée, add salt and pepper to taste and use as above.

SQUASH BLOSSOM SOUP
Sopa de Flor de Calabaza

The vegetable that is widely known as zucchini was being cultivated in Mexico as long ago as 7000 B.C. It is one of an enormous assemblage of plants of the genus *Cucurbita* which includes pumpkin and all manner of summer squashes. One of the extras that comes with zucchini is the edible blossom, pretty golden thing. Our zucchini are Mexican *calabacitas* and the flowers are *Flor de Calabaza* named after the mature vegetable, the *calabaza* which we often call pumpkin or West Indian pumpkin. Names get very confusing. The flowers are as popular today as they were in Aztec and Maya times and are sold fresh in all the markets. Fortunately they are increasingly available here, if not, start your own pumpkin patch.

1 lb squash blossoms

1 tablespoon butter

1 onion, finely chopped

6 cups chicken stock

Sprig *epazote*

Salt, freshly ground black pepper

Remove the stems and sepals from the blossoms and chop coarsely. In a frying pan heat the butter and sauté the onion until it is tender. Add the chopped flowers and sauté for a few minutes longer. Transfer the mixture to a food processor and process to a smooth purée. In a saucepan combine the purée and the chicken stock and simmer for 15 minutes. In the last 5 minutes add the *epazote*. Season the soup with salt and pepper to taste, remove and discard the *epazote* and serve. **SERVES 6.**

VARIATION:

To make this into a cream soup reduce the stock by 1 cup and make the soup as above. In the last 5 minutes add 1 cup heavy cream.

VERMICELLI SOUP
Sopa de Fideo

I think this must have been the first soup I had in Mexico when my husband and I stayed, on arrival, with my mother-in-law before going househunting. It is immensely popular and avoid it one could not, not that I wanted to, as it is very pleasant. It was with this soup that I learned that in Mexico there are wet and dry soups. This is the *aguada* version and there is also a *seca* one. The vermicelli comes in little bird's nest shapes making it easier to sauté without burning.

2 tablespoons olive or peanut oil

¼ lb vermicelli

1 onion, chopped

1 clove garlic, chopped

1 lb tomatoes, peeled, seeded and chopped

6 cups chicken stock

Salt, freshly ground black pepper

Pinch of sugar

1 tablespoon flat leaf parsley, chopped

¼ cup grated Parmesan cheese

Heat the oil in a frying pan and sauté the bundles of vermicelli until golden brown without breaking them up or letting them burn. Drain and set aside. Reserve the oil. Combine the onion, garlic and tomatoes in a food processor and process to a purée. Return the reserved oil to the pan, adding a little more if necessary and cook the purée, stirring constantly over moderate heat for

5 minutes. Combine the vermicelli, the purée and the stock in a large saucepan, taste for seasoning and salt if necessary, pepper, sugar and parsley. Simmer, over low heat, covered, until the pasta is tender, about 15 minutes. Serve immediately with the grated cheese on the side. **SERVES 6.**

ZUCCHINI SOUP
Sopa de Calabacita

The richness of cream and egg yolk are balanced neatly with the freshness of zucchini in this soup from central Mexico. Choose small, young zucchini where possible.

1 lb zucchini, coarsely chopped
1 large onion, chopped
6 cups chicken stock
1 large egg yolk
½ cup heavy cream
Salt, freshly ground black pepper

In a large saucepan combine the zucchini, onion and stock, bring to a simmer and cook until the vegetables are tender, about 15 minutes. Remove the solids from the soup and press them through a sieve or reduce to a purée in a food processor. Return the purée to the stock, stir to mix and season to taste with salt and pepper. Set aside. Beat the egg yolk and cream together and stir in about 1 cup of the hot soup then whisk it into the soup. Heat the soup but do not let it boil. **SERVES 6.**

SOUP MEXICAN-STYLE
Sopa a la Mexicana

Any dish called *a la Mexicana* is sure to have tomatoes, chilies and avocado among its ingredients. This soup is no exception in having them, and more besides making it hearty enough to be a main course if served in generous portions. If it is to be part of *comida* modest portions are appropriate. I defy even diners at a Mexican ranch to do better than that though it is amazing what can be got through given ample time with the promise of a siesta to follow. It evokes for me memories of a family ranch in Queretaro. It is splendidly warming and filling on a cold grey winter day.

3 chicken breasts, skinned, boned and halved

6 cups rich chicken stock

2 small zucchini, thinly sliced

3 baby carrots, peeled and thinly sliced

1 cup petit green peas

1½ lbs tomatoes, peeled, seeded and chopped fine

Salt and freshly ground black pepper

1 large avocado, sliced

Pickled *jalapeño* or *serrano* chilies

In a large saucepan combine the chicken breasts, the stock, zucchini, carrots and peas and cook over low heat for 10 minutes. Stir in the tomatoes and continue to cook until the tomatoes disintegrate and the other ingredients are tender. Season to taste with salt and pepper and serve so that each soup bowl has some of everything. Garnish with the avocado slices and serve the chilies on the side. **SERVES 6.**

BLACK BEAN SOUP
Sopa de Frijol Negro

Black beans are the preferred type of Mayan Mexico and have been for thousands of years. They are usually cooked with a sprig of the herb *epazote* and though bean soups are not common, I acquired this in the market on my visit to Yucatán's capital, Mérida on our way to visit the ruins of Uxmal and Chichén Itzá. I fell in love with the people, the ruins and the food. I remember thinking when I saw myself in a full-length mirror that I looked rather like a skinny young tree, far too tall. It was the Maya who looked right to me, short, finely made, dressed in white embroidered *huipils*, black hair in braids, the men in white trousers and special shirts.

1 cup black beans

8 cups chicken stock or water

¼ cup corn or peanut oil

1 onion, finely chopped

2 cloves garlic, chopped

1 teaspoon dried red *pequin* chili, crumbled

1 tomato (about 4 oz), peeled and chopped

½ teaspoon dried *epazote* or fresh sprig

Salt, freshly ground black pepper
¼ cup dry sherry (optional)

Rinse and pick over the beans. Put them into a large saucepan and pour in the stock or water. Bring to a simmer, cover and cook gently until the beans are almost tender. The time will vary according to the age of the beans, new season's beans will cook more quickly. Allow at least 2 hours.

Heat the oil in a frying pan and sauté the onion, garlic and *pequín* chilies, until the onion is soft. Add the tomato and *epazote* and cook until the mixture is well blended. Stir into the beans and season with salt and pepper. Simmer, covered, until the beans are very soft. Purée the solids in a food processor and return them to the liquid. Stir, and simmer to heat through. Stir in the sherry, if using. Serve in soup bowls. **SERVES 6.**

If liked accompany with quartered tortillas, fried crisp, crumbled fresh cheese, and quartered limes.

DRY SOUPS
Sopas Secas

No one quite knows why these dishes are called dry soups in Mexico. It is probable that when the Spanish introduced rice and the pastas a certain amount of confusion arose as to just where they fit into the emerging colonial meal pattern. A new category, the dry soups, was created and placed immediately after the wet or brothy soups. The Puerto Ricans developed their own rice dishes, the *asopaos* which are very soupy dishes of rice, chicken, prawns or beans with herbs that come halfway between soup and solid. What is interesting is the speed with which the New World embraced rice from Asia, and pasta which may have been brought to Italy by Marco Polo as a result of his 13th century journeys to China, compared with the slow acceptance of corn by Europeans. It is a fascinating evolution, and since Spanish cooks put both rice and pasta into soup the Aztecs may have concluded they were the operative part of the new dishes, hence "wet" soup and "dry" soup. Who knows and who knows if we will ever know? After the wet soup at the traditional Mexican late midday meal comes the dry soup, served as a separate course in the way Italians serve pasta or rice. In our meal pattern, dry soups would make admirable luncheon dishes or for dinner could be served as an accompaniment to grilled chops or other meats. Though some purists disagree, some tortilla dishes fit into this dry soupcategory and are another good way to use stale tortillas. I even had a cook who made a *sopa seca* of calf's brains. It was very special.

DRY SOUP MADE WITH BRAINS
Sopa Seca de Sesos

"Calf's brains form the most wholesome and reparative diet for all those who are debilitated by excessive head work, and the same remark applies to brains of ox and the sheep," wrote Escoffier in *A Guide to Modern Cookery*.

After giving his admirable recipe for cooking brains, M. Escoffier went onto point out a peculiarity of this organ meat, which is this: although brains take only 30 minutes to cook "until done" they may cook for as long as 2 hours, as the process only tends to make them firmer—which may be desirable.

2 pairs of calf's brains

Salt

1 tablespoon vinegar

Corn or peanut oil

1 onion, finely chopped

1 clove garlic, chopped

1 lb tomatoes, peeled, seeded and chopped

4 *serrano* chilies, chopped

Freshly ground black pepper

4 sprigs *epazote*, fresh or dried

18 5-inch day-old tortillas cut into strips

1 cup heavy cream

Grated Parmesan cheese

Carefully remove the membrane enveloping the brains and put them to soak in cold water for an hour. Drain and put into a saucepan with hot water to cover. Add salt and vinegar and bring to a simmer, cook, skimming as necessary for 30 minutes. Drain and chop coarsely. Set aside.

In a large frying pan heat 3 tablespoons of oil and sauté the onion and garlic until the onion is tender. Add the tomatoes, *serrano* chilies, salt, pepper and *epazote* and simmer, stirring from time to time, until the sauce is well blended, about 10 minutes. Set aside ¼ of the sauce. Mix the brains gently into the remaining sauce and keep warm.

Heat 6 tablespoons oil in a large frying pan and fry the tortillas on both sides for a few minutes without browning. Drain on paper towels. Grease an ovenproof casserole and cover the bottom with a thin layer of sauce. Follow this with a layer of tortillas topped with some cream and a layer of the brains mixed with sauce. Continue in this way until all the ingredients are used, ending with tortillas and cream. Pour the reserved sauce over the dish and sprinkle it with cheese. Bake in a preheated 350°F oven until heated through, 20-30 minutes. Day-old tortillas are preferred as fresh tortillas absorb too much liquid. Fresh tortillas can be dried for 5-10 minutes in a slow oven if necessary. **SERVES 6.**

VERMICELLI DRY SOUP
Sopa Seca de Fideos

This is a most accommodating dish. It may be flavorful but mild if made without chilies or quite *picante* with them. It may be made unctuous with sour cream or offer choices of Parmesan or Cheddar cheese. It depends how the cook is feeling.

2 tablespoons corn or peanut oil

½ lb vermicelli

1 onion, finely chopped

1 clove garlic, chopped

1 lb tomatoes, peeled and chopped

1 or 2 canned *chipotle* chilies, rinsed and chopped (optional)

Salt, freshly ground black pepper, pinch sugar

½ teaspoon oregano

1½ cups chicken stock

½ cup sour cream (optional)

¼ cup grated Parmesan or Cheddar cheese

Heat the oil in a frying pan and fry the bundles of vermicelli until they are golden brown turning them from time to time as they burn easily. Lift them out into an ovenproof casserole. In the oil remaining in the pan sauté the onion, garlic, tomatoes and chilies, if using, for about 5 minutes, stirring. Season to taste with salt, pepper, sugar and oregano. Stir in the stock, mixing well and pour the mixture over the vermicelli. Bake in a preheated 350°F oven for 25 minutes when the noodles will be tender and most of the liquid absorbed. Spread with the sour cream, if using and sprinkle with the cheese and continue to cook until the cheese has melted, about 5 minutes.

The dish can be cooked on top of the stove if preferred. Cook over low heat, uncovered, stirring from time to time, for about 30 minutes. The dish is ready when the noodles are tender and all the liquid has been absorbed. Sprinkle with cheese and run under the grill to melt the cheese. **SERVES 6.**

TORTILLA DRY SOUP WITH CREAM AND CHEESE
Sopa Seca de Tortilla con Crema y Queso

There were always leftover tortillas and dishes like these provided a good excuse for using them up. No one would have felt comfortable making tortillas then drying them out to pretend to have day old tortillas for the dish.

½ cup corn or peanut oil or 4 oz lard

1 onion, finely chopped

1 clove garlic, chopped

1 lb tomatoes, peeled, seeded and chopped

½ teaspoon oregano, crumbled

Salt, freshly ground black pepper

Pinch sugar

18 small tortillas, day old, cut into ½-inch strips

1 cup heavy cream

½ cup grated Cheddar cheese

Heat 2 tablespoons oil or the equivalent amount of lard in a frying pan and sauté the onion and garlic until the onion is soft. Add the tomatoes, oregano, salt, pepper and pinch of sugar and cook, stirring from time to time, until the sauce is thick and well blended, about 10 minutes. Set aside.

Rinse out and dry the frying pan and heat the remaining oil or lard. Sauté the tortilla strips quickly without letting them become crisp or brown, a matter of minutes. Drain on kitchen towels. Grease an ovenproof casserole and pour in a layer of sauce. Follow with a layer of tortilla strips, a layer of cream, one of sauce and one of grated cheese. Continue until all the ingredients are used up, ending with cheese. Put in a preheated 350°F oven and bake until heated through, about 30 minutes. **SERVES 6.**

TORTILLA DRY SOUP WITH *POBLANO* CHILIES
Sopa Seca de Tortilla con Chile Poblano

Poblano chilies have an exquisite flavor but are hard to find outside their native habitat, the state of Puebla in Mexico. They may be available in jars or canned and if so, use them, if not, use sweet green peppers or *jalapeños* which will be quite *picante*.

**6 canned *poblano* or *jalapeño* chilies, seeded and rinsed
 or 6 fresh sweet green peppers, seeded and chopped**

½ cup corn or peanut oil

1 onion, finely chopped

1 clove garlic, chopped

Salt, freshly ground black pepper

18 small, day old tortillas, cut into ½-inch strips

1 cup heavy cream

½ cup grated Cheddar cheese

Butter

Heat the oil in a frying pan and sauté the chilies, onion and garlic until they are soft. Season to taste with salt and pepper. Lift out and drain on kitchen towels and set aside.

In the oil remaining in the frying pan sauté the tortilla strips for a minute or two. They should not become crisp or brown. Drain on paper towels.

Grease a shallow ovenproof casserole and make a layer of tortilla strips then a layer of cream and the chili mixture, finishing with a layer of cheese. Repeat until all the ingredients are used up ending with a layer of cheese. Dot with butter and bake in a preheated 350°F oven just until heated through, about 30 minutes. **SERVES 6.**

DRY SOUP OF TORTILLAS WITH SPICY PORK SAUSAGES
Sopa Seca de Tortilla con Chorizos

This is a robust dish, admirable for a light supper or luncheon though traditionally it belongs in *comida*. Most of the *sopa secas* fit into modern meal patterns. They need little more than a salad and fruit or a light dessert. Perhaps guacamole and a fresh sauce like *salsa cruda* could happily accompany the casserole. Mexican food is splendidly adaptable.

Corn or peanut oil

3 chorizo sausages, skinned and chopped

1 onion, finely chopped

1 clove garlic, chopped

1 lb tomatoes, peeled, seeded and chopped

Salt and freshly ground black pepper

½ teaspoon oregano, crumbled

18 small, day old tortillas, cut into ½-inch strips

½ cup heavy cream

¼ cup freshly grated Parmesan cheese

Film a frying pan with oil and fry the sausages, stirring for about 5 minutes. Lift out and drain on paper towels. Set aside. Discard all but 2 tablespoons of the fat in the frying pan and sauté the onion and garlic until the onion is tender. Add the tomatoes and continue cooking, over moderate heat stirring from time to time, until the sauce is thick and well blended. Add salt and pepper to taste, and the oregano and set aside.

Rinse out and dry the frying pan and heat 4 tablespoons oil. Sauté the tortilla strips without letting them become crisp and brown. This takes only minutes. Lift out and drain on paper towels. Grease a shallow ovenproof casserole and make a layer of tomato sauce on the bottom. Top with a layer of tortillas, and a layer of sausage, repeating until all the ingredients are used up, finishing with a layer of tortillas. Pour over the cream and sprinkle with the cheese. Bake in a 350°F oven until heated through, about 30 minutes. **SERVES 6.**

EGGS

•

Huevos

Though the Aztecs and Mayans had turkey, duck, quail, pigeons and other birds for eggs, it was the Spanish who introduced the domestic hen. Hen's eggs were adopted into the Mexican colonial cuisine after the extraordinary culinary wedding created by the Conquest. The domestic hen, originally a wild fowl from the jungles of Burma, enjoys worldwide popularity and nowhere are its eggs more greatly esteemed than by the Spanish. Mexican cooks, with their usual ingenuity, combined the new eggs with local ingredients to create new and exciting dishes.

Before industrialization when Mexico had a largely rural economy, eggs were usually eaten at *almuerzo*, the second breakfast at about 11 A.M. which followed *desayuno*, the coffee and rolls or sweet breads of the dawn hours on ranches and haciendas. Today *Huevos Rancheros* (Country-Style Eggs), fried eggs on tortillas with a tomato-chili sauce, beans and avocado garnish are so popular they are served in just about every cafe and restaurant in the country but there are many other dishes, usually hearty, that are available. I remember the briefcase-carrying elegant young businessmen who breakfasted at Sanborn's restaurant enjoying a sustaining bite with coffee, chocolate or even beer before the serious intake of food later at *comida*, probably at home, followed by a siesta and a return to work. The tourists came for, what was for them, a late breakfast or early lunch for fortification against the rigors of sightseeing and shopping. They avoided *comida* as too heavy and an interruption into the main purpose of the visit. I was rather bewildered by it all. I found that meal hours aroused passions, mostly nationalistic, but what I most remember however is how very good the food was.

In all my years living in, or visiting Mexico on UN home leave, I only had one culinary disappointment with an egg. We had driven to Puebla, that lovely city of the Angels, home of a great deal of good food, where César had been asked to give a lecture, I think at the invitation of the Governor. I was allowed to tag along. We drove on the mountain road as the easier non-mountain road hadn't been built then. I am not very brave at coping with precipitous gorges and sheer drops. Looking down unnerves me. I managed without whimpering as César was a superbly safe driver and halfway I was emboldened to suggest we stop at a wayside *puesto* for *carnitas*, delicious bits of pork slow-fried until brown and tender. I should not have been so silly; I arrived in Puebla with *turista* or Moctezuma's revenge and took to my bed in the hotel, missing the lecture and the party after it. In the morning, somewhat recovered, I craved the familiar food of the nursery, a soft-boiled egg with "soldiers," fingers of buttered toast or bread to dip in the runny yolk. I was such a newcomer I reckoned without the effect of altitude and language. I asked for a *huevo tibio*, and got it. It was an egg dunked briefly in water that boiled at a much lower temperature than at sea level to bring it to lukewarm.

Though I sent it back to be cooked a mite more it didn't work and I went home content with toast. There were many other trips to Puebla especially after the new road was built and in time I got acclimatized to the local tummy bugs and still dote on *carnitas*, but I shall never forget my frustration trying to bridge the gap between a lukewarm egg and a soft-boiled one. Still there is a place in my life for a lukewarm egg. It is ideal for another Mexican dish, Caesar salad, only I call it a one-minute egg then. How perverse language is. I never did get a proper soft-boiled egg in a proper eggcup in Mexico but I went onto enjoy the egg dishes there which I cooked, ate and collected the recipes for here.

EGGS IN RED CHILI SAUCE
Huevos Adobados

Adobo, a mixture of chilies, herbs, spices and vinegar, is really a pickling sauce but makes a magnificent sauce for these eggs. The rice turns them into a satisfying main course dish for lunch or supper. I don't know if they are a northern dish though I first had them in a friend's house served with *Guacamole del Norte* (page 76).

6 *ancho* chilies

3 onions, chopped

2 cloves garlic, chopped

½ lb tomato, peeled and chopped

⅛ teaspoon ground cloves

¼ teaspoon ground cinnamon

1 tablespoon fresh coriander, chopped

½ cup chicken stock, about

Salt, freshly ground black pepper

½ teaspoon sugar

2 tablespoons corn oil or lard

1 tablespoon mild vinegar

12 large eggs

In a dry frying pan toast the *anchos*, turning them once or twice so that they do not burn. Remove the stems, slit them and shake out the seeds. Tear them in pieces and put them into a bowl covered with warm water. Let them soak until they are soft, about 30 minutes, and drain them. In a food processor combine the chilies, onions, garlic, tomato, cloves, cinnamon, coriander, salt,

pepper and sugar, and process to a coarse purée. If the purée is too thick, thin with a little of the chicken stock but do not make it runny. Heat the oil or lard in a large frying pan, add the purée and cook over moderate heat, stirring, for 5 minutes. Stir in the vinegar. The mixture should have a saucelike consistency. If necessary adjust it with a little more chicken stock. Set aside. Fill a large saucepan with water and bring to a boil. Carefully add the eggs, remove from the heat and let stand for 8 minutes. Drain and cover immediately with cold water. Let stand for 2 minutes. Shell the eggs carefully and add them to the prepared sauce. Heat gently until both eggs and sauce are hot. Serve on a bed of plain white rice with guacamole on the side.
SERVES 6.

EGGS WITH CHICKEN, CHICKEN LIVERS AND GIZZARDS
Higaditos

No festival in Oaxaca would be complete without this dish, a Zapotecan one. Ingredients vary as *higaditos* means "little livers" and sometimes pork livers are used and they are not little. They make a wonderfully robust breakfast. In the past only chicken livers and gizzards were used. Nowadays some recipes include pig's cheek or pork loin, but whatever is or is not included vast quantities of *higaditos* are eaten on market days in Oaxaca City and at weddings, and feast days and indeed on any festive occasion and not only in Oaxaca City but in nearby villages. When our Oaxacan cook Francisca did them for us we had them for Sunday supper as Sunday lunch with the family was a hearty affair and we usually skipped breakfast for it. Francisca's *higaditos* were lighter than most, using only chicken, chicken livers and gizzards.

Quarter breast of a chicken

4 chicken livers

4 gizzards

2 cups chicken stock or water

2 tablespoons corn or peanut oil

½ lb tomatoes, peeled and chopped

8 oz canned *tomatillos*, drained

1 sweet red pepper (pimiento), seeded and chopped

1 onion, finely chopped

3 cloves garlic, chopped

Salt, freshly ground black pepper

½ teaspoon saffron, ground
12 large eggs, lightly beaten

In a saucepan combine the chicken quarter, livers and gizzards with the water or chicken stock and bring to a simmer. After five minutes lift out and reserve the livers. Continue to cook until the chicken is tender, about 30 minutes in all. Lift out and reserve. Check if the gizzards are tender and lift out or cook a little longer until they are. Chop the livers, skin, bone and chop the chicken and chop the gizzards. Reserve the stock.

In a frying pan heat the oil and sauté the tomatoes, *tomatillos*, pepper, onion, and garlic. Season with salt, pepper and saffron. Add 1 cup of the stock and simmer, uncovered for 5-10 minutes or until the mixture is thick and well blended. Pour the eggs over the mixture. Do not stir them. Reduce the heat from moderate to low and cook just until the eggs have set. Serve immediately with *Salsa de Chile Pasilla* (*Pasilla* Chili Sauce).
SERVES 6-8.

PASILLA CHILI SAUCE
Salsa de Chile Pasilla

3 *pasilla* chilies
2 cloves of garlic, chopped
Salt
Corn or peanut oil
Lemon juice (optional)

Toast the chilies in a dry frying pan, turning to toast both sides, taking care not to burn them. Lift them out into a bowl and cover with warm water. Soak until softened about 15 minutes. Lift out, pat dry and remove the stems and if liked some of the seeds so that the finished sauce will be less *picante*. Put the chilies, roughly chopped with the garlic into a food processor or blender and ¼ cup of the soaking water, and reduce to a coarse purée as the sauce should have some texture. Season with salt and put into a bowl. Stir in enough oil to give a saucelike consistency. Add a few drops of lemon juice if liked.

SCRAMBLED EGGS WITH POTATOES
Huevos Revueltos con Papas

Perhaps this dish was inspired by the Spanish potato omelette, for though the potato is from the New World and was found growing wild in Mexico having found its way from the high Andes in South America, north to Mexico, they never even remotely challenged corn. Mexicans remained firmly corn people, not potato people. It is a good way to use leftover potatoes, or to give a vegetarian friend a pleasant meal.

¼ cup olive oil

2 potatoes, peeled and diced

1 onion, finely chopped

½ teaspoon *chile pequín*, crumbled

4 large eggs, lightly beaten

Salt

In a frying pan heat the oil and sauté the potato, the chili, and onion until the onion and potato are cooked. Stir in the eggs and cook, stirring with a wooden spoon, over moderately low heat until the eggs are set.
SERVES 2.
If using leftover cooked potatoes add them to the onion just to heat through. Any hot chili can be used in place of pequín, *either* jalapeño *or* serrano *to taste.*

EGGS SCRAMBLED WITH GREEN SAUCE
Huevos Revueltos con Salsa Verde

There is usually some *salsa verde* (green sauce) about in the Mexican kitchen and when we were skipping *comida* and having *almuerzo* late and calling it lunch, this was perfect. It was a much more convenient meal-hour pattern for my husband, though it was not usual for him to get away for the long midday break. We were always getting caught between two traditions as Mexican industrialization upset old rural ways for new-fangled city ones. I'd written about the changing meal patterns in 17th century England but it didn't make me any more flexible. Lunch I needed at lunchtime, not halfway through the afternoon. No wonder the family disapproved of my tiresome British ways.

2 tablespoons corn or peanut oil

1 cup *Salsa Verde* (page 80), about 1 recipe

8 large eggs, lightly beaten

In a frying pan, heat the oil. Combine the sauce and the eggs and pour the mixture into the frying pan over moderately low heat and cook, stirring with a wooden spoon until the eggs set, about 4 minutes. If the sauce seems watery, strain before using, or use the cooked version of the sauce or cook the uncooked version for 2-3 minutes in the oil and then scramble the eggs. It is very flexible. Serve with hot tortillas. **SERVES 4.**

EGGS WITH SPICY SAUSAGE
Huevos con Chorizo

Chorizo, a highly spiced and *picante* pork sausage from Spain, migrated to Mexico very early and is now a favorite in so many countries that the term chorizo is the accepted one. Not long ago cooks were told to substitute hot Italian sausage if chorizo wasn't available. The Italian sausage is very good but there is no longer any need for it to leave its own cuisine to substitute in another one. Mexican chorizos are different from the original Spanish ones because of the chilies used, *anchos* and *pasillas*. The Spanish version is milder, though heavily spiced with garlic and paprika. Of course the paprika uses a Mexican *chile*, the *pimiento*, which isn't hot but has a wonderful flavor and is also used in the Mexican version.

1 tablespoon corn or peanut oil

1 onion, finely chopped

3 chorizo sausages, skinned and coarsely chopped

1 lb tomatoes, peeled, seeded and chopped

Salt

6 large eggs, lightly beaten

Heat the oil in a frying pan and sauté the onion until it is tender. Add the chorizos and the tomatoes and continue to cook until the mixture is thick and well blended, about 5 minutes, stirring from time to time. Season with salt. Gently add the eggs, stirring with a wooden spoon to reach the entire surface of the pan, over moderately low heat. The eggs will set to a creamy consistency in 3-4 minutes. Serve immediately with hot tortillas. This and most other egg dishes can be accompanied by guacamole. **SERVES 4.**

EGGS WITH PRAWNS
Huevos con Camarones

We first enjoyed this for *almuerzo* when we were on holiday in Mazatlan, in Sinaloa on Mexico's Pacific coast. It wasn't built up or developed then and I shall never forget the oysters we ate between cooling dips into the ocean. They were large but delicate. I would have liked to stay there forever eating oysters and all the seafood in which the place abounded. But my husband's work called us back and saved me from the deadly sin of gluttony.

3 tablespoons corn or peanut oil

1 onion, finely chopped

2 cloves garlic, chopped

½ lb tomatoes, peeled and chopped

3 canned *jalapeño* chilies, rinsed, seeded and cut into strips

½ lb raw prawns, shelled and coarsely chopped

Salt, freshly ground black pepper

6 large eggs, lightly beaten

Lemon wedges

Heat the oil in a frying pan and sauté the onion and garlic over moderate heat until the onion is tender but not brown. Add the tomatoes and cook, stirring from time to time, for about 5 minutes or until the mixture is thick and well blended. Add the *jalapeños* and prawns to the skillet, season with salt and pepper, and stir in the eggs. Cook over low heat, stirring with a wooden spoon until the eggs have set, about 4 minutes. Cook for 1 minute longer and serve immediately sliding the eggs onto a warmed plate and cutting into wedges like a pie. Serve with lemon wedges. **SERVES 4.**

SCRAMBLED EGGS WITH GREEN BEANS
Huevos Revueltos con Ejotes

This is probably a family recipe invented by an enterprising family cook to liven up a vegetable dish to be served at *comida*. Whatever its origin it was a favorite and might even turn up at supper with ham on the side and *salsa verde*. I don't think it would be unfair to say that Tío Miguel was a food faddist, and though a mild mannered batchelor gentleman, the family never challenged his word because since the death of his father he was regarded as head of the household to his two widowed sisters, who lived with him. His crazes never lasted long and it was taken for granted that as a man he was inherently superior. It was an easy tyranny for though he was the youngest, he allowed my mother-in-law to assume that position so that she could put her age back a few years. This may have come from one of his chili obsessed periods. It's a good recipe.

1 lb green beans cut into 1-inch pieces

1 cup chicken stock

2 tablespoons corn or peanut oil

1 onion, finely chopped

1 *jalapeño* chili, seeded and chopped

Salt, freshly ground black pepper

6 large eggs, lightly beaten

Cook the beans in the chicken stock for about 8 minutes, or until they are tender. Drain and set aside. Reserve the stock for another use. Heat the oil in a frying pan and sauté the onion and *jalapeño* until they are tender. Add the beans, season to taste with salt and pepper and sauté for 2 minutes longer. Stir in the eggs and cook over low heat continuing to stir with a wooden spoon until the eggs have set lightly, 3-4 minutes. Serve, if liked, with ham and *salsa verde*. **SERVES 4.**

EGGS SCRAMBLED WITH BEEF JERKY
Machacado con Huevo

Machacado means "crushed" and this is what is done to the dried beef (jerky), traditionally using a special black stone, flat on one side and curved on the other which fits comfortably into the hand. This way the meat is pounded to shred it. The beef is called *cecina* or *charqui* which turns into "jerky" in English. Before refrigeration the best way to preserve beef in the northern cattle states was by salting and sun-drying it.

1 tomato, peeled and chopped

1 onion, finely chopped

2 cloves garlic, chopped

2 *serrano* chilies or 1 *jalapeño* chili, pickled and chopped

2 tablespoons corn or peanut oil

2 tablespoons beef jerky (dried beef), shredded

4 large eggs, lightly beaten

Salt, if necessary

Combine the chopped ingredients and sauté in a large saucepan in the oil until the mixture is thick and well blended, about 5 minutes. Stir in the beef and cook for 3-4 minutes longer. Add the eggs and stir with a wooden spoon until they have set. Because the dried beef is salty added salt will probably not be needed. Taste and add if necessary. **SERVES 2-3.**

EGGS WITH CACTUS PIECES
Huevos con Nopalitos

The cactus pieces here are from the *nopal*, or prickly pear cactus, whose spiny fruit, the tuna or prickly pear is now readily available, fortunately with the spines removed. The cactus pieces are the paddles, cleaned, chopped and canned. They are very rarely sold fresh as it is not easy to remove the spines that cover them. They are used in vegetable dishes and salads as they have a fresh, pleasant taste. The version here was from Queretaro and is the simplest. We found a slightly different recipe in Oaxaca, that exciting state of churches, Mayan ruins, markets and ancient customs. I was given the recipe in the market, while a third version came from a friend in Cuernavaca. It was interesting because the eggs were not scrambled but poached, described as *ahogados*, drowned, presumably in the sauce. We liked all three, so here they are.

1 cup canned *nopalitos,* chopped

3 tablespoons butter or corn or peanut oil

2 tablespoons heavy cream

6 large eggs, lightly beaten

Salt, freshly ground white pepper

Drain and rinse the *nopalitos* in cold water then drain again thoroughly. Pat dry with kitchen towels. Heat the butter or oil in a frying pan and sauté the *nopalitos* lightly. Whisk the cream into the eggs, season with salt and pepper and pour into the pan, stirring with a wooden spoon to reach the entire surface of the pan just until the eggs are set, about 3-4 minutes. They should have a creamy consistency. Serve immediately with hot tortillas. **SERVES 3-4.**

POACHED EGGS WITH CACTUS PIECES
Huevos Ahogados con Nopalitos

2 *pasilla* chilies, seeded

3 tablespoons corn or peanut oil

1 onion, finely chopped

1 lb tomatoes, peeled and chopped

1 clove garlic, chopped

1 cup *nopalitos* (canned cactus pieces) coarsely chopped

1 cup chicken stock

8 oz cream cheese, sliced

6 large eggs

Salt

In a small frying pan heat 1 tablespoon of the oil and lightly fry the *pasilla* chilies. Do not let them burn. Lift out onto kitchen towels and when they are cool enough to handle, cut them into strips. Set aside.

Put the rest of the oil into a large frying pan and sauté the onion until it is soft. Put the tomatoes and garlic into a food processor and reduce to a purée. Pour into the pan with the onion and cook, stirring for 5 minutes. Add the cactus pieces and chilies and simmer for 5 minutes longer. Stir in the chicken stock and cook just long enough to heat it through. Add the cream cheese, season with salt then break the eggs one by one into a saucer and slide into the pan. Cook until the whites of the eggs have set then serve immediately with the sauce. If the sauce seems that it will be too watery when cooking, reduce the amount of chicken stock. It should be the consistency of light cream. Serve with hot tortillas. **SERVES 3-4.**

EGGS OAXACA-STYLE
Huevos Oaxaqueños

1 lb tomatoes, peeled and chopped

4 fresh *serrano* chilies, seeded and chopped

1 onion, chopped

1 clove garlic, chopped

3 tablespoons corn or peanut oil

1 cup *nopalitos* (cactus pieces), chopped

6 large eggs, lightly beaten

Salt

In a food processor combine the tomatoes, chilies, onion and garlic and reduce to a purée. Heat the oil in a frying pan and pour in the purée. Add the cactus pieces and cook, stirring from time to time for 5 minutes. Season with salt. Stir in the eggs and continue to stir until the eggs are set. Serve immediately with hot tortillas. **SERVES 4.**

SCRAMBLED EGGS WITH VEGETABLES
Pisto

Who first invented this dish is a mystery. It turns up in Don Quixote country in Spain as a vegetable medley with fried or poached eggs served separately. In both the Spanish and Mexican versions most of the vegetables are from the New World so the question remains open. I was given it by family connections in Durango so my version is a northern Mexican one. Its origin doesn't really matter, it is more a question of curiosity, asking who was the genius cook who first put it all together. It is great for vegetarians who eat eggs if you omit the ham and for anyone who likes vegetables, and who doesn't?

3 tablespoons olive oil

1 onion, finely chopped

4 small new potatoes, cooked, peeled and cut into cubes

2 small zucchini, cooked and coarsely chopped

¼ lb cooked ham, chopped

1 sweet red pepper (pimiento), peeled, seeded and chopped

1 pickled *jalapeño* chili, chopped

2 tablespoons parsley, chopped

½ lb tomatoes, peeled and chopped

1 cup cooked green peas

Salt, freshly ground black pepper

6 large eggs, lightly beaten

Heat the oil in a large, heavy frying pan and sauté the onion until it is tender, but not brown. Add the potatoes, zucchini, ham, red pepper, chili and parsley. Sauté over moderate heat for about 5 minutes, stirring so that the mixture does not burn, and taking care not to break up the vegetables. Add the tomatoes and continue cooking for a few more minutes. Add the peas and season with salt and pepper. Fold the eggs into the vegetable mixture gently and cook until the eggs have set. **SERVES 4.**

SCRAMBLED EGGS
Huevos Revueltos

This is a northern way of cooking scrambled eggs, not as elaborate as *Huevos a la Mexicana* (Eggs, Mexican-Style), but not entirely plain either. They were a family favorite which I found intriguingly different from our own very French-style *Oeufs Brouillés* (Scrambled Eggs) where butter plays a dominant role. The family didn't like my eggs as my mother-in-law said they had "*demasiado mantequilla*" (too much butter). I did like theirs.

4 tablespoons butter

1 onion, finely chopped

3 tablespoons sour cream

6 large eggs, lightly beaten

3 tablespoons parsley, chopped

Salt

In a frying pan heat the butter and sauté the onion until it is tender but not browned. Set aside. Whisk the sour cream into the eggs and fold in the parsley. Season with salt. Reheat the onion mixture over low heat then add the egg mixture, stirring with a wooden spoon to reach the entire surface of the pan, for 3-4 minutes, or until just set. Serve immediately with fresh warm tortillas or toast. **SERVES 3.**

EGGS *"EN RABO DE MESTIZA"*
Huevos en "Rabo de Mestiza"

In Mexican cookbooks *"Rabo de Mestiza"* is always put in quotation marks—no one seems to know what it means. Actually it is a Spanish phrase dating back to the early days of the Conquest which means literally "in the rags and tatters of the daughter of a Spaniard and an Indian." It must be remembered that sixteenth century Spaniards were rather inclined to give bizarre names to food. *Ropa Vieja*, an honorable Spanish dish, means "old clothes" and the famous *Olla Podrida*, an excellent stew, means "rotten pot." Oh well, we have Toad in a Hole. *Poblano* chilies are the type that should be used for this but if they are not available, sweet green peppers are the best substitute. If liked, half a chopped *serrano* may be added to the sauce as the *poblanos* can be a little *picante*, and the sauce should not be bland.

3 *poblano* chilies or sweet green peppers, peeled and seeded
¼ cup olive oil
1 onion, finely chopped
1½ lbs tomatoes, peeled and chopped
½ *serrano* chili, seeded and chopped (optional)
Salt, freshly ground black pepper
6 oz cream cheese, sliced into 1-oz pieces
6 large eggs

Cut the chilies or peppers into strips. Heat the oil in a frying pan that has a lid. Add the chili or pepper strips and the onion and sauté them until the onion is tender. Add the tomatoes, season with salt and pepper and cook until the mixture is thick and well blended, about 10 minutes. It should not be smooth but retain some texture. Break the eggs, one by one, into a saucer and slide them gently into the sauce. Add the slices of cheese, cover and cook just until the whites of the eggs are set. If preferred, first add the cheese and slide the eggs on top. Serve egg, cheese, sauce and chili strips in shallow bowls. **SERVES 3.**

EGGS MOTUL-STYLE
Huevos Motuleños

These eggs are named after a small town in Yucatán though we had them in Mérida and I think at the hotel at Chichén Itzá. Sometimes we only got one egg, mostly two and sometimes the tortillas were crisp and sometimes just fried long enough to soften and warm them.

¼ **cup lard or corn oil**

6 **tortillas**

6 **tablespoons** *Frijoles Negros Refritos* (**Fried Black Beans**) (**see page 159**), **kept warm**

6 **large eggs**

1 **cup** *Salsa de Tomate Yucateca* (**Tomato Sauce, Yucatán-style**) (**page 56**), **kept warm**

2 **tablespoons grated Parmesan cheese**

1 **cup cooked green peas**

Heat the lard or oil in a frying pan and fry the tortillas on both sides until crisp. Spread three of the tortillas with a layer of the beans, using them all. Keep warm. In the fat remaining in the frying pan fry the eggs and put an egg on top of each of the tortillas. Gently lay a second tortilla on top of the egg and top with a second egg. Spoon the warm sauce over the eggs and sprinkle with cheese. Arrange the peas round each serving. **SERVES 3.**

SCRAMBLED EGGS MEXICAN-STYLE
Huevos Revueltos a la Mexicana

Once in a restaurant in Yucatán I saw these translated on the menu into "Screemble Mexican" and have wondered ever since what a "Screembled Mexican" would be like. Muddled, my husband said. However translated, the eggs are awfully good.

½ **cup** *Salsa de Jitomate* (**Tomato Sauce**) (**page 81**)

12 **large eggs, lightly beaten**

Salt, freshly ground black pepper

Pour the sauce into a large, preferably non-stick, frying pan and heat through over low heat.

Season the eggs with salt and pepper using the salt lightly as the sauce has salt. Pour the eggs into the sauce and cook them for 3-4 minutes stirring slowly and constantly with a wooden spoon to reach the entire surface of the pan. Serve immediately when eggs are set. **SERVES 6.**

Serve with fresh hot tortillas and beans, either plain or refritos *and with a bowl of pickled* serranos *or* jalapeños *on the side.*

COUNTRY-STYLE EGGS
Huevos Rancheros

This is Mexico's favorite egg dish. I could not imagine it without *Frijoles Refritos* (Refried Beans) but soupy beans are often preferred and the avocado garnish is dispensed with. Pickled *serranos* or *jalapeños* may be served as a side dish. The combined flavor of tortilla, sauce and egg are what gives the magic to this. There are few times when it would come amiss. It would be welcome for breakfast, light lunch or late supper.

2 recipes Country-Style Sauce (*Salsa Ranchero*) (page 77)

¼ cup corn oil or lard, or more if needed

12 small tortillas

12 large eggs

1 recipe Refried Beans (*Frijoles Refritos*) (page 159)

For the Garnish: 3 tablespoons grated Parmesan cheese (optional)

1 avocado, sliced (optional)

Warm the sauce and set it aside, covered to keep warm. In a frying pan heat the oil or lard and quickly fry the tortillas on both sides to soften them, just for a few seconds. Drain them on paper towels, wrap in foil and keep them warm. In the fat remaining in the frying pan, adding a little more if necessary fry the eggs just until the whites are set. The yolks should remain runny.

Assemble the dish. Put two tortillas on each of six warm plates and put an egg on each, two for each serving. Pour some of the sauce on the whites but do not mask the yolks with it. Sprinkle with cheese if liked and garnish the plates with sliced avocado. Serve the beans separately. Serve any remaining sauce separately. **SERVES 6.**

RICE

•

Arroz

When we were first in Mexico the rice available was of very poor quality, often broken, but the cooked rice was always superb, each grain separate and never mushy, well flavored, a tribute to the cook. I was surprised at the technique used. The rice was always soaked in hot water before cooking. I knew this was done by cooks in ancient Persia where cooking as an art is said to have begun, and since rice came to Mexico via Spain from Asia I supposed echoes of its cooking past came with it. I also wondered if the technique was adopted because of the altitude, for we were at almost 8,000 feet above sea level. Whatever the explanation, I adopted the method with admirable results. Later, from my friend and colleague Sri Owen, I picked up a useful kitchen trick. If the rice is to stand even a short time after it is cooked, put a folded tea towel on top of the saucepan, and replace the saucepan lid. This will prevent any moisture from condensed steam dropping back on the rice and spoiling it.

GREEN RICE
Arroz Verde

The dark green *poblano* chilies are the right ones to use for this but they are seldom available. The best substitute are sweet green peppers, sometimes called bell peppers from their almost square, rather squat shape. They lack the special flavor of the *poblano* but have an attractive flavor of their own.

4 *poblano* chilies or sweet green peppers, peeled, seeded and chopped (see page 18)

2 cups long or medium grain white rice

1 cup flat leafed parsley, chopped

1 onion, chopped

1 clove garlic, chopped

4 cups chicken stock

¼ cup olive or corn oil

Salt, freshly ground black pepper

Prepare the chilies and set them aside. Put the rice into a bowl and pour hot water over it to cover. Let stand for 15 minutes, drain, rinse in cold water, drain again and let it stand in a sieve to dry thoroughly. In a food processor combine the chilies, parsley, onion and garlic and process to a smooth purée. Heat the oil in a large saucepan or casserole and sauté the rice, stirring from time to time, until it is golden and all the oil absorbed. Stir in the chili mixture and sauté for 2-3 minutes longer. Pour in the stock, season to taste with salt and pepper, bring to a simmer, reduce the heat as low as possible, cover and simmer until all the liquid is absorbed and the rice is tender, about 15 minutes. **SERVES 6.**

YELLOW RICE
Arroz Amarillo

Although this rice cooks to a rosy red, for some curious reason it is always called *Arroz Amarillo* (Yellow Rice).

2 cups long or medium grain white rice

1 onion, chopped

2 cloves garlic, chopped

1 lb tomatoes, peeled, seeded and chopped

¼ cup olive or corn oil

4 cups chicken stock

Salt, freshly ground black pepper

Put the rice in a bowl and cover with hot water. Stand for 15 minutes, drain, rinse in cold water, drain again and let it stand in a sieve to dry thoroughly. Set aside.

In a food processor combine the onion, garlic and tomatoes and process to a smooth purée. Heat the oil in a large saucepan or casserole and sauté the rice until it is golden and has absorbed all the oil. Add the tomato mixture and cook, stirring, for 2-3 minutes longer. Pour in the stock, stir to mix, bring to a simmer, reduce the heat as low as possible and cook, covered, until the liquid has all been absorbed and the rice is tender, about 15 minutes. **SERVES 6.**

GOLDEN RICE
Arroz Gualdo

This recipe was given me by a friend's cook when we were travelling in the provinces. I think the cook came from Chiapas, certainly from the south where *achiote* is much used. I have never come across it in a book, or restaurant and I wonder if perhaps it was the cook's own creation. The rice has a deep golden color and very subtle flavor.

2 cups long or medium grain white rice

¼ cup corn oil

2 tablespoons annatto (*achiote*) seeds

1 onion, finely chopped

4 cups chicken stock

Salt

Put the rice into a bowl and pour over enough hot water to cover. Let it stand 15-20 minutes. Drain the rice, rinse in cold water, drain again and let it stand in the sieve to dry thoroughly.

While the rice is drying heat the oil in a small frying pan and add the annatto (*achiote*) seeds over low heat, stirring from time to time until the oil is a rich orange-red. This may take from 1 to 5 minutes according to how fresh the seeds are. Stale seeds will give up their color quickly and the oil will turn from orange to gold if the heat is continued. As soon as the color begins to lighten take the frying pan off the heat, cool the oil and lift out and discard the seeds.

Pour the oil into a casserole or saucepan and sauté the rice and onion over moderate heat, stirring from time to time, until the rice has absorbed all the oil. Pour in the stock, season with salt if necessary, bring to a simmer, reduce the heat as low as possible, cover and cook until the rice is tender and all the liquid absorbed, about 15 minutes. **SERVES 6.**

MEXICAN-STYLE RICE
Arroz a la Mexicana

This is the most popular of all the rice *sopa secas* enjoyed in homes, restaurants and *fondas* all over the Republic with slight variations but essentially the same. The peas can be left out though most cooks include them.

2 cups long or medium grain white rice

1 onion, chopped

2 cloves garlic, chopped

1 lb tomatoes, peeled, seeded and chopped

¼ cup olive oil

4 cups chicken stock

Salt

½ cup cooked green peas

For the Garnish: Fresh red chilies, cut into flowers

1 avocado, peeled and sliced

Coriander sprigs

Put the rice into a bowl and pour in hot water to cover. Stand for 15 minutes. Drain and rinse in cold water. Drain again and let it stand in a sieve to dry thoroughly. Set aside.

In a food processor combine the onion, garlic and tomatoes and process to a smooth purée. Heat the oil in a frying pan and sauté the rice over moderate heat, stirring from time to time until it is golden and has absorbed all the oil. Transfer to a saucepan and stir in the tomato mixture and the stock. Bring to a simmer, cover and lower the heat, and cook until almost all the liquid has been absorbed. Fold in the peas, and continue cooking until all the liquid is absorbed and the rice is tender. **SERVES 6-8.**

For the pepper flowers, choose tapering chilies about 4 inches long and slice them from the tip to the stem end in 4 or 5 sections. These will curl back forming flowers.

WHITE RICE
Arroz Blanco

This is the standard Mexican way of cooking everyday plain white rice. I have never found it to fail.

2 cups long or medium grain white rice

Hot water

¼ cup corn or peanut oil

1 onion, finely chopped

1 clove garlic, finely chopped

4 cups chicken stock

Salt if necessary

Put the rice into a bowl and pour over hot water to cover. Stand for 20 minutes. Drain the rice, rinse in cold water, drain through a sieve and leave to stand to dry.

Heat the oil in a casserole or saucepan and add the rice, sauté over moderate heat, stirring, until the rice grains are coated with oil, a matter of minutes. Stir in the onion and garlic and continue to sauté, stirring from time to time, until the rice is lightly colored, a pale gold. Stir in the chicken stock, bring to a simmer, cover and lower the heat as much as possible. Leave for 15 minutes or until the rice is tender and all the liquid absorbed. Continue cooking a little longer if necessary. The rice is now ready to be used. It will keep warm for about 15 minutes if necessary. In this case cover the casserole with a folded tea towel and place the pan lid on top to absorb any condensation.

The rice can be frozen. To reheat wrap it in aluminum foil and put into a 350°F oven until warm, about 45 minutes, or thaw, then reheat for about 15 minutes. **SERVES 6-8.**

VEGETABLES
AND SALADS

•

Verduras y Ensaladas

When, in the early days of the 16th century, Díaz del Castillo, a captain in Hernán Cortés's army first visited the great market in Tenochtitlán, the capital of Aztec Mexico, he wrote of his delight and astonishment at what he saw, all of it unfamiliar. Great piles of chilies, green, yellow and red, bright red tomatoes, corn, zucchini, avocados and beans, fresh runner beans and the dried beans like red kidney, pinto and black, and many more. Today in the great markets there are all the vegetables of the New World, as well as those of the rest of the world, in the jewel colors of red, green, yellow. I was an avid market-goer and in spite of this I got the false impression that Mexicans don't like green vegetables. What they don't like is plain green, or plain other colored vegetables, an attitude which goes a long way back as the Aztecs and Maya made vegetables part of dishes. For example you would not have meat or fish on a plate with potatoes and a plainly cooked green vegetable, instead wonderfully rich stews that Fray Sahagún found simmering in great *cazuelas* (earthenware casseroles) in the market, filled with vegetables and birds of some sort, or prawns. They still persist, using the greatly expanded range of food and modern cooking methods. I found it hard to understand the full role of vegetables in today's eating patterns as I was so used to the go-with patter. And salads, where do they belong?

Antojitos are always accompanied by shredded lettuce, sliced tomatoes, probably sliced onions, and radish flowers. Many families start *comida* with a leafy green salad and some serve salad at the same time as the main course. More robust salads of mixed cooked vegetables make good supper dishes and of course the on-the-table sauces like *salsa verde* and *salsa cruda* are made from vegetables, even though the tomato is, strictly speaking, a fruit. And guacamole is ever present. So the best way to put it is to say that vegetables and salads are integral to Mexican cuisine and if you eat Mexican you will eat vegetables.

STUFFED POTATOES
Papas Rellenas

The *chipotle* chili lifts this out of the ordinary with its quite extraordinary flavor. Though I was at home with other members of the family of cultivated *capsicums*, the *chipotle* posed problems. They taste like no other chili, I still cannot describe it. Also I found it hard to believe that it was just the *jalapeño* grown ripe, dried and smoked.

3 large baking potatoes

Béchamel sauce

½ cup freshly grated Parmesan cheese

½ cup sliced, cooked baby carrots

½ cup cooked petit peas

½ cup chicken breast, cooked and chopped

½ cup boiled ham, chopped

1 or more canned *chipotle* chilies, rinsed and chopped

Salt

For the Béchamel sauce:

1½ tablespoons unsalted butter

1½ tablespoons all-purpose flour

1 cup milk, or light cream

½ teaspoon salt

Pinch white pepper

Scrub the potatoes, rinse and dry thoroughly. Bake in a preheated 325°F oven until the potatoes are soft when gently squeezed, about 1½ hours. When they are cool enough to handle, cut the potatoes in half lengthwise and scoop out about three quarters of the flesh. Set the shell aside. Mash the potatoes until smooth, then beat in some butter and milk or until fluffy. Set aside.

Make the Béchamel sauce:

In a fairly small, heavy saucepan over low heat, melt the butter. Stir in the flour and stir constantly with a wooden spoon for 2 minutes. Remove from the heat and gradually stir in the milk until the mixture is smooth. Return the saucepan to the heat and cook, stirring over low heat, until the sauce has thickened. Stir in the salt and pepper.

To the hot Béchamel, add the grated Parmesan cheese stirring until well combined. Fold in the vegetables, chicken, ham and chili. Taste for seasoning. Spoon the mixture into the 6 potato shells, dividing it evenly, and spread mashed potato on top. Arrange on a baking sheet and bake in a preheated 325°F oven for 15 to 20 minutes or until the tops are lightly browned and the potatoes heated through. **SERVES 6.**

POBLANO PEPPERS WITH POTATOES
Poblanos con Papas

Potatoes were first cultivated in the Andean region of what is now Peru about 5,000 years ago, but had started to emigrate north sometime between then and the arrival of Hernán Cortés in Mexico in the early 16th century. There are records of potatoes and there are still wild potatoes to be found. This is a colonial dish with its cream and oil, but illustrates the point that plain vegetables are not much liked. In the north they might be served to accompany grilled meats. As a potato lover I found them irresistible though it was the Swiss *röesti* that César couldn't resist, which shows you what travel can do for you.

2 fresh *poblanos*
¼ cup mild Cheddar or similar cheese, grated coarsely
½ cup sour cream or *Crema Espesa* (page 314)
Salt
1 lb baking potatoes, peeled and cut into ½ inch cubes
¼ cup corn oil
1 onion, finely chopped
1 clove garlic, chopped

Toast the *poblanos* over a gas flame if possible, until they are charred all over. Put them into a plastic or brown paper bag, close it and leave to steam in their own heat for 15 minutes. Rinse off the charred skin under cold water, pulling off any bits that stick. Remove stems and seeds. Cut into strips ½ inch wide by 1½ inches long. Set aside. Put the potatoes into a saucepan with salted water to cover and bring to a boil over high heat. Reduce the heat and cook, covered, for 5 minutes. Drain and set aside.

In a frying pan heat the oil, add the onion and garlic and sauté over moderate heat until the onion is soft, about 3 minutes. Add the potatoes and cook stirring occasionally with a wooden spoon so as not to break them up, until they are golden. Add the *poblano* strips, cheese and cream and season to taste with salt. Cook just until the cheese melts and the cream is heated through. Serve with grilled meat or poultry. **SERVES 3-4.**

CHICK PEAS WITH SWEET RED PEPPERS
Garbanzos con Pimientos

The Spanish introduced chick peas to Mexico and although the Aztecs and Maya had their own beans they took to the newcomers, which are important in the food of Asia, the Middle East and Spain and Portugal. They go back so far that there is no record of the wild form, and they take forever to cook, so the wise thing is to buy them cooked and canned. César loved chick peas perhaps because his professional life in the Middle East as Information Chief to such peacekeepers as Count Bernadotte and Undersecretary Ralph Bunche with the United Nations had exposed him to the food of the region which he enjoyed. This is one of those family favorites that have become favorites because they not only taste good but are easy to cook.

¼ **cup olive oil**

1 **onion, finely chopped**

2 **cloves garlic, chopped**

3 **chorizo sausages, skinned and chopped**

4 **cups cooked canned chick peas, drained and rinsed**

2 **fresh *pimientos* (sweet red peppers) peeled, seeded and cut into strips**

½ **teaspoon dried oregano, crumbled**

Salt

Chicken stock if necessary

Heat the oil in a frying pan and sauté the onion, garlic and sausages until the onion is tender. Add the peppers and sauté for 3 minutes longer. In a saucepan combine the onion mixture, the chick peas and oregano, season to taste with salt, stir to mix and heat through. Add a little chicken stock if necessary. Serve with grilled meat. **SERVES 6.**

NOTE: *To cook raw chick peas, soak them overnight in water to cover. Drain, rinse, then cover with fresh water and put into a saucepan, bring to simmering point and cook, covered, until the chick peas are tender, anything from 2 to 6 hours. The time will vary with the age of the beans. As soon as they are tender, add salt, but not before. They keep their shape, even after long cooking.*

GREENS
Quelites

Quelites comes from the Nahuatl word *quilitl* meaning "any green herb" and is in fact the exact equivalent of our own word "greens." Díaz del Castillo writes of enduring a diet including herbs such as the leaves of species of *Chenopodium* and *Amaranthus*. Many of the best recipes are for greens we don't use but since it is the sauce and cooking method that are important I have included any that I have very much enjoyed, whether or not the particular *quelites* are available. I think it is perfectly legitimate in this instance to use any of our extensive list of greens: turnip greens, spring greens, kale, mustard, dandelion greens and endive. Some of the recipes are for greens which we have in common such as spinach and Swiss chard.

Green vegetables in Mexico, being elaborate, are served as a separate course though they may accompany plain roast or grilled meat, poultry or fish. They provide both vegetable and sauce and are popular in the north—cattle country and home of roast kid.

SWISS CHARD WITH POTATOES AND CHICK PEAS
Acelgas con Papas y Garbanzos

It is the combination of vegetables and flavorings that makes vegetables in Mexico such fun, so often so unexpected. It is also from a practical point of view, useful for coping with leftovers.

1½ lbs Swiss chard, green leaves only

1 onion, finely chopped

1 clove garlic, chopped

½ teaspoon *pequín* or other hot dried chilies, crumbled

1 lb tomatoes, peeled, seeded and chopped

3 tablespoons corn oil or lard

Salt, pinch of sugar

6 small new potatoes, cooked and peeled

1 cup chick peas, cooked

Grated Parmesan cheese or any fresh cheese

Put the chard into a saucepan of briskly boiling salted water, and cook for three minutes. Drain and chop. Heat the oil or lard in a frying pan and sauté the onion and garlic until the onion is soft. Add the chilies and tomatoes and cook, stirring from time to time until the mixture is thick and well blended, about 5 minutes. Season to taste with salt and a pinch of sugar. Stir in the potatoes, chick peas and chard and cook just long enough to heat through. Serve with cheese. If liked add 1 cup cooked corn kernels instead of chick peas, or as well as. **SERVES 6.**

GREENS IN *MULATO* CHILI SAUCE
Quintoniles con Chile Mulato

The *mulato* is an essential in the national dish, *Mole Poblano de Guajolote*. It looks like the *ancho* but is less wrinkled, larger, and sweeter in flavor. It is rich flavored rather than hot.

1½ lbs any greens
Salt
3 dried *mulato* chilies
1 onion, chopped
1 clove garlic, chopped
3 tablespoons corn oil or lard
3 hardboiled eggs, sliced

Cook the greens in the usual way in briskly boiling salted water, drain, chop and set aside. Toast the *mulatos* in a dry frying pan, lightly, take out, remove the stems and shake out the seeds. Tear the chilies into pieces and put into a bowl with warm water to cover and soak for 20 minutes. Take out and reserve the soaking water. In a food processor combine the chilies, onion, and garlic and process to a purée. In a frying pan heat the oil or lard and cook the purée for 5 minutes over a moderate heat, stirring from time to time. Stir in the greens. If the mixture is too dry add a little of the reserved soaking water from the chilies. Heat the mixture through, taste for seasoning and serve garnished with the sliced eggs. **SERVES 6.**

GREEN BEAN SALAD
Ensalada de Ejotes

1 lb cut green beans, cooked

3 *pimientos* (sweet red peppers) peeled, seeded and chopped (if available canned or bottled, drain and chop)

1 small white onion, finely chopped

½ cup finely chopped flat leafed parsley or fresh coriander

¾ cup oil and vinegar dressing (page 184)

Lettuce leaves

Toss all the ingredients except the lettuce in a bowl with the dressing. Arrange on a bed of lettuce leaves. **SERVES 6.**

GREEN BEANS WITH SWEET RED PEPPERS
Ejotes con Pimientos

Surrounded with so much that was new, it was fun to meet up with the scarlet runner bean and to find out that it had first seen the light of day as a cultivated vegetable in Mexico. I thought of all those London back gardens with fences festooned with the bright red flowers that give the scarlet runner its name.

1 lb fresh green beans, cut into 1½ inch pieces

3 tablespoons corn oil

1 onion, finely chopped

3 *pimientos* (sweet red peppers) peeled, seeded and coarsely chopped (page 18, note on *poblano*)

Salt

Bring a large saucepan of salted water to the boil and add the beans. Bring back to the boil and cook for 5 to 8 minutes. Drain. Heat the oil in a frying pan and sauté the onion until it is soft. Add the beans and the peppers, season with salt and heat through, stirring. Serve immediately. **SERVES 6.**

CAULIFLOWER IN *ADOBO* SAUCE
Coliflor en Adobo Rojo o Adobo Verde

There was sometimes leftover *adobo* or it was sometimes convenient to make an extra quantity, and since we got splendid cauliflowers this became a favorite recipe. Just by itself it can make an adequate luncheon, easily adapted for vegetarians.

1 large head cauliflower, about 1½ lbs
1 recipe *Adobo* Sauce (page 175)
Salt
Butter

Trim away any tough leaves and the woody base from the cauliflower. Have ready a large saucepan of briskly boiling, salted water and put the whole cauliflower face down and simmer for 15 minutes. Drain. Butter a flameproof casserole and add the cauliflower. Have the *adobo* sauce heated and pour it over the vegetable and cook, uncovered, over a very low heat for 5 minutes, or until the cauliflower is tender. When making the *adobo* sauce use chicken stock instead of pork stock. **SERVES 6.**

PURSLANE WITH *CHIPOTLE* CHILI
Verdolagas con Chipotle

This is *Portulaca oleracea* and just how it reached the New World from the old as far back as the first millennium is a mystery. It is a succulent little plant but if it is not available, use any greens. The extraordinary flavor of *chipotle* makes the recipe worthwhile no matter what green is used.

1½ lbs any greens
3 tablespoons corn or peanut oil
1 onion, finely chopped
2 cloves garlic, chopped
1 or more canned *chipotle* chilies, rinsed and chopped
½ lb cooked pork, cut into ½-inch pieces
Salt

Cook the greens in the usual way in briskly boiling salted water. Drain and chop. Heat the oil in a frying pan and sauté the onion, garlic, *chipotle* and pork until the onion is tender. Stir in the greens, mix well, season with salt if necessary and heat through. **SERVES 6.**

PURSLANE IN GREEN SAUCE
Verdolagas en Salsa Verde

As purslane is not likely to be available, use any green of your choice. The subtle green sauce marries as well with greens as the exotic *chipotle* sauce. Choose a mild flavored green.

1½ lbs any greens
½ recipe Cooked Green Sauce (*Salsa Verde Cocida*) (page 80)
Salt

Cook the greens in the usual way in briskly boiling salted water, drain and chop. Combine the greens and the sauce in a saucepan and gently heat them through. **SERVES 6.**

MEXICAN GREEN TOMATOES WITH CHEESE
Tomatillos con Queso

I don't know where this recipe came from. I had it on César's cousin Humberto's ranch, the inspiration I think of China, his wife. She was called China because she was beautiful, and because she didn't like her name Marta Eugenia. She was a wonderful mother, and a very brilliant cook. When they make complimentary remarks on my books I think of how much I owe them, endlessly generous in imparting information, the Ortizes and their friends and children. Some of the ingredients are a little difficult to find, but it is worth the effort.

2 tablespoons butter or oil
1 onion, finely chopped
8 oz *tomatillos*, if canned, drained weight
2 Anaheim or similar green chili pepper, peeled, seeded and chopped
1 cup fresh coriander sprigs, chopped
Salt

8 oz cottage or similar cheese, cubed

¾ cup *Crema Espesa* (page 314)

Heat the butter or oil in a large frying pan and sauté the onion, garlic and Anaheim chili until the vegetables are soft. Add the *tomatillos*, coriander and salt to taste and simmer, uncovered, over low heat for 5 minutes. Add the cheese and as soon as it begins to melt stir in the cream. Cook just long enough to heat through. Serve as a dip with tortilla chips, or as a sauce over eggs.

GREENS WITH *POBLANO* CHILIES
Quelites con Chile Poblano

Any greens you are cooking will be suitable for this recipe as the sauce will not be overpowering. If you are a lover of the *poblano*, this is a good excuse for using it.

1½ lbs greens, cooked and coarsely chopped

2 *poblano* chilies

3 tablespoons corn or peanut oil

1 onion, finely chopped

1 clove garlic, chopped

¾ lb tomatoes, peeled, seeded and chopped

Salt

Set the greens aside to keep warm. Toast the *poblanos* over a gas flame or under a grill until they are blackened all over. Put them into a brown paper, or plastic bag and let them steam for 15 minutes. Rinse off the charred papery skin, remove the stems and seeds and slice thinly. Heat the oil in a frying pan and sauté the onion and garlic until the onion is tender but not brown. Add the *poblanos* and tomatoes and cook, stirring from time to time, for 5 minutes. Add the prepared greens, taste for seasoning, stir and heat through.
SERVES 6.

ROMERITOS

I should subtitle this "Pride Goeth Before a Fall." It was in my earliest days in Mexico and, aided by the market women, I was having considerable success cooking local dishes. Then I heard about *romeritos* which translates as "rosemary" but was clearly not rosemary as I knew it. In my quest for knowledge I frequently came upon problems as to what was what. I recall César's aunt, I am sure in an endeavor to put me in my place, asking me if in England we had a spice called macey. Pompously I said that yes, we did and that it was called mace, in Spanish *macis*. How, at such times, they must have disliked me. But to *romeritos*. I acquired a recipe and, since it was Lent decided to surprise the family with a dish of *romeritos* which were the "rosemary" in a rich sauce served with dried shrimp fritters. I took off for the market at a rather late hour for buying green stuff and a wily lady was ready to offload her last bunch of the things to me. It was naughty of her as the skinny little leaves should have been stripped off their woody stems. It was a complicated recipe and I slaved mightily over it, so it was a mortification of the spirit to be told when I served it that it was inedible as the woody stems should not be there. They ate the dried shrimp fritters. Apparently *romeritos* are usually sold ready to cook which is probably why none of the cookbooks I consulted said to strip the leaves from the stems. I suppose I felt a bit better but all the same I did feel that common sense should have told me that a woody stem is less than appetizing.

I never found this vegetable outside Mexico. The best thing to do is substitute 12 oz of canned *nopalitos* (cactus paddles) as these are used in the dish. The canned paddles need only be rinsed to be ready to use and they should be available from shops selling Mexican ingredients or by mail order. If defeated in the search for *nopalitos*, it might be possible to substitute very young French beans and I even heard of a cook who used finely chopped spinach for the *romeritos*. After all the Aztecs called edible green herbs *quilitl* greens, so why not?

Romeritos turn up in cookbooks in a more accessible form titled *Revoltijo* (Scrambled) and is popular in the vigils before Easter and also Christmas. Instead of making the sauce for *Mole Poblano* specially, keep some refrigerated when the holiday dish is made. There is always abundant sauce and instead of using spinach as a substitute for *romeritos* here I use the green part of Swiss chard (*acelgas*).

1 lb Swiss chard, green part only, chopped

Salt

10 oz *nopalitos*, chopped

½ lb new potatoes, boiled, peeled and quartered

½ lb dried shrimp, cleaned

¼ cup breadcrumbs

2 eggs, lightly beaten

Corn or peanut oil for frying

2 cups *mole* sauce

In a saucepan of briskly boiling salted water cook the chopped chard for 3 minutes, drain and set aside with the *nopalitos*, if canned rinsed and chopped, if fresh, cooked in briskly boiling water for 10 minutes, drained and chopped. Add the potatoes. Simmer half the dried shrimp for about 10 minutes, drain and set aside with the vegetables. Put the other half of the shrimp in a food processor and reduce to a purée. In a bowl combine the shrimp purée, breadcrumbs and eggs adding more breadcrumbs if necessary to give a fairly firm mixture. Heat oil in a frying pan and fry the mixture by the tablespoon until delicately brown on both sides. Drain on paper towels.

Combine all the other ingredients in a saucepan with the *mole* sauce and cook just to heat through. Just before serving add the shrimp fritters.
SERVES 6.

GREENS WITH *ANCHO* CHILI SAUCE
Quelites con Chile Ancho

A fairly robust green like Swiss chard is a good one to balance the full, round flavor of the *anchos*.

3 *ancho* chilies
1½ lbs Swiss chard, green part only
1 onion, chopped
1 clove garlic, chopped
2 tablespoons corn or peanut oil
Salt

Toast the *anchos* lightly on both sides, in a dry pan. Lift out, remove the stems and shake out the seeds. Tear into pieces and put into a small bowl with warm water to cover. Let soak for 20 minutes. Strain and reserve the soaking water. Cook the Swiss chard leaves in a large saucepan of briskly boiling salted water for 3-5 minutes. Drain and chop coarsely. Set aside in a saucepan. Combine the *anchos*, onion and garlic in a food processor and reduce to a purée. Heat the oil in a frying pan and cook the purée, stirring, over moderate heat for 5 minutes. Stir in the reserved soaking water and stir to a smooth sauce. Season with salt. If more liquid is needed use chicken stock. Add the sauce to the greens and heat through, stirring. **SERVES 6.**

BEANS
Frijoles

When Cortés arrived in Mexico they found everyone eating, not the beans they were used to but *Phaseolus vulgaris*, the common bean, essential to the Mexican diet. It was the red kidney, which had been cultivated since 5000 B.C. and was the earliest cultivated bean in the Americas, and one of the earliest in the world. The country rejoices in beans. There is the pinto, a sort of light brown speckled bean, the most popular one for *Frijoles Refritos* (Refried Beans), that triumph of bean cookery; the *frijol negro*, the black bean, the Mayan favorite, always cooked with the herb *epazote*; the *canario* (yellow bean); *bayos* (brownish), and probably many others I never met up with. For all practical purposes there are only a few recipes: *Frijoles de Olla*, literally beans cooked in a pot, sometimes described as Soupy Beans, Brothy Beans, or more accurately Boiled Beans; *Frijoles Refritos*, cooked beans mashed and fried with lard or sometimes oil; *Frijoles Charros*, named for the Charros, the elegant horseman of Mexico; and *Frijoles Borrachos*, Drunken Beans which are Charro beans cooked with beer. These are both from Monterrey which has great beer and horsemen. Both of Césars uncles, army generals, were cavalry and the elder of the two introduced the army to polo though I don't know if they were keen on *Frijoles Charros* or *Borrachos*. Beans are eaten at *almuerzo*, the second and hearty breakfast, at *comida*, and if hunger persists, at supper.

The Spanish were not beanless, they too had their legumes, *habas*, the broad bean, and *garbanzos* (chick peas), the bean family being universal with Oriental soya and adzuki, African black-eyed peas.

Doña Carmelita graciously taught me to cook beans her way, the right way. I called them Seven Precious Beans so that I would not forget the seven important things to do in the right sequence. The grandmother insisted right off that though you should pick over the beans and rinse them, they must not be soaked. They should be put into an earthenware *cazuela* with a finely chopped onion, a clove of garlic, chilies if liked and a bay leaf and enough cold water to cover by about 1 inch, brought to a simmer, covered and cooked until the beans begin to wrinkle, in about 20 minutes. Then some lard must be added, the beans covered again and left to simmer. They must be checked from time to time to see if they are cooking dry in which case 1 cup boiling water should be added, and if necessary this step repeated at intervals. As soon as the beans are soft, salt to taste should be added, but not before. The beans should then be cooked, covered, over low heat for 30 minutes. By this time there should not be a great deal of liquid left. The beans are fine to eat whenever you want but there is one more refinement that may have belonged to the family, or been a northern extra, or for that matter what all Mexican cooks do.

Heat 1 tablespoon of lard in a frying pan and sauté an onion and a clove of garlic, both finely chopped until they are soft then add a medium size tomato, peeled and chopped and cook until the mixture is well blended, then mash half a cupful of beans and their liquid with them into a heavy paste and stir into the bean pot to thicken what liquid is left. I've always cooked beans this way, the grandmother's only correct way, and served them after the main course and before dessert, accompanied by a tortilla or two. At *comida* in my mother-in-law's apartment which she shared with her brother and sister, beans were always served to Uncle Miguel but never to the rest of us. We weren't even asked if we wanted any. Herlinda would be summoned from the kitchen and told to bring the señor's beans and that was that. I wondered why I never questioned the practice? Never until now have I even wondered about it.

BOILED BEANS
Frijoles de Olla

2 cups black, pinto or red kidney beans

2 onions, finely chopped

2 cloves garlic, chopped

Sprig *epazote* (for black beans) or 1 bay leaf for others

2 *serrano* chilies, seeded and chopped or 1 teaspoon dried *pequín* chilies, crumbled (optional)

3 tablespoons lard or corn oil

Salt

1 tomato, peeled, seeded and chopped

Pick over the beans but do not soak. Put them into a casserole, preferably earthenware with enough water to cover and one of the onions and cloves of garlic, the *epazote* or bay leaf and the chilies if using. Bring to a boil, reduce the heat, cover and simmer over low heat. As soon as the beans wrinkle, in about 20 minutes, stir in 2 tablespoons of the lard or oil and continue to simmer the beans. Be ready to add boiling water, 1 cup at a time as the water is absorbed. As soon as the beans are soft, add salt to taste. The time will vary according to the age or type of bean. Continue to cook for another 30 minutes. There should not be much liquid when the beans are done. ★

Heat the remaining lard or oil in a small frying pan and add the remaining onion and garlic and sauté until the onion is soft. Add the tomato and continue to cook until the mixture is thick and well blended. Add 4 tablespoons beans and any liquid with them and mash them into the onion mixture until there is a smooth paste. Stir this into the beans over low heat to thicken the remaining liquid. **SERVES 6.**

REFRIED BEANS
Frijoles Refritos

Frijoles Refritos translates as "refried beans" which they aren't. They are only fried once. There are a number of explanations none of them absolutely fool-proof. I can give you mine for what it is worth. Spanish is a very euphonious language and *frijoles fritos* is not euphonious. Change it to *refritos* and it sits sweetly on the ear.

1 recipe Boiled Beans (*Frijoles de Olla*) (page 158)

6 tablespoons lard, about

For garnish: Parmesan cheese, or crumbled cottage or similar cheese

Tortilla chips

Cook the beans to the point marked with a star (★) in the previous recipe. Omit the step to thicken the liquid.

In a large, heavy frying pan heat 2 tablespoons of lard and gradually mash in the beans, spoonful by spoonful. Add lard from time to time and continue over low heat until the beans form a heavy paste. Form into a roll on a serving platter and sprinkle with the cheese then stick a row of tortilla chips along their length. Serve as a side dish. If using for *antojitos*, simply spread the bean paste as needed. **SERVES 6-8.**

NUEVO LEÓN-STYLE BEANS
Frijoles Charros

This is often translated as "cowboy beans" which seems a rather inadequate, not to say down-putting name for the elaborately dressed horsemen of Mexico, the *Charros*, so I have named them for the state, Nuevo León, from which they come. The first time I watched the Independence Day parade from a building in Reforma, that grand Avenue that gave us a superb view, I have been an awe-stricken admirer of the *caballeros*, the horsemen. Alas, that building fell down in an earthquake, but memory stays green and how, with in-laws from Nuevo León could one forget? Also I'm too greedy to forget *agujas* (beef ribs) and *cabrito* (kid) that goes so well with the beans.

1 cup pinto or pink beans

¼ lb boneless pork, cut into ½-inch pieces

1 onion, chopped

2 cloves of garlic, chopped

¼ lb thickly sliced bacon, rind removed and cut into ½-inch pieces

Salt

¾ lb tomatoes, peeled, seeded and chopped

2 fresh *poblanos*, peeled, seeded and chopped, or 3-4 fresh *serranos*, seeded and chopped

½ cup chopped fresh coriander leaves

Oil, if necessary

Pick over and rinse the beans and put them into a pot, preferably earthenware, with the pork, onion and garlic and enough water to cover by about 2 inches. Bring to a boil, reduce the heat to low, cover and simmer until the beans are tender, about 1½ hours. The time may vary according to the age of the beans. Season to taste with salt and set aside.

In a frying pan sauté the bacon over moderate heat, adding a little oil if necessary, until it has given up all its fat. Add the tomatoes, chilies and coriander and cook for about 5 minutes. Stir the mixture into the beans and cook, uncovered, over low heat for 15 minutes to blend the flavors and reduce the liquid. Serve separately, in small bowls, with grilled meats or as a course in *comida*, or at any other time. **SERVES 6-8.**

VARIATION:

For Frijoles Borrachos *(Drunken Beans) cook the beans as for* Frijoles Charros *(Nuevo León-style) but reduce the amount of water in the beginning. When the beans are getting soft and need more liquid to finish cooking pour in ½ bottle of any one of the Monterrey beers. These are small bottles. Then continue to cook the beans in the usual way.*

POBLANOS IN FRESH WALNUT SAUCE
Chiles en Nogada

The *poblano* chili comes into its own with this dish to celebrate Mexican Independence Day on September 15. It also celebrates St. Augustine's Day on August 28 in honor of the patron saint of Augustin de Iturbide, leader of the forces that finally liberated Mexico from Spanish domination. The colors are those of the Mexican flag, green for the *poblano*, white for the walnut sauce and red for the garnish of pomegranate seeds. This is a particularly joyous festival. The night before there was the official celebration at the National Palace and at embassies all over the world, when Father Hidalgo initiated the revolution with the *grito* calling on the nation to rise and throw out the invaders, or rather, their descendants. That year a rare treat awaited us. One of the members of César's staff at the United Nations Information Center had a wife known for the excellence of her *chiles en nogada*. The fact that she was a Spanish lady married to a Mexican gentleman bothered no one. Sensibly, attention was focused on her cooking skills. Also invited were César's mother, his aunt and his uncle. We were surprised at the early hour of the invitation to *comida*, 12:20 P.M., but as we were staying with the family at the time, we all set off in good time and were good and hungry. We were the first guests to arrive but others soon followed, and we were settled in comfortable chairs at tables in the large and rustic garden of our hosts. There was lots of tequila and beer and wine, few if any nibbles, and the guest of honor had not yet arrived. He was a very distinguished man who lived conveniently just across the way. He was in government but his great distinction was that he had decoded the Aztec calendar proving it to be an astrological one that predicted, accurately, to the year 2000, the transit of Venus. Time passed, we waited for food, our hostess looking anxious as she and the maids fussed off to the kitchen at regular intervals. More nibbles appeared, little red radishes, olives (green and black), corn chips, peanuts. Happy guests downed more tequila, we did our best, but the looks on the family faces grew ever more glum and their complaints louder. Elenita, César's mother, grew tight-lipped, an ominous sign. There were suggestions that the missing guest of honor might be telephoned or approached by a quick trip across the street to his house, but to no avail. At 2:30 P.M. Elenita gathered up her brother and sister, and, instructing us to remain, swept out tersely saying to her host that they were off to get some food.

Wits were a little fuddled when the guest of honor swept in at 5 P.M., saying that he did not care to have *comida* before that hour, so had not arrived earlier. The *Chiles en Nogada* and accompaniments, beans, guacamole, salad, sauces, *chiles en escabeche*, arrived with commendable speed and, miraculously, in perfect condition. All those trips to the kitchen had not been in vain. The festive stuffed *poblanos* were superb. I acquired the recipe and César and I made our break for freedom at about 8 P.M. By then we were hungry again and found an excellent Swiss restaurant nearby. César had been given an important book on archaeology and of course we left it behind in the restaurant, which meant a trip the following morning after anxious phone calls. Altogether a memorable Independence Day.

6 *poblanos*

Picadillo

Walnut sauce

For the Garnish: flat leaf parsley
Pomegranate seeds from 1 pomegranate

For the *poblanos*:

Impale the chilies with a toasting, or similar fork, and toast over direct heat turning so that the skin is charred. Put the chilies as they are done into a plastic or brown paper bag and leave for 20 minutes. The charred skin will come off easily, run under cold water. Slit the chilies carefully lengthwise and remove the stems, seeds and veins. Do not cut them through. Set aside.

For the *picadillo*:

2 tablespoons olive or corn oil

2 lbs lean, boneless pork, finely chopped

1 onion, finely chopped

1 clove garlic, chopped

1 lb tomatoes, peeled and chopped

Salt

1 pear, peeled, cored and chopped

1 peach, peeled, pitted and chopped

2 tablespoons seedless raisins

2 tablespoons blanched, slivered almonds

Heat the oil in a large frying pan and sauté the pork until it is lightly browned. Add the onion and garlic, and cook, stirring from time to time, until the onion is soft. Add the tomatoes, stir, season to taste with salt and cook over low heat for 15 minutes. Add the fruit, raisins and almonds and cook for 10 minutes longer. Set aside until ready to stuff the *poblanos*.

For the sauce:

Fresh walnuts are available in Mexico at the time of Independence Day festivities. They are briefly soaked and the skin rubbed off. If using walnut meats soak them overnight in milk to cover.

1 cup walnut meats, soaked, peeled,
    patted dry and finely ground

4 oz cream cheese, softened

1½ cups *Crema Espesa* (page 314) or sour cream

1 tablespoon sugar (optional)

¼ teaspoon ground cinnamon (optional)

Work the walnuts into the cream cheese and the *Crema Espesa* or sour cream until the mixture is smooth and has the consistency of mayonnaise. If liked stir in the sugar and cinnamon. Set aside.

For the batter:

2 large eggs, separated
¼ teaspoon salt
Flour for dusting the *poblanos*
Oil for deep frying

In a bowl beat the egg yolks until they are light and lemon colored. In a separate bowl beat the egg whites with the salt until they stand in peaks. Fold the whites into the yolks.

To assemble the dish:

Stuff the *poblanos* with the *picadillo*, dust with the flour, and dip in the egg. Have ready a large frying pan with the oil to about ½ inch depth and sauté until they are golden brown all over. The batter (egg) will seal the pepper preventing the filling coming out. Transfer to a platter, mask with the walnut sauce and garnish with pomegranate seeds and a few parsley leaves.
SERVES 6.

If poblanos *are not available, the best substitute is the sweet green pepper. Remove the papery skin by charring in the same way as for the* poblanos *but do not slit them open. Cut off the tops, carefully scoop out the seeds and use the tops as a lid.*

STUFFED PEPPERS
Chiles Rellenos

After the drama that accompanied my learning about the Independence Day *Chiles en Nogada* making a dishful of *Chiles Rellenos* was child's play, or almost. It is no good pretending the dish doesn't take time, it does, but it is worth it.

6 *poblanos*, or 6 sweet green peppers

1 recipe for *picadillo* preferably the pork one used for *Chiles en Nogada* (page 160), or if preferred *picadillo* made with beef

1 recipe for Tomato Sauce (*Salsa de Jitomate*) (page 81)

1 cup stock from cooking *picadillo* or use chicken stock

¼ teaspoon salt

2 large eggs, separated

Flour for dusting the chilies

Lard or corn oil for frying

Prepare the *poblanos* or green peppers as in the previous recipe and set aside. Make the *picadillo* and the tomato sauce. In a bowl beat the egg yolks until they are light. In another bowl beat the egg whites with the salt until they stand in firm peaks. Gently fold the whites into the yolks. Dust the chilies with flour and dip them into the eggs. Heat enough fat in a large frying pan to reach a depth of ½ inch and sauté the chilies until they are golden on both sides. Drain on paper towels.

In a casserole heat the tomato sauce with the cup of stock to a texture halfway between a sauce and a broth. Stir to mix and add the chilies. The tomato sauce will come about halfway up the chilies. Cook for 2-3 minutes over low heat and serve immediately, preferably in rimmed soup plates so the chilies can be surrounded by the sauce. **SERVES 6.**

VARIATION:

For Chiles Rellenos de Frijoles *(Peppers Stuffed with Beans) follow the instructions for* Chiles Rellenos *(Stuffed Peppers) until they are fried, using 1 recipe* Frijoles Refritos *(Refried Beans) (page 159) instead of* picadillo. *Arrange the chilies in an ovenproof dish and mask with 1 cup* Crema Espesa *(page 314) or sour cream and sprinkle with grated cheese such as Cheddar and bake in a preheated 350°F oven just until the cheese melts.* **SERVES 6.**

ZUCCHINI WITH *POBLANO* CHILIES
Calabacitas con Poblanos

We had these in Puebla where we had gone to buy the candied fruits in which the region excels and to lunch at a restaurant whose name I have, alas, forgotten, to eat *Mole Poblano de Guajolote*, the great national dish for which they are famous. Puebla is the gastronomic center of Mexico and since its full name is Puebla de los Angeles I think it is legimate to say it serves heavenly food. It is a beautiful city, a colonial gem and I sometimes tried not to think quite so much about food when we visited it. Never succeeded though. The dark green, almost black green, *poblano* is one of Puebla's achievements. I wish we had a word for chili hot to distinguish it from hot weather hot, or food served hot not cold. *Picante* would do nicely but isn't quite right.

Anyway if the *poblano* is too hot, soak it for 20 minutes in salt water, to take the heat out. I like it hot, but it is a matter of taste. If there are no *poblanos* to be had, sweet green peppers can be used instead.

**3 *poblanos*, peeled, seeded and cut into strips,
  ½ inch by 1½ inches**

1 onion, chopped

3 tablespoons corn oil

1 lb young zucchini, cut into ½-inch diagonal slices

Salt

¾ cup *Crema Espesa* (page 314) or sour cream

Prepare the *poblanos*. Heat the oil in a frying pan and sauté the chili strips for about 5 minutes. Lift out to a bowl and set aside. Purée the onion and garlic in a food processor and sauté in the oil remaining in the frying pan. Add the zucchini and enough water barely to cover, about ½ cup, cover and simmer until the zucchini are tender, about 10 minutes. Pour in the cream, season with salt and gently fold in the reserved *poblano* strips. Cook just long enough to heat through. **SERVES 6.**

CHAYOTES

The pear-shaped *chayote* (*Sechium edule*), is one of the squashes that originated in Mexico a very long time ago, perhaps even as early as 7000 B.C. There are three types; small light-green ones, very light green ones almost creamy in color, and dark green ones with spines. The usual type available in markets is the very light green one and they usually weigh about 1 lb. They have spread from their original homeland to the tropical regions of the world. As a result of their travels they are known by a number of names, in Spanish, English, French and Brazilian they are *chayote*, cho-cho, *christophene* and *chu-chu*. There are probably others. They taste rather like zucchini, but with a crisper and finer texture. They have a large edible seed which the cook usually gets, at least I did. *Chayotes* are stainy and best peeled under running water unless they are to be stuffed, in which case they are left unpeeled.

STUFFED CHO-CHOS
Chayotes Rellenos

3 *chayotes*

Salt

3 tablespoons butter or oil

1 onion, finely chopped

2 cloves garlic

½ lb cooked ham, finely chopped

3 tablespoons fresh coriander leaves, chopped

⅔ cup sour cream or *Crema Espesa* (page 314)

6 oz Cheddar, coarsely grated

Halve the *chayotes* and put into a saucepan with boiling water just to cover and simmer, for 10 minutes. Lift out and drain then carefully scoop out the flesh taking care to leave the shell intact. Mash the flesh and set aside. In a frying pan heat the butter or oil and sauté the onion and garlic until the onion is soft. Add the ham, coriander and the reserved mashed *chayote*. Cook, stirring, for 3-4 minutes. Season to taste with salt and fill the *chayote* shells. Top with the cream and cheese and put into an ovenproof dish. Bake in a preheated 350°F oven just until the cheese has melted. Serve as a first course or to accompany plainly cooked meat or poultry. **SERVES 6.**

CHO-CHOS WITH CREAM
Chayotes con Crema

3 *chayotes* (cho-cho) peeled under running water and
　　cut into ½ inch cubes

4 tablespoons corn oil

1 onion, finely chopped

1 fresh *serrano* chili, seeded and chopped

4 oz Cheddar cheese, coarsely grated

2 cups *Crema Espesa* (page 314) or sour cream

¼ teaspoon dried oregano, crumbled

2 tablespoons fresh coriander leaves, chopped

Salt

Remove the pits (seeds) from the *chayotes* and chop them coarsely. Add to the diced *chayotes*. In a frying pan heat the oil and sauté the *chayotes*, onion and chili, stirring from time to time over moderate heat for about 10 minutes or until the *chayote* is tender. In a bowl mix together the cheese, cream and oregano and pour it into the frying pan, stirring to mix and cook over low heat just to melt the cheese and heat the cream. Taste for seasoning and add salt if necessary. Sprinkle with the coriander and cook for 1-2 minutes longer. Serve separately before the main course in *comida* or as a supper dish. **SERVES 6.**

YOUNG PEAS OR GREEN BEANS IN RED OR GREEN ALMOND SAUCE
Chicharitos o Ejotes en Salsa de Almendra Roja o Verde

I was most impressed in Medellín market to find that the green peas were already released from their pods saving us the chore of shelling them. That is an advance equal to the triumph of creating green beans to replace string beans.

For each vegetable make 1 recipe of the sauce (pages 85-86)

For the beans:
Trim 1½ lbs green beans and cut into 1½ inches. Have ready a saucepan of briskly boiling salted water. Add the beans and cook for 5 minutes, or until tender. Drain and add to the sauce. If necessary heat through. **SERVES 6.**

For the peas:
Have ready a pan of briskly boiling salted water. Add 1½ lbs peas, bring to a boil and cook for 2-5 minutes, according to the age of the peas. Drain and add to the chosen sauce. If necessary heat through. **SERVES 6.**

SWISS CHARD WITH CREAM
Acelgas con Crema

1½ lbs Swiss chard, green part only

Salt

2 tablespoons butter or corn oil

1 onion, finely chopped

3 *poblano* chilies, peeled, seeded and chopped

1 cup *Crema Espesa* (page 314) or sour cream

Wash the Swiss chard in cold water then cook in a large saucepan of briskly boiling water for 2-3 minutes. Drain and chop coarsely. In a frying pan heat the butter or oil, add the onion and sauté until it is soft. Put the *poblano* in a food processor and reduce to a purée. Add to the onion and cook, stirring, for 3-4 minutes. Add the Swiss chard and stir in the cream. Season to taste with salt and cook just long enough to heat through. **SERVES 6.**

POTATO CAKES
Tortas de Papa

Potatoes, though they were eaten in pre-Columbian Mexico, grew wild; they were not cultivated until after the Conquest, when potatoes from Peru, where they had originated in the high Andes, focused attention on this extraordinary vegetable. Mexican potatoes are of superb quality yet the country has never taken to them as enthusiastically as it has to rice which the Spanish introduced from Asia. Although the rice is inclined to be poor, Mexican cooks perform miracles with it. I have never eaten badly cooked rice in Mexico. As a result, there are few original recipes for potatoes.

2 lbs boiling potatoes
2 cloves garlic, crushed
½ cup light cream
Salt, freshly ground black pepper
2 large eggs, lightly beaten
Oil for frying

Put the potatoes into a large saucepan with cold water to cover and simmer until they are tender when pierced with the point of a small sharp knife. When cool enough to handle, peel the potatoes and mash with the garlic. Beat in the cream and season with salt and pepper. Beat in the eggs. Form the potatoes into 12 cakes about 1 inch thick. Pour into a saucepan enough oil to reach a depth of ½ inch and when it is hot fry the potato cakes until they are lightly browned on both sides. Serve with *Salsa de Jitomate* (Tomato Sauce) (page 81). **SERVES 6.**

LENTILS WITH PORK, COASTAL-STYLE
Lentjas Costenas con Puerco

I was pleased, though a little surprised, when I went to Mexico to find that lentils were extremely popular. I like lentils, so did César and as brown lentils were available I set about finding local recipes for them. This one came from the cook of friends who lived at sea level, the coastal kitchen very different from the cooking of the high plateau. Coastal-style usually means dishes with the addition of fruits, many of them tropical, like bananas and pineapple. I'd spent all my life to that point at or near the sea and I found mountains rather alien and having to adjust to altitude cooking was irritating as it meant I had to let the cook cook when I wanted to be at the stove myself. Such selfishness.

½ lb lean, boneless pork cut into 1-inch pieces

1½ cups brown lentils

½ cup seedless raisins

¼ cup olive oil

1 onion, finely chopped

2 cloves garlic, chopped

1 apple, peeled, cored and chopped

1 large, firm banana, peeled and sliced

2 slices fresh pineapple, cut into chunks, or 12 oz pineapple chunks canned in their own juice

1 lb tomatoes, peeled, seeded and chopped

1 or more fresh *jalapeño* chilies, seeded and chopped (optional)

Salt

Put the pork into a large casserole and pour in enough water barely to cover. Bring to a simmer, cover and cook over low heat for 1 hour. Drain, reserve the stock and set the pork aside. Rinse out the casserole, return the stock, stir in the lentils and raisins and add water, if needed, to cover. Simmer, covered for 40 minutes or until tender. Set aside. Meanwhile, heat the oil in a frying pan and sauté the pork, onion and garlic until the pork pieces are very lightly colored. Lift everything out with a slotted spoon and add to the lentils. In the oil remaining in the frying pan sauté the apple, banana and pineapple for a few minutes. Add the tomatoes and the chilies, if using, season with salt and cook until most of the liquid has evaporated. Add to the lentils, stirring gently to mix. Simmer over very low heat, uncovered, for 10 minutes to blend all the flavors. The finished dish should be fairly dry, with the lentils creamy. This makes a good luncheon dish. **SERVES 6.**

CACTUS PADDLES WITH CHEESE
Nopales con Queso

Nopales are the paddles of the prickly pear cactus, *Opuntia ficus indica* and other *Opuntia* species which originated in northwest Mexico. They have a light pleasant taste that is said to be reminiscent of green beans and green peppers but taste is notoriously hard to define. Fresh *nopales* bought in Mexican markets are usually cleaned of the eyes and prickly spines which are a menace to the unwary. They range in size from small oval paddles to large plate-size ones. The small ones are the nicest. It is better if someone in the market cleans them though I am told it is quite easy. I have never even tried, and go one step further buying my *nopalitos* canned with all the anguish and trouble removed as they can exceedingly well. All that has to be done is drain and rinse them and check what is their drained weight. *Nopalitas*, that is small *nopales* are sometimes eaten raw in salads but I prefer them cooked which the canned ones are anyway.

12 oz canned *nopalitos*, rinsed and drained

2 tablespoons butter

1 onion, finely chopped

½ teaspoon dried *epazote*, crumbled

3 *serrano* chilies, seeded and chopped or 1-2 *jalapeño* chilies, seeded and chopped

8 oz cottage or ricotta cheese, mashed

2 tablespoons *Crema Espesa* (page 314), optional

Salt

Chop the *nopalitos* coarsely. Heat the butter in a frying pan and sauté the onion until it is soft, add the *nopalitos*, *epazote* and chilies and cook until the vegetables are soft. Add the cheese and the *Crema Espesa* if using. Season with salt and continue to cook until the cheese begins to melt. Serve at once.
SERVES 4.

CACTUS PADDLES WITH *PASILLA* CHILI
Nopales con Chile Pasilla

Chile Pasilla is one of those amazing chilies that is transformed when ripe and dried. It begins life as a long, narrow, black-green chili named a *chilaca*. It is flavorful and very hot and a must with *Mole Poblano*. It is popular in the northwest and César's family used it both dried and fresh.

1 or 2 *pasilla* chilies
12 oz canned *nopalitos*, rinsed and drained
2 tablespoons olive oil
1 onion, finely chopped
½ teaspoon dried *epazote*
Salt

Toast one or two chilies according to how hot you want the dish to be, in a dry pan, remove from the pan, pull off the stems and shake out the seeds. Tear the chilies in pieces and put them in a small bowl with warm water to cover. Leave for 20 minutes, then drain and purée in a food processor. In a frying pan heat the oil and sauté the onion until it is soft. Add the chili purée and cook, stirring constantly for 5 minutes over moderate heat. Add the *epazote* and the *nopalitos*. Season to taste with salt and heat through. **SERVES 4.**

MUSHROOMS WITH *CHIPOTLE* CHILI
Hongos con Chipotle

It took me some time to like the very foreign taste of the *chipotle* but eventually I became addicted to it. And it took me some time to learn that it was my favorite *jalapeño*, ripe and smoked. One would never know they are related so different are their flavors. There is no end to learning about the family of the domesticated *capsicums* which I was trying to do before Dr. Jean Andrews had written and illustrated her book on these peppers, which has been described as a treasure trove. I never did learn about Mexico's wild mushrooms beyond *huitlacoche*, the corn fungus, but I found "ordinary" mushrooms perfectly adequate.

1 lb mushrooms, large ones quartered, small ones left whole
1 onion, chopped
1 clove garlic, chopped

½ teaspoon dried *epazote* or sprig fresh

1 or 2 canned *chipotle*s, rinsed and coarsely chopped

2 tablespoons tomato purée

¾ cup chicken stock

4 tablespoons olive oil

1 tablespoon butter

2 tablespoons lemon juice

Wipe the mushroom caps with a damp cloth. Remove and chop the stems coarsely and put them into a food processor with the onion, garlic, *epazote*, *chipotle* and tomato purée, and reduce to a smooth purée. In a frying pan heat 2 tablespoons of the olive oil, add the purée and cook, stirring, over medium heat for 5 minutes. Taste for seasoning and salt as needed.

Heat the remaining olive oil and the butter in a large, heavy frying pan, add the mushrooms and cook over fairly high heat, tossing and shaking the pan, for about 5 minutes until the mushrooms are lightly browned. Reduce the heat to low, pour in the *chipotle* mixture and heat through but do not cook further. Stir in the lemon juice and serve immediately. **SERVES 6.**

MUSHROOMS MEXICAN-STYLE
Hongos a la Mexicana

1 lb mushrooms, quartered if large, small left whole

3 tablespoons corn oil

1 tablespoon butter

2 cloves garlic, chopped

½ teaspoon dried *epazote*

1 or 2 canned *jalapeño* chilies, rinsed and sliced

Salt

Wipe the mushrooms with a damp cloth. In a large, heavy frying pan heat the oil and butter. Add the garlic, mushrooms, *epazote*, *jalapeño* and salt to taste. Cook, stirring from time to time over moderate heat until the mushrooms are lightly browned, 6-8 minutes. **SERVES 6.**

BROAD BEANS OR FRESH LIMA BEANS
Habas Verdes

Broad beans (*habas*) are another of the ancient beans of the Old World that the New World accepted with enthusiasm. They can be used in recipes instead of the South American lima bean from Peru, which reached Mexico about 1500 B.C.

1½ lbs fresh lima beans

2 tablespoons butter or corn or olive oil

1 onion, chopped

1 clove garlic, chopped

½ lb tomatoes, peeled and chopped

1 *jalapeño* chili, peeled, seeded and chopped
    (see note on *poblano*, page 18)

Salt, freshly ground black pepper

3 hardboiled eggs, sliced

½ cup fresh coriander leaves or flat parsley, chopped

Boil the beans in briskly boiling salted water for 5-10 minutes according to age. Drain and keep warm. In a frying pan heat the butter or oil and sauté the onion and garlic until the onion is soft. Add the tomatoes and *jalapeño*, season to taste with salt and pepper and simmer over low heat, stirring from time to time until the ingredients are blended into a sauce. Pour over the beans and serve garnished with the sliced eggs, and sprinkled with the coriander or parsley. **SERVES 6.**

CHILIES WITH CHEESE
Chile con Queso

This is a quintessentially Chihuahuan dish though it has become so popular in the American Southwest and in California that it is often thought of as Texan. The favorite chili for it is the Anaheim, which has an interesting history as it is believed that Captain General Don Juan de Oñate took the peppers from Mexico to New Mexico in 1597 after the Conquest when he colonized the state and founded Santa Fe. It is a large, fleshy light green chili that ranges from mild to hot. The cheeses that are used are *Queso de Chihuahua* and *asadero* for which mozzarella is a good substitute, while a mild Cheddar can substitute for *Queso de Chihuahua. Poblanos*, which are sometimes used instead of Anaheims are not usually available so the easiest substitute is a sweet green pepper. The dish is eaten as a vegetable with grilled meats and is good with either corn or flour tortillas.

6 fresh sweet green peppers

2 tablespoons lard or corn or peanut oil

1 clove garlic, chopped

1 onion very thinly sliced

3 large tomatoes, skinned and thinly sliced

6 oz mozzarella cheese, cut into small dice

6 oz Cheddar, cut into small dice

1 cup light cream

Impale the peppers, one at a time, on a toasting fork and toast them over a gas burner turning them constantly until they are charred all over. Put them into a plastic or brown paper bag and leave for 20 minutes. Rinse off the charred skin. Remove the stems and seeds. Cut into ½ inch strips. Heat the lard or oil in a frying pan and sauté the garlic and onion over moderate heat until soft but not brown. Add the tomato slices and the pepper strips and cook for 5 minutes. Add the cheese and as soon as it starts to melt pour in the cream. Season with salt and cook just long enough to heat through. **SERVES 6.**

CABBAGE IN *ADOBO* SAUCE
Adobo de Col

Cabbage is amazingly popular for an introduced vegetable but it seems to have a natural affinity with tomatoes and chilies. I had great fun making the *adobes* and *moles* but I used to get very uppity because instructions told me to *freir* (fry) the purée. "You can't fry a liquid," I would cry, to everyone's annoyance. In time I learned that I made the mixture too liquid when it should have been paste like. The end result was the same so no one bothered to tell me, letting me work it out for myself. They thought I was rather perverse having this passion for seeking out the secrets of the Mexican kitchen. The *adobo* here is similar to one that is used for pork.

1 firm cabbage weighing about 3 lbs

Salt

For the *Adobo*:

4 *ancho* chilies

1 onion, chopped

1 clove garlic, chopped

½ teaspoon dried oregano, crumbled

½ teaspoon ground cumin

½ lb tomatoes, peeled, seeded and chopped

2 tablespoons lard or corn oil

For the garnish: 2 hard-boiled eggs, sliced

Shred the cabbage finely then toss it into a large saucepan of briskly boiling salted water and boil, over high heat, for 5 minutes. Drain thoroughly, return to the saucepan and set aside. Reserve the cooking water.

In a dry frying pan lightly toast the *anchos*. Tear off the stems and shake out the seeds. Remove the veins and tear the *anchos* into pieces. Put into a bowl with warm water barely to cover and soak for 30 minutes, turning from time to time. Drain the *anchos* and put them into a food processor with the onion, garlic, oregano, cumin and tomatoes and reduce to a heavy purée. Heat the lard or oil in a frying pan, add the purée and cook, stirring for 5 minutes. The sauce should be thick but if necessary thin it a little with the reserved cooking water from the cabbage. Taste for salt and pour it over the cabbage. Stir to mix and warm it through. Turn into a warmed vegetable dish and garnish with the eggs. **SERVES 4-6.**

ROOSTER'S BEAK *JICAMA* SALAD
Pico de Gallo Ensalada de Jicama

I first tasted *jicama* (HEE-ka-ma), a crisp juicy root vegetable, usually eaten cooked, in a salad at a lunch at the home of the governor in the small west-central state of Colima. A most curious visit that. We were only recently married and César being in charge of the United Nations Information Center in his own country was a great challenge. It was an official visit but he was allowed to take me along. The governor took one look at my naturally blond hair and light grey-blue eyes and resolutely addressed me as "Señorita," a most deadly insult as I was Señora accompanying my husband. Every time he said "Señorita," I said "Señora." To no avail. César making serious UN discourse, which my Spanish was not up to, tended to bounce on the peculiarly sprung sofa we were parked on so I went up and down gently as the governor called me what, in those days (still is) was the equivalent of "foreign whore." His wife served us lunch but did not sit with us, and then she waded in. I could follow her Spanish, she said I was self-ish. I had no children preferring to traipse about with my husband when a decent woman would be at home breeding. I retaliated by pointing out that I had not yet had time to produce living young, and that where I came from if you had a baby before you had been married for two years, you would be suspected of having been practicing ahead of time. Insults or no, I managed to get more than one recipe, and we got a good laugh after we escaped. Same thing happened in reverse when César took me and a female house guest of ours to Puebla when he was on an official trip as the guest of the governor. The doorman of the hotel where they were meeting thought César was our tourist guide and that the car was ours. A Mexican gentleman with a blond and redhead and he was the boss! He went in to see the governor, we wandered off sightseeing, and the doorman marveled.

As to *jicama* (*pachyrzuserosus*), also known as yam bean. It started life in Mexico, is a tuber that looks a bit like a large turnip, has a thin light brown skin and a juicy, crunchy sweetish ivory flesh. A favorite way to eat it is thinly sliced, sprinkled with lime juice, salt, and chili powder, eaten raw to accompany drinks.

For the salad:

Jicama **weighing about 1 lb peeled and cut into**
 ¾ inch cubes
½ cup Seville (bitter) orange juice
Salt

4 navel oranges, peeled, sectioned, pitted and chopped

Hot paprika, cayenne or hot chili powder

In a bowl combine the *jicama*, Seville orange juice and salt to taste and refrigerate for an hour. Toss in the oranges and season with hot chili. **SERVES 6.**

If Seville oranges are out of season use a mix of equal amounts of grapefruit juice, orange juice and lemon juice.

CHO-CHO SALAD
Ensalada de Chayote

3 *chayotes* each weighing about 1 lb

½ lb tomatoes, peeled, seeded and chopped

2 fresh *jalapeño* chilies or 3 *serranos*, peeled, seeded and finely chopped

Vinaigrette made with 3 parts olive oil to 1 part mild vinegar or lemon juice, salt and freshly ground black pepper

Lettuce, shredded

Peel the *chayotes* under running water. Halve them and put in a saucepan with salted boiling water to cover. Boil for 10 minutes. Drain, remove the seeds and cut the *chayotes* into ½-inch cubes. Chill lightly. In a bowl combine the *chayotes*, tomato, *jalapeño* or *serranos*. Toss with the vinaigrette. Line a salad bowl with lettuce and add the salad. **SERVES 6.**

PRAWN SALAD
Ensalada de Camaron

Mexico produces prawns that are superlatively good, whether they are delicate little ones or the jumbo prawns that are as flavorful and tender as the small ones. César's family on his mother's side, the Tinoco Sarabias, were more than partial to prawns. The two prawn salads are both family recipes. I use cooked, frozen North Atlantic ones as I find tropical jumbo prawns tough, always a disappointment.

Lettuce leaves

½ cup mayonnaise

½ cup *Crema Espesa* (page 314) or sour cream

1 lb cooked prawns, coarsely chopped

2 ribs celery (½ cup), chopped

6 small new potatoes, freshly cooked and diced

1 cup cucumber, unpeeled and diced

3 hard-boiled eggs, coarsely chopped

½ teaspoon cayenne pepper

Salt

Line a large salad bowl with lettuce leaves. Mix the mayonnaise and *Crema Espesa* together. In a bowl combine the prawns, celery, new potatoes, cucumber, eggs, cayenne and salt. Mix gently then fold in the mayonnaise mixture and put the salad into the prepared salad bowl. **SERVES 6.**

ANOTHER PRAWN SALAD
Otra Ensalada de Camaron

4 teaspoons lemon juice

Salt, freshly ground black pepper

¾ cup olive oil

1 lb cooked prawns, coarsely chopped

1 small white onion, finely chopped

½ lb tomatoes, peeled and chopped

1 large avocado, peeled, pitted and cubed

2 teaspoons fresh coriander, finely chopped

2 oz *pimiento*-stuffed green olives, halved

2-3 canned *jalapeño* chilies, seeded and cut into strips

Lettuce leaves

In a small bowl combine the lemon juice, salt and pepper and whisk in the olive oil. In a larger bowl combine the prawns and onion and pour the dressing over them. Marinate for 2 hours. Add the tomato, avocado, coriander, and olives and toss lightly to mix. Line a salad bowl with the lettuce leaves, add the prawn mixture and garnish with the chilies. **SERVES 6.**

ZUCCHINI SALAD
Ensalada de Calabacitas

The chilies are equal both in flavor and heat. Choose the one that most suits your palate, the *poblano* is the most subtle, the *chipotle* the most exotic.

6 young zucchini, trimmed and thickly sliced

Salt

1 bunch spring onions

2 canned *poblano*, *jalapeño* or *chipotle* chilies, rinsed, seeded and cut into strips

2 avocados, peeled, seeded and cubed

1 cup oil and vinegar dressing (vinaigrette) (page 184)

Lettuce leaves

Drop the sliced zucchini into a large saucepanful of briskly boiling salted water, bring back to the boil over high heat and cook for 6-8 minutes. The zucchini should be crisp but not hard. Drain thoroughly and chop coarsely. Cool. Combine all the ingredients except the lettuce leaves in a bowl and toss with the dressing. Chill in the refrigerator. Line a salad bowl with the lettuce and arrange the salad in the center. **SERVES 6.**

CAULIFLOWER SALAD
Ensalada de Coliflor

This salad looks quite splendid on a buffet. The guacamole lifts the flavor of the bland cauliflower. I prefer *guacamole del Norte* as the *tomatillos* take the dish right out of the ordinary.

1 medium cauliflower, about 1 lb
Salt
1 recipe Guacamole or *Guacamole del Norte* (page 76)
¼ cup freshly grated Parmesan cheese

Trim away any tough leaves and the woody base from the cauliflower. Have ready a large saucepan of briskly boiling salted water and put the cauliflower into it face down and simmer for 15 minutes. Drain thoroughly and cool. Place in a suitable dish and mask with guacamole. Sprinkle with the cheese. Chill slightly, if liked, before serving. **SERVES 6-8.**

ANOTHER CAULIFLOWER SALAD
Otra Ensalada de Coliflor

4 tablespoons oil and vinegar dressing (page 184)
Florets from 1 medium cauliflower, cooked
Lettuce leaves
1 recipe Guacamole (page 74)
Freshly grated Parmesan cheese (optional)

Put the cauliflower florets into a bowl and pour the dressing over them, and marinate for 1 hour. Chill lightly and when cold arrange the florets in mounds on the lettuce leaves. Mask with guacamole and sprinkle with the cheese, if liked. **SERVES 6.**

STUFFED AVOCADOS
Aguacates Rellenos

3 large, ripe avocados
Fresh lime or lemon juice
3 (4 oz) cans sardines in olive oil
Salt, freshly ground black pepper
Mild wine vinegar
3 hard-boiled eggs, halved and finely chopped
Freshly grated Parmesan cheese
Strips of *pimiento* (sweet red pepper)
Lettuce leaves, ripe olives, tomato slices and sliced radishes

Peel and halve the avocados and discard the seeds. Sprinkle with lime or lemon juice and set aside. In a bowl mash the sardines and the oil from the cans. Season to taste with salt, pepper and a little vinegar. Fold in the chopped eggs. Stuff the avocado halves with the mixture. Line 6 plates with lettuce leaves and put a halved avocado, cut side up, on each one. Sprinkle with grated cheese and strips of sweet red peppers (*pimientos*, canned if possible). Garnish the plates with ripe olives, tomato slices, and radishes either sliced or cut into flowers. **SERVES 6.**

TOMATO AND AVOCADO SALAD
Ensalada de Jitomate y Aguacata

When César first told me of the contributions Mexico's pre-Columbian agriculture had made to the world's larder, practically doubling it, I found there was some controversy about the tomato. One source said they came from Peru, another said Mexico. Naturally I sided with those who said Mexico. Also it seemed more plausible as I felt Peru had too much altitude territory to have given birth to fruit that doesn't like cold nights, which is what the Peruvian uplands have. None of this prepared me for the sight of tomatoes in San Juan market. There were enormous stands of tomatoes classified by their use, those for salads, those for sauces and so on. And the prices for those red ripe flavorful enormous beauties were, as far as I was concerned, a gift. I made juice from some of them as one couldn't buy it in the local supermarket at that time, and I made soups, and sauces and so it went. It was a great wonder I didn't turn orangey-red from my enthusiastic intake. They tasted as I was sure tomatoes ought to taste, and looked as they should look. Not like the pale pink cotton wool I had so often met. These are two of my favorite salad recipes using the kind of tomato that I can get here now which proves that not all progress is bad after all.

3 large avocados, peeled and pitted

3 large tomatoes (about ½ lb), peeled and seeded

Lettuce leaves

Chives, finely chopped

Oil and lemon juice dressing, or mayonnaise

Cut the avocados and tomatoes into an equal number of thick slices. Arrange the tomato slices on a bed of lettuce leaves, put the avocado slices on top. Sprinkle with the chives and pour on some of the dressing or serve with the mayonnaise separately. **SERVES 6.**

TOMATOES STUFFED WITH GUACAMOLE
Jitomates Rellenos de Guacamole

6 medium tomatoes

Salt

1 recipe Guacamole or *Guacamole del Norte* (page 76)

Lettuce leaves

Peel the tomatoes, cut a slice off the top of each and carefully scoop out the pulp with a spoon leaving a thick shell. Sprinkle the inside with salt, turn upside down, and drain for 15 minutes. Stuff the tomatoes with guacamole and arrange on individual plates on a bed of lettuce leaves. **SERVES 6.**

CACTUS PADDLE SALAD
Ensalada de Nopalitos

Cactus paddles with the spines and eyes removed are available in Mexican markets, but not so far as I know elsewhere. However shops or markets selling Mexican ingredients often have them canned. All that has to be done is to drain and rinse them. This is a very Mexican salad, very refreshing.

10 oz cans *nopalitos* (cactus paddles)

¾ lb tomatoes peeled, seeded and chopped

1 small white onion, finely chopped

1 teaspoon fresh coriander leaves, finely chopped

½ cup oil and vinegar dressing (page 184)

Rinse and drain cactus pieces and cut them into ½ inch pieces. In a salad bowl combine the cactus with the tomatoes, onion and the dressing. Chill in the refrigerator and serve. **SERVES 6.**

COLD ROAST BEEF SALAD
Ensalada de Carne de Res

This is one of my favorite salads and I have enjoyed it with slight variations in countries all over the world. The first time I had it was in a restaurant in Mexico City, the next was in Paris in a wonderful Dijon mustard vinaigrette and the next Bangkok where our cook, a Thai young man Tongdee Pholomai surprised us with a splendid version with the flavors of lemongrass and nam pla and other things I didn't know about then. I have often meant to collate all the roast beef salads I have enjoyed and where they came from. Such a traveller this one, always the same and always different.

1½ lbs rare roast beef, cut into strips

1 large Bermuda-type onion, very thinly sliced

2 navel oranges, peeled and thinly sliced

1 cup vinaigrette (oil and vinegar dressing) (page 184)

Lettuce leaves

Fresh hot red chilies, cut to form flowers

Sprigs of fresh coriander or 2 tablespoons chopped coriander leaves

In a bowl combine the beef, onion and orange slices and pour the vinaigrette over them. Leave to marinate at room temperature for 2 hours or in hot weather marinate in the refrigerator. Line a large platter with the lettuce leaves. Make the chili flowers. Cut 4 or 5 strips from the tips to the stems ends but without severing them completely. They will curl back into flowers. Arrange the beef, onion and orange slices on the lettuce, with the dressing poured over. Garnish with the chilies and coriander. Serve with crusty bread and butter. **SERVES 6.**

OIL AND VINEGAR DRESSING
Salsa Vinaigrette

This is sometimes called *Salsa Francesa* (French Sauce) just as it is sometimes called French dressing in English-speaking countries. Mexican cooks add all sorts of things to the basic vinaigrette and call it *Vinaigrette Especial* (Special Vinaigrette) or just another vinaigrette. These are changed by adding herbs and peppers for the most part.

In a bowl whisk together 3 or 4 parts of oil with 1 part vinegar, add salt and freshly ground pepper to taste. Different oils and vinegars may be used and lime or lemon juice instead of vinegar.

CHRISTMAS EVE SALAD
Ensalada de Noche Buena

This is a very popular salad traditionally a part of the special dinner served on Christmas Eve after midnight mass and after the series of parties called the Posadas (Inns) held to commemorate the search by Mary and Joseph (Los Santos Peregrinos, the Holy Pilgrims) for room at an inn at Bethlehem for the birth of the infant Jesus. This is not very popular outside Mexico or rather among non-Mexicans who know about local food, but there you are, I have heard it described as baroque, and as eye-catching, a kinder description. It is colonial, exotic and colorful and Christmas Eve dinner would not be the same without it. All the same I am less than enthusiastic about the hard candies that are sometimes added. In colonial time the dressing used was simply ½ cup sugar mixed with 4 tablespoons wine vinegar. Not my favorite.

3 medium-size cooked beets, chopped

2 oranges, peeled and thinly sliced

2 *jicamas*, peeled and chopped, or 2 tart cooking apples, peeled, cored and chopped

2 large bananas, peeled and sliced diagonally

3 slices fresh pineapple, cubed

Lettuce leaves

1 tablespoon toasted peanuts, coarsely chopped

Seeds from 1 pomegranate

1 cup mayonnaise

1 stick sugar cane, peeled and chopped (optional)

In a large bowl mix together the beet, oranges, *jicamas* or apples, bananas and pineapple and chill thoroughly in the refrigerator. Line a salad bowl with the lettuce leaves and pile on the chilled salad mixture, garnish with the peanuts and pomegranate seeds. Serve the mayonnaise separately. Add the sugar cane, if available and if using, to the salad when mixing it. **SERVES 6-8.**

CHOPPED ZUCCHINI
Calabacitas Picadas

But for Elizabeth David, we would not have had zucchini growing in Britain as soon as we did. They are not hard to grow and I grew some accidentally in my back garden to my astonishment. The name has always amused me. They were first cultivated in Mexico, as far back as 7000 BC, members of the huge family of *cucurbitaceae*, the squashes. If left alone the *calabacita* would grow into the *calabaza*, which we should probably call pumpkin. The Italians and Americans call these babies zucchini, the French call them courgettes, and every cook in Mexico has her own special recipe for *calabacitas*. They are best when only 3-4 inches long. Tio Miguel's housekeeper/cook Antonia had her own *Calabacitas Picadas* which she would vary from time to time as the mood took her. Her cooking was never dull.

Other cooks contributed their own recipes until I don't quite know who should be credited with which. It really is a wonderful vegetable, we can eat the flowers, the young fruit and the mature *calabaza* (West Indian pumpkin) as soup, vegetable and dessert.

2 tablespoons corn or peanut oil

1 onion, finely chopped

1 clove garlic, chopped

1 lb tomatoes, peeled, seeded and chopped

2 sprigs *epazote*

1 fresh *jalapeño* **chili, seeded and chopped**

**1½ lbs zucchini, trimmed and cut into
    ¾ inch slices, diagonally**

Salt

Heat the oil in a frying pan and sauté the onion and garlic until the onion is soft. Add the tomatoes, *epazote*, *jalapeño* and zucchini, season with salt, cover and cook over very low heat, stirring from time to time, until the zucchini are cooked, about 30 minutes. The acid in the tomatoes slows the cooking of the zucchini, which explains why the cooking time is so long, when, if they are cooked in boiling salted water they will be done in 5-10 minutes. **SERVES 6.**

VARIATION:

For Calabacitas con Jitomate *(Zucchini with Tomatoes) use 2 tablespoons fresh coriander leaves, chopped, instead of* epazote, *2* serranos *instead of the* jalapeño, *and add 1¾ cups corn kernels (if frozen, thoroughly defrosted), and cook as for* Calabacitas Picadas.

FISH AND SHELLFISH

•

Pescados y Mariscos

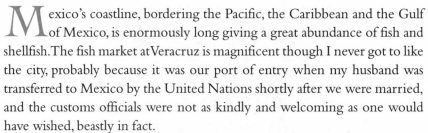

Mexico's coastline, bordering the Pacific, the Caribbean and the Gulf of Mexico, is enormously long giving a great abundance of fish and shellfish. The fish market at Veracruz is magnificent though I never got to like the city, probably because it was our port of entry when my husband was transferred to Mexico by the United Nations shortly after we were married, and the customs officials were not as kindly and welcoming as one would have wished, beastly in fact.

Still the fish market ranks with, and often surpasses, fish markets I have visited all over the world which is something, as I "collect" fish markets. Another bonus was enjoying the country's most famous fish dish, *Huachinango a la Veracruzana*, Red Snapper Veracruz-style, hard to better. We were on our way to Mexico City and stopped off in Fortín de las Flores to get used to the altitude. This is the vanilla capital of Mexico and the air is perfumed by the orchid whose seed pods give us vanilla. It was an extraordinary experience staying in an old colonial building breathing the exotically scented air in the gently warm climate, far enough above semitropical sea level to be close to perfection. And it was a long way from fish which I wanted to learn about. I recognized the Caribbean ones though the names were different but others were completely strange. I had to wait until Mexico City and the fish market at La Merced or was it San Juan? I was newcomer enough to get mixed up. Years later Elizabeth David asked César if he could give her anything about ice for her book and he translated a piece from Fray Sahagún's *A General History of the Things of New Spain* on the importance the Aztecs gave to frost, snow and hail, and it took me right back to fish and Veracruz.

Ancient chronicles of the Spanish conquistadores and many modern history books recall the fact that when Hernán Cortés entered Mexico City, then called Tenochtitlán, and met the great Aztec emperor Moctezuma he learned that the emperor and his court received fresh fish from the sea by courier, from what is now Veracruz, to the capital in the high plateau or Valley of Mexico. The couriers ran the 250 mile route from sea level to the high plateau situated at 8,000 feet in two or three days, by relays, and kept the fish fresh by packing it in snow brought down first from the volcano now called Pico de Orizaba—about halfway to Tenochtitlán—and then at the mountain pass between the volcanoes Popocatepetl and Ixtaccihuatl.

Father Bernadhino de Sahagún, in his great work, records the following:

> They fixed a certain time of the frost (in the high plateau), saying that frost appeared 120 days of the year, from the month which they called *Ochpaniztle* to the month called *Tititl*, and it was during the latter month that the people (farmers) said that it was time to prepare and sow the land, plant the corn (maize)

and other seeds, and so they all worked together. When the snow falls almost like rain, they call it *Cepayauitl*, which means ice that becomes like a mist, and when this happened it was a sign of good harvest and a rich and fertile forthcoming year. But when the thick clouds covered the high mountains, they said that it was the beginning of what they called the *Tlaloque*, or gods of water. When these people saw very white clouds covering the mountains, they said it was a sign that hail would come and this would destroy the planted fields and so they feared it very much, but it (the hail) was very good for the hunters because it killed an infinite number of birds. And in order to keep away the hail there were witch doctors called *Teciuhtlazque*, which means interferers of hail; and they had certain magical arts to cast away the hail and keep it from the corn fields and send it to deserts or uncultivated parts.

The fish market in the capital was full of fish and shellfish all of which had arrived by a more expeditious method than the one the emperor had used. I began to learn. There were a number of types of flatfish (*lenguados*) but they weren't sole, they were flounders. However to my mother-in-law all flatfish were not just sole, they were *filete de sole* and they were her favorite fish. I almost began to believe that delicate sole fillets, lightly floured and seeking butter were swimming in our oceans. Elenita travelled the world but she never ate a true sole, fobbed off with flounder, poor soul. Flounder is a very fine fish and perhaps I was unkind being a purist in insisting, sole it is not. Once in Cancún I saw on the menu of a small restaurant *filete de sol*, the "e" having got lost. It was translated into fillet of sun fish.

Though the fish in Mexico's waters are different from the fish that swim in ours, we have many in common and there are also adequate substitutes. There are oysters, prawns and the moro crabs of Yucatán, squid, octopus, clams, abalone, conch, turtle, mussels, frogs' legs and crawfish as well as snapper, flounder, mackerel, *corvina* (bass) and *albacore* (tuna). Unless an oily fish is specified it is always right to use a non-oily, firm fleshed white fish. There is a great array of dishes to choose from, *escabeche* and *seviche*, and the Mexican versions of dried cod dishes from Spain, as well as dishes of great subtlety using saffron, coriander and various nuts as thickeners, these clearly going back to Spain's own period under the Arabs.

Many recipes depend upon the *Court Bouillon* that follows.

COURT BOUILLON FOR FISH

Fish trimmings (head, tail, fins, bones)

2 cups dry white wine

7½ cups water

1 onion, halved and stuck with a clove

1 carrot, peeled and thinly sliced

1 bay leaf

3 sprigs flat leaf parsley, chopped

¼ teaspoon dry thyme or 1 sprig fresh

10 black peppercorns, bruised

1 teaspoon salt

Put all the ingredients into a large saucepan and bring to a simmer, covered, over moderate heat. Uncover and cook, skimming from time to time, for 30 minutes. Strain through a sieve lined with dampened cheesecloth.
MAKES ABOUT 6 CUPS. *Freezes successfully.*

RED SNAPPER VERACRUZ-STYLE
Huachinango a la Veracruzaña

This is the best known and probably the most popular fish dish in Mexico and rightly so for it is delicious. There are many versions of it, one quite spectacular where a whole large red snapper is cooked. I prefer it made with snapper fillets and this is the version I have chosen as it is my favorite and I never tire of it.

6 large red snapper fillets

Salt, freshly ground black pepper

¼ cup lime or lemon juice

½ cup olive oil

2 onions, finely chopped

2 cloves garlic, chopped

2 lbs tomatoes, peeled, seeded and chopped

2 tablespoons large capers

20 small *pimiento*-stuffed green olives, halved

2 pickled *jalapeño* chilies, seeded and cut into strips

12 freshly cooked small new potatoes, kept warm

3 slices white bread, cut into triangles

Butter for frying

Season the fish with salt, pepper and lime juice and set aside. Heat the oil in a large frying pan and sauté the onions until they are tender. Add the tomatoes, capers, olives, and chilies and simmer over low heat until the mixture is thick and well blended, about 10 minutes. Add the fish fillets and cook for about 10 minutes longer. While the fish is cooking heat butter in a frying pan and fry the bread triangles until they are golden on both sides. To serve arrange the fish on a platter and pour the sauce over it, and surround it with the potatoes, with the bread as a garnish round the edge.

SERVES 6 AS A MAIN COURSE.

SEVICHE

Though its origins remain obscure it is generally accepted that *seviche* is of Polynesian origin. It is sometimes spelled *ceviche* but *seviche* is generally preferred. Like all migratory dishes, it has undergone changes that make this version genuinely Mexican, very different from the *seviches* of Peru and Ecuador. Mexicans prefer to use mackerel for this but any fish can be used, oily or non-oily. Lime juice is best but lemon juice can be used instead, just make sure there is enough of it to cover the fish as it is the citric acid in the juice that "cooks" the fish. This is a fine first course, especially in hot weather.

1 lb fillets of mackerel, cut into ½ inch pieces

1½ cups of lime or lemon juice

½ lb tomatoes, peeled and chopped

1 onion, finely sliced

2 pickled *jalapeño* chilies, rinsed and chopped

¼ cup olive oil

1 tablespoon mild white vinegar

2 tablespoons chopped coriander or flat parsley

¼ teaspoon dried oregano, crumbled

Salt

Green olives

Put the fish into a deep glass dish and pour over the lime or lemon juice. Refrigerate for about 6 hours, turning once, about halfway through the process. By this time the fish should have lost its translucent look. Drain and reserve the juice. Combine all the remaining ingredients, except the green olives, add the reserved lime or lemon juice and pour over the fish. Toss gently to mix and refrigerate until ready to serve. It should not be very cold so let it stand outside the refrigerator for about 15 minutes before serving. Garnish with the olives. **SERVES 6.**

PICKLED OR SOUSED FISH
Pescado en Escabeche

This cooking method came to the New World from Spain and is popular throughout Latin America. In Mexico it is most popular in Veracruz, Yucatán, Tampico and Tabasco, which boasts an incredibly luxurious version, *Ostiones en Escabeche* (Soused Oysters). It makes a fine first course and a great many fish are suitable, mackerel, bass and any white fish. Its merits do not end there, it is easy to make and the ingredients are readily accessible, the sort of things most store shelves will have.

**2¼ lbs mackerel, bass or any white fish cut into 6 slices
about 1 inch thick**

¼ cup lime or lemon juice

Flour for dusting

Salt, freshly ground black pepper

½ cup corn or peanut oil

1 onion, thinly sliced

2 fresh *jalapeño* chilies, seeded and cut into strips

3 cloves garlic, chopped

1 teaspoon oregano, crumbled

½ teaspoon ground cumin

¼ teaspoon ground allspice

2 bay leaves

1 cup mild vinegar, such as cider vinegar

Lettuce

Green olives

Put the fish pieces into a shallow dish and pour the lime or lemon juice over them. Set them aside for 30 minutes, turning once. Lift out the fish and pat dry with kitchen paper. Dip the fish in flour seasoned with salt and pepper, shaking to remove the excess. Heat the oil in a large frying pan and sauté the fish lightly until it is just golden on both sides. It should be barely cooked. Rinse out and dry the shallow dish in which the fish was marinated and arrange the fish in it.

In the oil remaining in the pan sauté the onion until it is tender. Add all the ingredients except the lettuce and olives, and bring to a simmer. Pour over the fish, cover and set aside to season for 3-4 hours or if preferred, refrigerate overnight. Serve garnished with lettuce leaves and olives. **Serve with tortillas. SERVES 6 AS A MAIN COURSE.**

FISH WITH CORIANDER
Pescado con Cilantro

I am addicted to coriander. It is a funny herb because people either love or hate it. It is a close relative of the innocent parsley which no one would think of hating, and is the "stinking" herb of Gerard who says the name derives from the Greek for "bed bug" and smells like that bug does when crushed. When I was working on the *Foods of the World* series for Time-Life the kitchen would divide into two groups when the big bunches of coriander arrived for our day's testing for the book of Latin American cooking. Those of us who wanted to bury our noses in the stuff could not understand those who emitted cries of "Ugh, ugh." I had thought it was a Mediterranean herb introduced into Mexico by the Spanish conquerors but my husband's Aunt Tere said no, it existed only in Mexico and though her view was a little extreme and inaccurate I did find that most people in Mexico thought it was indigenous. I had marvelled that an introduced herb had become so integrated into the nation's cooking in so short a time, as the Spanish had been around only since 1521. Ultimately I solved the crushed bed bug problem. This was clearly *Erygium foetidum*, broad leafed coriander, the stronger, bolder and stinkier relative of *Coriandrum sativum*, the gentler cultivated coriander we most of us dote on. It is called *cilantro* in Mexico and is sometimes known as Chinese parsley and there are even some pig-headed people who claim they can't tell it from flat leafed parsley, though it is a lighter green and more feathery. It is not very popular in modern Spain, though it is in modern Portugal and in the Middle East, the Far East, the Indian subcontinent and so on. Here in London I get wonderful *cilantro* from Cyprus and try as I may I cannot grow it though I have grown both parsley and chervil successfully. Maybe it knows I am going to eat it in lavish amounts as in this delicate and lovely fish dish.

**3½ lbs fillets of sea bass, grouper, flounder
    or any firm white fleshed fish**

Salt, freshly ground black pepper

½ cup lime or lemon juice

¼ cup olive oil

1 onion, finely chopped

1 tablespoon chopped fresh coriander (*cilantro*) leaves

2-3 pickled *jalapeño* chilies, rinsed, seeded and chopped coarsely

Season the fish fillets with salt and pepper and pour the lime or lemon juice over them. Set them aside. Heat 3 tablespoons of the oil in a frying pan and sauté the onion until it is soft. Film a shallow ovenproof casserole with oil. It should be just large enough to hold the fish, in more than one layer if necessary. Arrange the fish in the casserole and pour over any liquid that has collected. Cover the dish with the onion and any oil in the pan, the coriander and *jalapeños* and the remaining 1 tablespoon oil. Bake the fish in the preheated 350°F oven for 20 minutes, or until it has lost its translucent look. Serve with plain white rice as a main course. **SERVES 6.**

FISH IN SAFFRON AND PECAN SAUCE
Pescado en Salsa de Azafrán y Nuez

Nuez (nut) in Mexico usually means walnut but sometimes it means pecan probably because the pecan is often thought of as the Mexican walnut. Mexican cooks love to play variations on a theme, given saffron, parsley, coriander and a number of nuts, they mix and match, coming up with a number of dishes superficially alike but very different in flavor. I tasted and tested them and marvelled at the ingenuity of cooks who never, like me, wrote anything down, who knew the right amount of each ingredient simply because it was the right amount, and who often wondered what the fuss was all about when I went chasing flavors with such enthusiasm.

3 lbs fillets any non-oily, firm fleshed white fish

2 cups *Court Bouillon* (page 190)

1 onion, chopped

1 clove garlic, chopped

1½ tablespoons pecans, finely chopped

2 teaspoons flat leafed parsley, chopped

½ teaspoon saffron threads ground in a mortar

1 canned *chipotle* chili, rinsed and chopped

Salt

Lemon juice (optional)

Arrange the fillets in a large frying pan or shallow flameproof casserole and pour the *court bouillon* over them. Bring to a simmer and cook just until the fish loses its translucent look, about 5 minutes. Do not overcook. Lift out to a heated platter, cover and keep warm. Reserve the stock.

Combine the onion, garlic, pecans, parsley, saffron and the *chipotle* chili in a food processor with 1 cup of the fish stock and reduce to a smooth purée. Transfer to a saucepan and heat through. Season to taste with salt and pour over the warm fish. If liked stir in a squeeze of lemon juice into the sauce. Serve immediately. Serve with plain white rice. **SERVES 6.**

FISH IN ALMOND AND CORIANDER SAUCE
Pescado en Salsa de Almendra Verde

In the colonial period when the modern Mexican cuisine was being created, almonds became very popular especially for the delicacy of sauces using them. This one with coriander and *serrano* or *jalapeño* chilies is a favorite of mine though I like it less well with parsley, but then I am hooked on coriander.

3 lbs fillets any non-oily, firm fleshed white fish

2 cups *Court Bouillon* (page 190)

3 tablespoons olive oil

1 clove garlic

1 slice white bread

1 tablespoon finely ground almonds

**3 *serrano* chilies, seeded and chopped or
  1-2 *jalapeño* chilies, seeded and chopped**

½ cup fresh coriander leaves, chopped

Salt

Arrange the fish in a large frying pan or shallow flameproof casserole and pour in the *court bouillon*. Bring to a simmer over moderate heat and cook just until the fish loses its translucent look, about 5 minutes. Be careful not to overcook. Lift the fish out to a warm platter and set aside. Pour the stock into a jug. Heat the oil in a small frying pan and fry the garlic with the bread over moderate heat until the bread is golden on both sides. Discard the garlic and chop the bread coarsely. Combine the bread, almonds, chilies, and coriander in a food processor and process to a purée. Thin to sauce consistency with the reserved stock, heat and pour over the fish. Serve immediately. Serve with plain rice. **SERVES 6.**

FISH IN HAZELNUT SAUCE
Pescados en Salsa de Avellanas

The use of nuts to thicken sauces came to Spain from its Moorish conquerors and since nuts were used in Aztec-Maya cooking it is easy to see how a dish like this would have evolved in the colonial period. Almonds, walnuts and hazelnuts were all brought in by the Spanish. Native nuts were peanuts, cashews and pecans.

3 lbs fillet of any non-oily, firm fleshed white fish

2 cups *Court Bouillon* (page 190)

3 tablespoons olive oil

1 slice white bread

1 clove garlic, chopped

1 tablespoon hazelnuts, skins removed

½ cup flat parsley or fresh coriander leaves

1 teaspoon saffron threads, ground in a mortar

Salt, freshly ground black pepper

Arrange the fish in a frying pan or shallow flameproof casserole and pour in the *court bouillon*. Bring to a simmer and cook just until the fish loses its translucent look, about 5 minutes. Do not overcook. Lift out to a platter, cover and keep warm.

In a small frying pan heat the oil and fry the bread with the garlic until the bread is lightly golden. Take care not to burn the garlic as it will taste bitter and discolor the sauce. Chop the bread coarsely. Combine the bread, garlic, nuts, parsley or coriander in a food processor adding a little of the liquid used to poach the fish. Pour the mixture into a saucepan, season with salt and pepper and thin to sauce consistency with more of the fish stock. Heat and pour over the fish. Serve with rice. **SERVES 6.**

COLEY IN SAUCE
Mero en Mac-Cum

Mac-Cum is the name in the Mayan language for this sauce but I have lost the translation though not the recipe. We had come back from the market to our hotel and were having a drink before lunch in the bar where the barman was telling us, me particularly, what he thought of the *Meshicanos* of the high plateau. I can't remember why but there was some ill-feeling between the races at the time and our barman had an unusual reason for his umbrage. The Aztecs, he said, could not learn to speak English properly as their native tongue lacked the sound of the short "i" and the "th," whereas the Mayan had both. "If," he said to me leaning across the bar "I asked you out to dinner, I would lean across the table and say "Miss, would you like some fish" but if a Meshicano asked you out he would say "Mees would you like some feesh." His smile was triumphant. No one ever asked me out to dinner and asked if I would like some fish, not even my husband and I have lost my notes on *Mac-Cum* but if I ever heard someone say "Dis feesh" I shall know they are not from Yucatán.

**2 lbs coley or any firm fleshed, non-oily
   white fish cut into 4 steaks**

Salt, freshly ground black pepper

6 cloves garlic, crushed

½ teaspoon ground cumin

½ teaspoon oregano, crumbled

1 tablespoon ground *achiote* (annatto)

½ cup Seville (bitter) orange juice

½ cup olive oil

1 onion, thinly sliced

2 cloves garlic, chopped

½ lb tomatoes, peeled and sliced

2 *pimientos* (sweet red pepper), peeled and cut into strips

2 *habañero* chilies, seeded and chopped

2 tablespoons chopped coriander

Arrange the fish steaks on a platter large enough to hold them in a single layer. In a bowl combine salt, several grinds of pepper, garlic, cumin, oregano, annatto and enough orange juice to make a mixture of spreadable consistency. Coat the steaks on both sides with the mixture and let stand at room temperature for 30 minutes.

Film a shallow baking dish, large enough to hold the fish in a single layer, with olive oil. Arrange the fish, with any marinade, in the dish. Top the fish with sliced onion, chopped garlic, tomatoes, *pimientos*, and *habañeros*. Pour the remaining olive oil over the fish, cover the foil and bake in a preheated 350°F oven for about 15 minutes or until the fish has lost its translucent look. Serve sprinkled with the coriander and accompanied by plain white rice and fresh hot tortillas. **SERVES 4 AS A MAIN COURSE.**

SMOTHERED SEA BASS
Tapado de Robalo

Sea bass or striped bass can both be used for this. The fish that swim in Mexican waters are not the same as those that swim in our waters but for all practical purposes they are not so radically different that substitutes cannot be found. I have had the Mexican *robalo* in various references attributed to a number of diverse fish families. I have learned not to be too nitpicky about this but to make sure the dish tastes right and here my husband was of inestimable help as he would taste whatever I had cooked and tell me if it tasted right or not. He had a wonderful palate and a marvellous memory for flavors. So bass is the fish to use for Mexican *robalo* which has borrowed its name from the Portuguese. I don't think knowing the Nahuatl or Maya language names would help.

3 lbs bass fillets

Flour for dusting

Salt

½ cup corn or peanut oil

1 onion, finely chopped

2 cloves garlic, chopped

½ cup flat parsley or fresh coriander leaves, chopped

1 lb tomatoes, peeled and chopped

8 oz *tomatillos*, chopped

1 or 2 dried *guajillo* chilies, peeled, seeded and chopped

Dust the fish with flour seasoned with salt. Heat the oil in a large frying pan and sauté the fish lightly on both sides just until it is golden. Lift out onto a heated serving dish and keep warm, covered.

In the oil remaining in the frying pan sauté the onion until it is soft. Add the garlic, parsley or coriander, tomatoes, *tomatillos*, and chilies and cook over moderate heat until the sauce is thick and well blended, stirring from time to time. Season with salt. The sauce should have the consistency of heavy cream. Pour over the fish and serve. Serve with rice or with fresh hot tortillas and guacamole. **SERVES 6.**

DRUNKEN FISH
Pescado Borracho

Anything cooked with any form of alcohol in Mexico is called "drunken" and some timid souls may fear being overtaken by a similar fate if they indulge in the dish. It is quite safe as the alcohol cooks out and even the large number of chilies are safe from assaulting the timid palate as *anchos* are rich tasting but mild. A useful rule for timing how long whole fish should cook is to measure their depth and cook for 10 minutes to the 1 inch. The fish looks quite spectacular served on a large platter with its sauce. Bream is our best substitute if snapper is not available.

6 *ancho* chilies

5 lbs to 6 lbs whole snapper

Flour for dusting

Salt

¼ cup olive oil

1 onion, finely chopped

2 cloves garlic, chopped

½ cup fresh coriander or flat parsley, chopped

1 lb tomatoes, peeled and chopped

¼ teaspoon ground cumin

½ teaspoon dried oregano, crumbled

6 oz *pimiento*-stuffed green olives, halved

2 tablespoons large capers

2 cups dry red wine

Toast the *anchos* in a dry frying pan, turning once. Do not overcook. Remove from the pan, remove the stems and shake out the seeds. Tear into pieces and put into a bowl with warm water just to cover. Soak for 30 minutes. Drain and purée in a food processor.

Dust the fish with flour that has been seasoned with salt. Heat the oil in a frying pan large enough to hold the fish and sauté it lightly on both sides just long enough to color it golden. Transfer it to a large ovenproof casserole and set it aside when making the sauce. In the oil remaining in the frying pan sauté the onion and garlic until the onion is tender. Drain and add the *anchos*, the coriander or parsley, tomatoes, cumin, oregano and salt to taste. Cook over moderate heat, stirring from time to time, for 5 minutes. Add the olives, capers and red wine, mixing well. Pour over the fish, cover the casserole and cook in a preheated 350°F oven for about 30 minutes according to the 10 minutes to the 1 inch rule. Serve with rice and fresh, hot tortillas. **SERVES 6.**

FISH IN WHITE WINE
Pescado en Vino Blanco

This was a family dish cooked when they were feeling fancy, especially if the guests included someone French. The cook thought it was too dull and added a little pickled *serrano* chili and a little oregano without telling anyone and served it with *Arroz Verde* (Green Rice) instead of plain white rice. And tortillas and guacamole. I think that cook's name was Hermila, not a very jolly type but a great cook who preferred her own way to that of others. She could make tortillas by hand patting them out with great skill, but seldom deigned to do so, and though she promised to teach me how to do this, went blank when I asked for an exact time for a lesson.

4 lbs bass, whole with head and tail on

Flour for dusting

Salt

¼ cup corn oil

2 onions, finely chopped

1 clove garlic, chopped

Large pinch freshly grated nutmeg

½ teaspoon oregano, crumbled

1-2 pickled *serrano* chilies, rinsed and chopped

1 tablespoon fresh coriander, chopped

2 cups dry white wine

Measure the depth of the fish and calculate its cooking time as 10 minutes to the 1 inch. Dust the fish with flour seasoned with salt, shaking to remove the excess. Heat the oil in a frying pan large enough to hold the fish and sauté it lightly on both sides. Transfer it to a lightly oiled ovenproof casserole. In the oil remaining in the pan sauté the onions and garlic until the onions are soft. Add the pan contents to the casserole.

In a saucepan combine the nutmeg, oregano, *serranos*, coriander and wine and season with a little salt. Pour the mixture over the fish, cover and bake in a preheated 350°F oven according to the 10 minute rule. Serve with *Arroz Verde* (Green Rice). **SERVES 6.**

FISH YUCATÁN-STYLE
Pescado Yucateco

Hot chilies are not used a great deal in Mayan cooking which seems contradictory when this kitchen has the hottest chili sauce of them all, using the fiercely fiery little *habañero* with its exquisite flavor matching its fire. Served separately, it allows the timid to proceed with caution and uncautious to repent at leisure.

5 lbs to 6 lbs whole red snapper or similar fish with head and tail left on

3 tablespoons lime, or lemon juice

Salt, freshly ground black pepper

¼ cup corn or peanut oil

1 onion, finely chopped

3 oz pitted green olives

2 *pimientos* (sweet red peppers), peeled, seeded and chopped

1 tablespoon *achiote* (annatto), finely ground

2 tablespoons fresh coriander or flat parsley, chopped

½ cup Seville (bitter) orange juice

2 hard-boiled eggs, chopped

Measure the depth of the fish and be ready to cook it for 10 minutes to the 1 inch. Sprinkle the fish with the lime or lemon juice and season with salt and pepper. Lightly oil an ovenproof casserole and add the fish with any liquid. Heat the oil in a frying pan and sauté the onion until it is soft. Add the olives, red peppers (*pimientos*), *achiote* and coriander and cook over moderate heat for 3-4 minutes. Pour in the Seville orange juice and taste for seasoning. Pour the hot sauce over the fish and bake in a 350°F oven until cooked following the 10 minute rule. Serve garnished with the eggs. If liked accompany with *Ixni-Pec* (page 78) sauce and fresh hot tortillas. **SERVES 6.**

FISH IN *ADOBO* SAUCE
Pescado en Adobo

This translates into "fish in pickling sauce" which is not fair to this well flavored main dish but as a friend said to me, "when was life or translation meant to be fair?" The *ancho* chilies give this *adobo* a very rich flavor and a fine red color.

5 lbs bass, snapper or sea trout with head and tail on

Flour for dusting

Salt, freshly ground black pepper

½ cup corn or peanut oil

6 *ancho* chilies

1 onion, chopped

2 cloves garlic, chopped

¼ teaspoon ground cloves

¼ teaspoon ground cinnamon

½ teaspoon each ground cumin, thyme, oregano

1 teaspoon sugar

1 lb tomatoes, peeled and chopped

Measure the depth of the fish and be ready to cook it for 10 minutes to the 1 inch. Dredge the fish in flour which has been seasoned with salt and pepper, shaking to remove the excess. Heat the oil in a large frying pan and sauté the fish lightly on both sides and transfer to an ovenproof casserole that has been greased. Set aside.

Toast the *anchos* lightly in a dry frying pan, take out and remove the stems and shake out the seeds. Tear into pieces and put into a bowl with warm water barely to cover. Soak for 30 minutes, turning from time to time. Drain reserving the soaking liquid. Combine the *anchos* with the onion, garlic, herbs and spices, the sugar and tomatoes and process to a fairly coarse purée. It should have some texture. Heat the oil remaining in the frying pan and sauté the mixture for 5 minutes over moderate heat stirring from time to time. Pour the sauce over the fish and bake in a 350°F oven for the time following the 10 minute rule. Serve with rice, and hot tortillas and guacamole on the side. **SERVES 6.**

VARIATION: *Prawns may be used instead of fish.*

MACKEREL IN *PASILLA* SAUCE
Sierra en Chile Pasilla

Very popular ripe and dried, the *pasilla* chili is much less used in its fresh form when it is called *chilaca*. I never came across *chilacas* though I knew the *pasilla* well for its role in *Mole Poblano*. I often find it hard to recognize the fresh and dried chilies as being the same fruit, as the change is quite dramatic, the *poblano* turning into the *ancho* for instance. The *pasilla* is long and slender, only about 1 inch wide to 6 inches long, wrinkled and so dark a red it is some-times called *chile negro* (black chili). It is full-flavored and hot. It is particularly good with oily fish.

6 *pasilla* chilies

2 cups *Court Bouillon* (page 190)

3 lbs mackerel fillets

3 tablespoons corn or peanut oil

1 slice white bread

1 onion, chopped

1 clove garlic, chopped

½ teaspoon ground cumin

Salt

1 tablespoon lime juice

Toast the *pasillas* lightly in a frying pan on both sides. Remove the stems and shake out the seeds and tear into pieces. Put to soak in a bowl with warm water barely to cover and leave for 30 minutes, turning from time to time. Set aside.

Put the mackerel into a frying pan and pour the *court bouillon* over them. Bring to a simmer over moderate heat and cook just until the fish is opaque. Lift out onto a serving dish and cover to keep warm. Reserve the cooking liquid. Rinse out and dry the frying pan. Heat the oil in the pan and fry the bread until it is golden on both sides. Lift out and chop coarsely. Transfer to a food processor with the drained chilies, onion, garlic, cumin and the reserved *court bouillon*. Process to a purée, transfer to a saucepan, taste for seasoning and simmer for 10 minutes to blend the flavors. Stir in the lime juice and pour over the mackerel fillets. If necessary add the fish to the sauce to heat through. Serve with rice, if liked, and fresh hot tortillas. **SERVES 6.**

PRAWNS IN PUMPKIN SEED SAUCE
Pipián de Camarones

Fray Bernadhino de Sahagún, the Spanish priest who arrived in Mexico shortly after the Conquest (1519-21) and wrote the monumental *Historia General de las Cosas de Nueva España* (*A General History of the Things of New Spain 1558-69*) gave us brilliant descriptions of the huge market at Tenochtitlán, the Aztec capital of Mexico. He described with enthusiasm, relish and detail the foods he found simmering in huge earthenware *cazuelas* (casseroles) so faithfully I was able to work out an approximate version of the dish. I have used a little sugar where honey would have been used, as sugar was introduced by the Spanish and there are other differences. Different types of onion and garlic and no oil or lemon juice are others. Sahagún's descriptions of Mexican foods are of especial interest as they tell us a great deal about the cuisine before the foods of Europe and Asia were introduced following the Conquest. *Pipián* is a classic Aztec sauce made from ground pumpkin seeds, chilies and tomatoes, as popular today as it was back then.

2 lbs raw prawns, unshelled

1 cup hulled *pepitas* (pumpkin seeds) (page 22)

1 onion, finely chopped

2 cloves garlic, chopped

½ lb tomatoes, peeled and chopped

½ teaspoon ground allspice

3 fresh *serrano* chilies, seeded and chopped

2 *pimientos*, seeded and chopped

Salt

½ teaspoon sugar

3 tablespoons corn or peanut oil

Drop the prawns in boiling water to cover and cook for 2-3 minutes according to size, or just until they turn pink. Lift out and as soon as they are cool enough to peel remove the shells. Set aside. Return the shells to the cooking water and cook at a simmer for 5 minutes. Strain, discard the shells and reserve the liquid.

Grind the *pepitas* in a food processor or nut grinder as fine as possible then shake through a sieve. Set aside. Combine the onion, garlic, tomatoes, allspice, chilies and *pimientos* in a food processor and process to a purée. Season to taste with salt and add the sugar. Add the *pepitas*. Heat the oil in a frying pan and cook the mixture over moderate heat for 5 minutes, stirring. Stir in

1 cup of the reserved prawn stock. The sauce should be the consistency of cream. Add more stock if necessary. Add the prawns and cook just to heat through. Serve with plain rice and hot tortillas. **SERVES 6.**

VARIATION:

I prefer fresh coriander, about 1 tablespoon, to the allspice though allspice is closer to the original. The mixture would almost certainly not have been fried as this was not an Aztec/Maya technique, instead it would have been cooked very gently in the altitude of the altiplano.

RICE AND CRABS YUCATÁN-STYLE
Arroz con Jaibas Yucateco

The moro crabs of Yucatán are famous and as far as I am concerned would live out their lives in peace as I have neither the courage nor skill to kill them. I eat crab with relish provided someone else is the killer. I was once told by a famous chef that the humane way to kill a lobster was to stroke its chest which would anesthetize it but even this was beyond me. I am a coward so I buy lump crabmeat, fresh or frozen. It works very well. A small nut grinder or coffee grinder works best for the *achiote* which is very hard.

2 cups long grain raw white rice

½ cup corn or peanut oil

2 onions, chopped

2 cloves garlic, chopped

1 lb tomatoes, peeled and chopped

1 tablespoon *achiote* (annatto), finely ground

5 cups chicken stock, about

Salt

1½ lbs lump crabmeat, broken up

3 *pimientos* (sweet red peppers) peeled, seeded and cut into strips

1 cup raw young peas

Sprig *epazote* or 1 bay leaf

½ cup dry sherry (optional)

Put the rice into a bowl with hot water to cover and soak for 20 minutes. Drain, rinse thoroughly in cold water and put into a sieve to drain and dry thoroughly. Heat the oil in an ovenproof casserole and sauté the rice over moderate heat until it is lightly golden. Set aside.

In a food processor combine the onions, garlic, tomatoes and *achiote* and process to a purée. Pour into a measuring jug and add enough stock to bring the quantity up to 6 cups. Stir to mix, season with salt and pour over the rice in the casserole. Fold in the crabmeat, the pepper strips, *epazote* or bay leaf, and peas.

Cover the casserole and cook in a preheated 350°F oven for 30 minutes or until the rice is tender and all the liquid has been absorbed. If liked stir in the sherry gently. Serve with fresh hot tortillas, and guacamole and a hot chili sauce like *Ixni-Pec* (page 78) on the side. Prawns or lobster can be used instead of crabmeat. **SERVES 6-8.**

DRIED SALT COD
Bacalao

The great popularity of dried salt cod (*bacalao*) in both Spain and Portugal with their extensive sea coasts and abundant fresh fish is a paradox. About the time Columbus was "discovering" the Americas, Portuguese fishermen were making the hazardous journey each spring to the Grand Banks of Newfoundland to fish for cod which they salted and dried at sea and brought home in the autumn. They almost certainly discovered North America without recognizing the fact. The cod dries into board-like pieces of pale yellow which need only soaking to turn back into edible fish. *Bacalhau* (salt cod) is so popular in Portugal that there are said to be 365 different ways to cook it, one for every day of the year. The Spanish Basques especially rejoice in *bacalao*. An even more astonishing paradox is that love of salt cod has migrated to the New World, especially to Mexico which has its own version of the favorite Basque dish, *Bacalao a la Vizcaina* (Salt Cod Basque-Style) while Jamaica's national dish is Salt Fish and Ackees.

I happen to have a passion for salt cod and I had a favorite restaurant in Lisbon that had a cod specialty cooked to perfection, and in Mexico there was a Basque restaurant whose salt cod were memorable, but to my husband it was anathema. So I waited until he was away on some United Nations work to test recipes. I was, I am afraid, not quite so considerate in everything I cooked but his detestation of salt cod merited respect. It was not just a hangover from childhood when the days of fasting turned it into hated Friday food or that he bitterly resented the Spanish Conquest and the destruction of Mexico's ancient cultures, he just plain downright hated the taste. Can't quarrel with that. Here are three salt cod recipes which show how the genius of Mexican cooks adapted something as foreign as *bacalao*.

To prepare salt cod for cooking soak it for 24-36 hours in cold water, changing the water several times. For less heavily salted fish the soaking time can be shortened. Drain, rinse and blanch the cod, putting it into a saucepan with cold

water to cover and bringing to a boil over heat. Drain and remove the skin and bones. The cod is now ready to be used according to recipe instructions.

SALT COD, BASQUE-STYLE
Bacalao a la Vizcaina

Mexico has a considerable Basque population and they introduced their greatest dried salt cod dish to the country, where it underwent a change without losing its original character altogether. In Spain sweet, dried, smooth-skinned, medium-sized *ñoras*, which are of Mexican origin, would be used. In Mexico *pimientos* (sweet red peppers) plus a small, dried hot chili, seeded and chopped, would be used, or even *quajillos* leaving out the hot chili.

1 lb dried salt cod

¼ cup olive oil

1 onion, chopped

2 cloves garlic, chopped

1 lb tomatoes, peeled and chopped

3 *pimientos* (sweet red peppers), peeled, seeded and chopped

Salt, freshly ground black pepper

1 small, dried hot chili, seeded and chopped

12 small new potatoes, freshly cooked and peeled

3 slices white bread, cut into triangles

Olive oil for frying

2 tablespoons flat parsley, chopped

Stuffed green olives

Prepare the salt cod in the usual way (see page 206) and put it into a saucepan with fresh cold water to cover, bring to a simmer over moderate heat and cook until the fish is tender, about 15 minutes. Drain, remove any skin and bones and cut into 1 inch pieces. Heat the oil in a frying pan and sauté lightly on both sides. Transfer to shallow, fireproof casserole. Reserve the oil. Combine the onion, garlic, tomatoes, *pimientos* and chili in a food processor and process to a purée. Heat the reserved oil and cook the purée over moderate heat, stirring from time to time, for 5 minutes. Season to taste with salt and pepper and pour over the fish. Add the potatoes and cook for about 5 minutes to heat through. Fry the bread in the frying pan with more oil if needed until golden. Serve the cod with the sauce, garnished with the bread, parsley and green olives. **SERVES 6.**

SALT COD IN CREAM
Bacalao con Crema

This is almost definitely inspired by a Portuguese salt cod dish. It is almost certainly from Yucatán or Campeche but I had it in Mexico City with the family at one of the Sunday *comidas* when we went to a restaurant chosen by Tío Miguel, though I often wonder how much choice he had when flanked by his sister Tía Tere and my mother-in-law, his sister Elenita. The cream used in Mexican cooking is rich and heavy, well-matured and more like French crème fraîche than anything else. Sour cream is a good substitute, or make your own *Crema Espesa,* page 314.

2 lbs sait cod

Flour

½ cup olive oil

2 onions, finely chopped

6 medium-size new potatoes, freshly boiled, peeled and sliced

¾ cup stock from fish

1 cup sour or heavy cream (see headnote)

2 sprigs fresh *epazote* chopped, or ½ teaspoon dried

2 teaspoons fresh flat parsley, chopped

Prepare the salt cod fish in the usual way (page 206) and put into a saucepan with fresh cold water to cover, bring to a simmer over moderate heat and cook until the fish is tender, about 15 minutes. Drain, pat dry and cut into 2 inch pieces. Reserve the stock. Dredge the fish with flour, shaking to remove the excess. Heat the oil in a frying pan and sauté the onions until tender. Push them to one side of the pan and sauté the cod until it is golden on both sides. Add the potatoes. Pour in the fish stock, cream, *epazote* and parsley and simmer over very low heat to blend the flavors, for 5 minutes. Serve with fresh hot tortillas, and if liked a fresh hot sauce. **SERVES 6.**

SALT COD IN CHILI AND ALMOND SAUCE
Bacalao con Chile y Almendra

This is a typically colonial dish. The Aztecs took to the delicate almond which the Spanish introduced with relish but lost none of their enthusiasm for their *anchos* and tomatoes. It makes a wonderful combination of flavors and is a fine main course with rice, another introduced food that had an instant welcome.

3 *ancho* chilies

2 lbs dried salt cod

2 oz blanched almonds, chopped

1 onion, chopped

½ lb tomatoes, peeled and chopped

½ teaspoon dried oregano, crumbled

3 tablespoons olive oil

Salt, freshly ground black pepper

Toast the *anchos* lightly on both sides in a dry frying pan. Take out of the pan and remove the stems and shake out the seeds. Tear into pieces and put into a bowl with warm water barely to cover and soak for 30 minutes, turning from time to time. Drain and set aside.

Prepare the salt cod in the usual way (page 206) then put into a saucepan with fresh cold water to cover, bring to a simmer and cook for 15 minutes or until the fish is tender. Drain, remove any skin and bones, pat dry and cut into 2 inch pieces. Reserve the stock. Combine the *anchos*, almonds, onion and oregano in a food processor and process to a purée. Heat the oil in a large frying pan and cook the mixture for 5 minutes, stirring from time to time until it is well blended and the consistency of cream. If it is too thick, thin with a little of the reserved stock. Season to taste with salt and pepper. Add the cod and cook over low heat until the fish is heated thoroughly, about 5 minutes. Serve with plain white rice. **SERVES 6.**

WHITE FISH OF LAKE PÁTZCUARO
Pescado Blanco de Pátzcuaro

As well as its enormous wealth of seafood, Mexico also has freshwater fish including catfish, carp and the famous, little white fish, the *pescado blanco*, transparent with a silver stripe down each side from the two largest lakes, Pátzcuaro in Michoacán and Chapala in Jalisco. Michoacán means "Land of Fish" in Tarascan Indian and this region is their territory. Apart from *Caldo Michi*, a fish soup made with lake fish, the best way to cook the white fish is to pat them dry and fry them quickly in oil. They need nothing more than perhaps a squeeze of lime or lemon juice, with fresh tortillas and guacamole on the side to make a small feast.

I was very privileged on my first visit to the lake. César was there for some cultural event, connected I think with UNESCO. It was on or about November the second, All Souls' Day, *Día de los Muertos*, when the Mexicans visit the graves of their loved ones as a mark of affection and respect, and this is marked especially on the little island of Janitzio in the lake. Of course the island is not open to the public but we were aware of the celebrations which are elaborate and certainly include rites belonging to the pre-Christian era. It was my first Day of the Dead in Mexico and I was taken a little aback to be given a candy skull with my name on it. "Who wants me dead?" was my first thought but as everyone got a skull to nibble on, I nibbled too. The region is very lovely and I remember the intense blue sky, bright sun and the huge bunches of vivid orange marigolds, *zempazuchitl*, being taken to the graves. It was amazingly joyous. And I remember the small *pescados blancos*, with their pointed heads and delicate flavor. There were other November seconds but none quite like that one, when I learned how the men of the village had gone duck hunting to get the wild duck for the special *tamales* for the women to make and take with them when they go with their children to keep vigil all night at the gravesides, while the men keep vigil at home. The dead feast in a mystical way that night, and the next day families feast too, but not mystically. And they add beer, pulque, and tequila to the menu.

My second experience of the freshwater lake fish was quite different. The family, that is Uncle Miguel, had organized a few days' excursion to the lake resort near Veracruz, Lake Catemaco, with a young Tinoco cousin, Berta and us. They had fish, not I think the same as the little transparent ones, but good to eat all the same, provided it was not just the "all" to eat. Each day we had fish for *comida*, and each evening *merienda* with the usual light things and if we three hungry younger ones wanted more, there was fish. The family said we should not eat at night. It was bad for one in the altitude, ignoring the fact that from its very beginning Veracruz had been at sea level. César finally persuaded the management that if we did not have a change from the lake fish for supper we would die. The management relented, the chef promised chicken, fried, for supper. I was served first with a wing with a bone almost as thick as my arm. The other two had equally robust portions. It was tender and tasted fine but as we tried to work out what manner of bird had so generous a wingspan, or be of a size to match its other noble parts, we fell into helpless giggles. We talked of the great bird of Catemaco, was it a buzzard, a vulture, and the more the elders looked scandalized, the more we were caught in those awful giggles. We ate the great bird, or rather the areas of it served to us, and were glad we were going home in the morning. We went to bed under a cloud, not to be forgiven for a long time for our *escandalosa* behavior. Bad enough to sink so low as to laugh in public, but to giggle, and giggle and giggle like tourists or naughty children!

MEAT

•

Carnes

Meat plays an important role in the colonial Mexican kitchen, with pork taking first place. The Aztecs had peccary, a wild pig that was hunted as boars were hunted in Europe in the Middle Ages. However, when the Spaniards introduced a domestic pig after the Conquest, it was adopted with enthusiasm and immediately supplanted the wild pig. There are a great many good and unusual pork dishes in Mexico, perhaps because the pork is of an excellent quality, which doubtless encourages the cooks. These three are especially distinctive: *Tapado de Cerdo* (Smothered Pork), *Mancha Mateles de Cerdo* (Pork Tablecloth Stainer) and *Puerco con Piña* (Pork with Pineapple).

Steak is probably the most popular cut of beef, particularly fillet cooked in what might be the international way. There are some distinctive beef recipes where old and new worlds meet. One of the most interesting is *Carne de Res con Nopalitos* (Beef with Cactus Pieces). Meat balls, using a mixture of meats, are highly esteemed. They are not fried but poached in a thin sauce flavored with chili so that they taste of the sauce as well as their own ingredients. *Picadillo* (Minced or Chopped Meat), an inheritance from the Middle East and popular throughout all of Latin America, is used in all sorts of ways, very much for filling *empanadas* (turnovers) and in the corn kitchen.

There are not a great many veal dishes but the ones there are among the most delicately flavored in the whole cuisine. Veal takes extremely well to *tomatillos* (green tomatoes) and fresh coriander.

Lamb is not very popular but goat, introduced at the same time by the conquerors, is. In northern Mexico *Cabrito al Horno* (Roast Kid) is a great favorite and is served with flour tortillas, guacamole, *salsa verde* or *salsa cruda* and beans, often black beans.

Offal, terrible word, is another favorite in the kitchen. I'd rather we called offal, organ meats but no matter, there are wonderful tripe dishes and the dishes with tongue show the genius of the cooks for creating a whole series of flavors around a single ingredient. *Lengua Ahumada con Tomatillos* (Smoked Tongue with Green Tomatoes) is one of my greatest favorites.

BEEF WITH CHILIES
Chile con Carne

Mexican *Chile con Carne* is very different from Texas chili and at least a little older. The Spanish introduced beef to the country's north, good cattle country, and presumably the dish was born then, a mixture of New World cooking technique with an old world four-footed animal. It could be older using wild boar or some such beast but I don't think so. The dish permits some variations, pork may be used instead of beef, cumin may be used instead of or with oregano, and tomatoes added to the chili mixture which is mild and fully-flavored and not incendiary like Texas chili. Properly speaking this should be called *Carne con Chile Colorado* (Meat in Red Chili Sauce).

6 *ancho* chilies

2 lbs beef chuck cut into ½-inch cubes

1 onion, chopped

2 cloves garlic, chopped

2 tablespoons lard or corn oil

½ teaspoon dried oregano, crumbled

Salt, freshly ground black pepper

2 cups cooked red kidney beans (see method)

To cook beans for *Chile con Carne* put the beans in a large saucepan with 1 teaspoon salt and cold water to cover, bring to a boil and boil hard for ten minutes, then reduce to a simmer, cover and cook for about 2 hours, or until the beans are tender. Add a little hot water if the beans dry out.

Toast the *anchos* lightly in a dry frying pan, tear off the stems, shake out the seeds and tear into pieces. Put them in a small bowl and cover with hot water. Leave to soak for 30 minutes. Put the beef into a large flameproof casserole or saucepan, add water to cover, cover and simmer over low heat for 1 hour. Skim off any scum that rises to the surface. In a food processor combine the onion, garlic and *anchos* and process to a coarse purée. In a frying pan heat the lard or oil, add the purée and cook, stirring for 5 minutes. Add the oregano, cumin and salt and pepper to taste. Add to the beef and cook, covered at a gentle simmer for an hour longer. Add the beans, cover and cook for 15 minutes longer. **SERVES 6.**

VARIATION:
Instead of beef use shoulder of pork cut into ½-inch pieces. If liked add 1 lb tomatoes, peeled, seeded and chopped though this is unorthodox. Some cooks add a potato weighing about 8 oz cut into ½ inch pieces cooked until just tender but still firm.

BEEF WITH CACTUS PIECES
Carne de Res con Nopalitos

This is the modern version of a colonial recipe where the foods of old and new worlds combined. There were no canned versions of anything then as there are now and this would have been available only in Mexico and taken quite a lot of work cleaning the cactus paddles. I always bought my cactus canned as I was quite bad at cleaning the beast. My cook did it with great facility and marvelled at my ineptitude.

3 tablespoons corn oil or lard

2 lbs beef chuck cut into 1-inch pieces

1 large onion, finely chopped

2 cloves garlic, chopped

8 oz canned *nopalitos*, drained

6 canned *serranos*, or 6 fresh, seeded and chopped

10 oz canned *tomatillos*, drained or 8 oz fresh

3 tablespoons tomato purée

1 cup beef stock

2 tablespoons fresh coriander, chopped

Salt, freshly ground black pepper

Heat the oil or lard in a frying pan and brown the beef pieces a few at a time. Put the beef into a flameproof casserole and set aside. In the fat remaining in the pan sauté the onion and garlic until the onion is soft, and add to the casserole. Add the *nopalitos*, thoroughly rinsed, the chilies, *tomatillos*, tomato purée, beef stock, coriander, and salt and pepper to taste. Cover and simmer over low heat until the beef is tender, about 2½ hours. **SERVES 6.**

BEEF STEW, DURANGO-STYLE
Caldillo Durangueño

This is a family recipe as well as a regional one. It is simple but because of the chilies very richly flavored. Now that so many of the dried chilies are available it is no longer out of reach. A friend of mine once wrote a book on stew and heading them should be the beef stews and this one among the top. Until I tasted beef with chilies, I would not have expected these two to get together so happily in the stew pot.

3 *ancho* chilies

3 *mulato* chilies

2 tablespoons corn oil

1 large onion, finely chopped

2 lbs lean beef cut into ½-inch cubes

2 cloves garlic, chopped

1 lb tomatoes, peeled, seeded and chopped

1½ cups beef stock

Salt, freshly ground black pepper

½ teaspoon oregano

Fresh lemon juice

Toast the chilies in a dry frying pan, pull off the stems, shake out the seeds, reserving ½ cup. Tear the chilies into pieces and put into a bowl with warm water to cover. Let stand for 30 minutes.

Heat the oil in a frying pan and brown the beef quickly over a fairly high heat. Transfer the beef into a flameproof casserole and set aside. In the oil remaining in the pan sauté the onion and garlic until the onion is soft. Add the tomato and continue to cook, stirring, until the mixture is thick and well blended. Add the mixture to the beef. In a food processor combine the chilies and the seeds and blend until smooth. Add to the beef. Add enough beef stock to cover, salt and pepper and the oregano. Cover and simmer over low heat until the beef is tender, about 2 hours. Squeeze in the lemon juice and serve. There should be abundant gravy as this is quite a soupy stew.
SERVES 6.

SMALL STUFFED BREAD ROLLS
Pambacitas

I don't know where this recipe rightly belongs. I first had *pambacitas* in Yucatán when César took me to see the ruins at Uxmal and Chichén Itzá which he knew very well. He told me a story of frightening himself half to death on his first trip there when he was still a teenager. Intrigued by the great monuments, he returned to the ruins after nightfall and was wandering around about midnight in the eerie moonlight of the near tropics, when he heard voices and was certain they were those of the ancient Maya-Toltecs. He fled. While telling me about this experience he ate *pamabacitas* and drank wonderful Yucatán beer while I drank tequila and tried to work out what was in the filling, and absorb a lesson in archaeology at the same time.

Lard or corn oil

3 chorizo sausages, skinned and chopped

¾ lb potatoes, freshly cooked, peeled and diced

1 onion, finely chopped

Salt, freshly ground black pepper

1 large egg, lightly beaten

12 small, round, bread rolls

Finely shredded lettuce, preferably romaine

Oil and vinegar dressing

1 cup mashed kidney beans (*Frijoles Refritos*) (page 159)

***Salsa Verde* (page 80) or *Salsa de Jitomate* (page 81)**

Freshly grated Parmesan cheese

Radishes, thinly sliced

Heat 1 tablespoon lard or corn oil in a frying pan and add the sausages and onion. Sauté until the onion is soft. Season with salt and pepper to taste. Stir in the beaten egg and cook over moderate heat until the egg is set. Cut the tops off the rolls and set them aside. Pull the crumbs out of the bottom half of the rolls and fry both parts in hot lard oil. Toss the lettuce in the dressing to coat lightly and put a layer in the bottom of each roll. Top with a layer of beans, a layer of the sausage mixture, a little sauce, a sprinkling of cheese and a slice or two of radish. Replace the tops and eat immediately while still hot. **SERVES 12.**

BEEF WITH ORANGES
Carne de Res con Naranjas

Mexican cooks were enthusiastic adopters of old world foods and the orange must have been one of the most exciting. It had been an exciting immigrant into Europe where the Seville (bitter) orange was the principal type at first and it was certainly this that was used to create the dish. When I met this at a summer buffet luncheon the sweet orange was the one used. It would be fun to experiment with Seville oranges instead.

3½ lbs chuck or top round or similar cut in one piece

Salt, freshly ground black pepper

1 large onion, chopped

2 cloves garlic, chopped

¼ teaspoon ground cloves

¼ teaspoon ground cinnamon

½ teaspoon thyme, finely chopped if fresh, half as much if dried

1½ cups strained fresh orange juice, about

Rind ½ orange cut into julienne

1 envelope unflavored gelatine

½ cup dry sherry

For garnish: Orange slices, capers, pitted green olives, shredded lettuce

Season the beef with salt and pepper and place into a flameproof casserole. Add the onion, garlic, cloves, cinnamon and thyme. Pour in enough orange juice to cover the beef. Add the orange rind. Cover and simmer over low heat until the beef is tender, about 2½ hours. Cool the beef in the stock, lift out and pat dry with kitchen towels and cut into thin slices. Arrange on a chilled platter in overlapping slices. Set aside. Clarify the stock (page 92). Add the sherry and enough orange juice to bring the amount up to 2 cups. Sprinkle the gelatine over ¼ cup cold water in a small bowl. Pour the stock into a saucepan and add the softened gelatine, stir over low heat until dissolved. Chill in the refrigerator until mixture is syrupy then pour over the beef slices and refrigerate until set. Garnish the platter with the lettuce, orange slices, capers and olives. **SERVES 6-8.**

POT *MOLE* FOR BEEF
Mole de Olla para Carne de Res

The best way to explain a *mole* is a stew with chilies. It is the main meat and poultry cooking method of the Aztecs, ideally suited to the high altitude of the region. It is wonderfully versatile, adapting to Old World foods with no problems.

3 *ancho* **chilies**

1 *pasilla* **chili**

2 lbs beef chuck or similar cut, cut into 2-inch pieces

Sprig *epazote*

2 onions, chopped

1 clove garlic, chopped

1 lb tomatoes, peeled, seeded and chopped

2 tablespoons corn oil or lard

1 lb young zucchini, trimmed and sliced

12 small new potatoes

Salt, freshly ground black pepper

Toast the chilies lightly in a dry frying pan, pull off the stems, shake out the seeds and tear into pieces. Put into a small bowl with warm water to cover and soak for 30 minutes. Put the beef and *epazote* into a flameproof casserole with enough water to cover, bring to a simmer, cover and cook over low heat for about 2 hours or until almost tender. Add the zucchini and potatoes and continue cooking until the beef and vegetables are tender, about 10-15 minutes longer. Combine the chilies, onions, garlic and tomatoes in a food processor.

Heat the oil or lard in a frying pan and cook the mixture over moderate heat, stirring, for 5 minutes or until it is thick and well blended. Season with salt and pepper and pour into the beef. Simmer over very low heat to blend the flavors and heat through. The chili mixture can be added earlier with the vegetables. **SERVES 6.**

PORK TABLECLOTH STAINER
Mancha Manteles de Cerdo

The Aztecs took to the domesticated pig when the Spanish, great pork lovers, introduced it. In the first place they did not have to hunt it as they had the wild and fierce peccary, and secondly it gave them lard which became their preferred cooking fat and introduced them to the technique of frying, unknown in their cuisine before the Conquest.

6 *mulato* chilies

4 *ancho* chilies

2 *pasilla* chilies

3½ lbs boneless shoulder or loin of pork cut
    into 2-inch pieces

1 bay leaf

½ teaspoon dried thyme, crumbled or twice the amount fresh,
    chopped

½ teaspoon dried oregano, crumbled, or twice the amount fresh,
    chopped

1 whole clove

Salt

1 onion, roughly chopped

1 clove garlic, chopped

1 tablespoon fresh coriander, chopped

1 cup walnuts chopped

8 oz Mexican green tomatoes (*tomatillos*), fresh or canned

3 tablespoons corn oil or lard

Freshly ground black pepper

3 tart apples, cored, peeled and sliced

3 pears, peeled, cored and sliced

3 large firm bananas, peeled and sliced

3 slices fresh pineapple, cut into chunks

3 young zucchini, trimmed and sliced

1 cup raw, fresh, green peas or frozen, thawed

Toast the chilies lightly in a dry frying pan, tear off the stems, shake out the seeds and tear in pieces. Put into a bowl with warm water to cover and soak for 30 minutes. Set aside.

Put the pork into a flameproof casserole with the bay leaf, thyme, oregano, clove and enough salted water just to cover. Bring to a simmer, cover and cook over low heat for 1½ hours. Drain, strain and reserve the stock. Rinse out the casserole and return the pork.

In the food processor combine the onion, garlic, coriander, walnuts, *tomatillos* and prepared chilies and blend until smooth. Heat the oil or lard in a frying pan, add the mixture and cook, stirring for 5 minutes over moderate heat. Season to taste with salt and pepper and thin with the reserved stock. Add all the fruits and vegetables to the casserole arranging them in layers. Pour the chili mixture over all, cover, and simmer over a low heat to blend flavors and heat through. **SERVES 6-8.**

BEEF WITH MEXICAN GREEN TOMATOES
Carne de Res con Tomatillos

This is a regional dish from Saltillo. It is well flavored and extremely easy to cook. The sort of dish you can forget about once it is on the stove. It is the combination of *tomatillos* with fresh coriander and the heat of the *serranos* that lifts it out of the ordinary.

2 tablespoons corn oil or lard

2½ lbs round steak, in one piece

1 onion, sliced

1 clove garlic, chopped

1 chorizo sausage, skinned and chopped

8 oz *tomatillos*, canned or fresh

2 or more *serrano* chilies, seeded and chopped

½ cup fresh coriander leaves, chopped

Salt, freshly ground black pepper

1 cup beef stock

12 small new potatoes, freshly cooked and peeled

Heat the oil or lard in a frying pan and brown the steak on both sides. Transfer it to a flameproof casserole. In the fat remaining in the pan sauté the onion, garlic and sausage, add them to the steak together with the *tomatillos*, chilies and coriander. Season with salt and pepper and pour in the beef stock. Cover and simmer over low heat until the steak is tender, about 2 hours. Add the potatoes and cook just long enough to heat them through. **SERVES 6.**

SEASONED CHOPPED BEEF
Picadillo

This is popular throughout Latin America and in Mexico as a filling for tacos, *tamales*, *empanadas* and for *poblano* peppers for the Independence Day dish, *Chiles en Nogada*.

In the north *Picadillo de la Costa* comes from the high plateau, the altiplano, this recipe from the semitropical coastal regions. It came to the New World via Spain from the Arabs, an inheritance from the almost 800-year Moorish occupation of Spain which was nearing its ending with the *Reconquista* when Spain upped and conquered Mexico and lots of the Caribbean and Central and South America. I once saw it on a menu in a small restaurant as *pecadillo*, little sin. Misspelling can create philosophical wonders.

¼ cup olive oil

2 lbs chopped lean beef

2 onions, finely chopped

1 clove garlic, chopped

2 tart apples, cored, peeled and chopped

1 lb tomatoes, peeled, seeded and chopped

3 canned or fresh *jalapeño* chilies, seeded and chopped

½ cup seedless raisins

12 *pimiento*-stuffed green olives, halved

¼ teaspoon ground cinnamon

¼ teaspoon ground cloves

Salt, freshly ground black pepper

¼ cup slivered almonds

Heat the olive oil in a large frying pan and brown the meat then add the onions and garlic. When the onions are cooked add all the other ingredients except the almonds. Season to taste with salt and pepper and simmer over low heat, uncovered until cooked, about 20 minutes, stirring from time to time. Fry the almonds for a minute or two in a little oil and sprinkle over the *picadillo*. If preferred substitute thyme and oregano for the cinnamon and cloves. **SERVES 6.**

CHOPPED MEATS COASTAL-STYLE
Picadillo de la Costa

Geographically, Mexico consists of a series of high valleys ringed by mountain peaks, the largest of which is the altiplano, the high plateau where Mexico City is situated. The mountains run down to coasts lapped by the waters of the Gulf of Mexico, the Pacific Ocean and the Caribbean. Dishes from the coastal regions, though they vary widely, are traditionally referred to simply as *de la costa*, of the coast. This *picadillo* is from Guerrero, home state of the famous beach resort of Acapulco.

2 tablespoons olive oil

1 lb ground pork

1 lb ground veal

2 onions, finely chopped

1 clove garlic, crushed

1 lb tomatoes, peeled, seeded and chopped

Salt, freshly ground black pepper

3 thick slices fresh pineapple, cut into chunks, or pineapple canned in its own juice

3 bananas, peeled and sliced

3 pears, peeled, cored and cut into chunks

¼ teaspoon ground cinnamon

¼ teaspoon ground cloves

¼ cup slivered almonds

Heat the oil in a large, heavy frying pan and brown the meats. Add the onions and garlic and sauté until brown. Drain off any excess fat. Add the tomatoes, and salt and pepper to taste and cook, uncovered, for 15 minutes. Add the fruits and spices and simmer gently for another 15 minutes. The fruits should blend into the *picadillo* but should not disintegrate. Fry the almonds until golden in a little olive oil and sprinkle over the top of the *picadillo*. Cook for a minute or two longer. **SERVES 6.**

PORK WITH PINEAPPLE
Puerco con Piña

The pineapple is indigenous to Brazil but rapidly spread through tropical America and Mexico, and after Columbus, to the rest of the world. It is widely used in Mexico as an ingredient in meat dishes, as well as in desserts and drinks. This, and similar dishes, come from the Huasteca, the region embracing the coasts of Veracruz and Tamaulipas, states which border on the Gulf of Mexico. The region takes its name from the Huastecs, a Toltec Indian group. This may explain why *Puerco con Piña* is so different in its cooking from the *mollis* of the high plateau which originated with the Aztecs, the dominant tribe of the Nahuas and conquerors of the Huastecs, with a far-flung empire before the discovery of the Americas.

1 tablespoon corn oil or lard

3 lbs boneless shoulder or loin of pork cut into 2-inch pieces

2 large onions, thinly sliced

½ teaspoon *chile pequín*, crumbled

¼ cup dry sherry

1 medium-sized pineapple, peeled and cut into chunks

1 large *pimiento* (sweet red pepper), peeled and cut into chunks

1 large *pimiento* (sweet red pepper), peeled, seeded and coarsely chopped, or canned *pimiento morrón*

6 fresh mint leaves, chopped

Salt, freshly ground black pepper

1 cup beef stock

In a frying pan heat the oil or lard and brown the pork pieces, a few at a time, drain and transfer to a flameproof casserole. Brown the onions in the remaining fat, add the chilies and sauté for 1 minute longer over moderate heat, and add it to the pork. Pour off any fat from the frying pan and rinse it out with the sherry scraping down all the brown bits that cling to the pan. Pour over the pork. Add all the remaining ingredients. Cover and cook at a gentle simmer over low heat until the pork is tender, 2-2½ hours. **SERVES 6-8.**

TRIPE MEXICAN-STYLE
Tripas a la Mexicana

Tripe is extremely popular in Mexico and deserves to be as it is of very good quality, not over-processed so that it cooks to a mush. There are also very good recipes for it. César would not eat kidneys, flinched from liver and recoiled from brains even *au beurre noir* in France. But he doted on tripe and was saddened when it became hard to get and its quality diminished.

3 lbs honeycomb tripe

1 onion, sliced

1 onion, finely chopped

1 tablespoon lard or corn oil

3 cloves garlic, chopped

6 *pequín* chilies, crumbled

½ teaspoon ground cumin

½ teaspoon dried oregano, crumbled

Salt, freshly ground black pepper

1 cup canned, cooked chick peas (*garbanzos*)

Cut the tripe into strips or squares, combine in a flameproof casserole with the sliced onion and enough salted water to cover and simmer, covered, until tender. Tripe varies enormously from one supplier to another and it is wise to nibble a piece so as to gauge how much cooking it will need. Heat the lard or oil in a frying pan and sauté the onion, garlic and chili until the onion is lightly browned. Add to the tripe with the cumin, oregano and salt and pepper to taste. Add the chick peas and cook long enough to heat through. Serve in soup bowls with side dishes of chopped onion, chopped coriander and warm tortillas. **SERVES 6-8.**

NOTE:

Chick peas take a long time to cook. If using raw chick peas soak 4 oz overnight and cook in salted water until tender, several hours. A quicker method is to boil them for 5 minutes in salted water, remove them from the heat and let them stand for 1 hour. Drain, cover with fresh cold water and cook for 1 hour longer.

SMOTHERED PORK
Tapado de Cerdo

I don't know what region this comes from, only that it came to me from a gifted cook who told me this was a traditional recipe from her region whenever that was. The use of *pasilla* chilies on their own makes it interesting as the long, dark brown wrinkled chili is not only very hot but very rich in flavor. Six of them, as here, gives a very lively dish.

6 *pasilla* chilies

3 lbs boneless shoulder or loin of pork, cut into 2-inch pieces

3 cloves garlic, chopped

3 tablespoons lard or corn oil

2 onions, finely chopped

1 lb tomatoes, peeled, seeded and chopped

8 oz *tomatillos* (Mexican green tomatoes), canned or fresh

Salt

2 chorizo sausages, skinned and chopped

¼ cup toasted slivered almonds

¼ cup green *pimiento*-stuffed olives, halved

½ cup dry sherry (optional)

Toast the chilies lightly in a dry frying pan, tear off the stems and shake out the seed. Tear them in pieces and put into a bowl with water to cover and soak for about 30 minutes. Put the pork pieces into a flameproof casserole and cook in salted water, covered, until tender, about 2 hours. Drain well discarding the stock. In a food processor process the *pasillas* and garlic to make a heavy paste. Heat 2 tablespoons of the lard or oil in a frying pan and sauté the paste for 5 minutes, stirring constantly. Stir thoroughly into the pork in the casserole. Rinse out and dry the frying pan, heat the remaining lard or oil and sauté the onions until they are soft, add the tomatoes and *tomatillos* and cook, stirring from time to time, until they form a smooth sauce. Season to taste and set aside. Fry the chorizos in a little fat and drain. Set aside. Cover the pork with the sausage, followed by the ham and the almonds and olives. Pour on the tomato mixture and finish with the sherry, if using. Cover and heat through, taking care not to let the thick sauce catch. If necessary add a little liquid stock, water, tomato juice or whatever. **SERVES 8.**

RED *ADOBO* OF PORK
Adobo Rojo de Cerdo

This is another of the recipes that make the cooking of Oaxaca so attractive. Just when I thought Yucatán was the love of my life I got hooked on Oaxaca. Not that Monte Alban is a ruin with the same allure as Chichén in Uxmal.

6 *ancho* chilies

2 lbs boneless pork shoulder or loin cut into 1-inch pieces

Salt

1 onion stuck with a clove

1 onion, chopped

1 clove garlic, chopped

½ teaspoon ground oregano

½ ground cumin

Freshly ground black pepper

½ teaspoon sugar

½ lb tomatoes, peeled, seeded and chopped

¼ cup cider vinegar

2 tablespoons lard or corn oil

Toast the *anchos* lightly in a dry frying pan, pull off the stems, shake out the seeds and tear into pieces. Put into a bowl with warm water to cover and soak for 20-30 minutes. Put the pork into a flameproof casserole with the whole onion and enough salted water to cover and cook, over low heat, until tender, about 1½ to 2 hours. Pour off the stock and reserve. Discard the onion.

In a food processor combine the *anchos*, chopped onion, garlic, oregano, cumin, salt and pepper, sugar, tomatoes and process to a heavy purée. Heat the lard or oil in a frying pan and sauté the mixture over low heat, stirring, for 5 minutes. Thin the mixture with 1 cup of the pork stock, and the vinegar. Pour over the pork and cook, uncovered, over low heat for 30 minutes, the sauce should be very thick. **SERVES 6.**

BEEF STEAK WITH CARROTS
Guisado de Carne de Res con Zanahorias

The baby carrots—only about 2 inches—that are sold in San Juan and other markets in Mexico City are a deep, deep orange, and so clean they look as if they have never associated with anything as grubby as soil. Larger ones are available for anyone who wants them. The miracle is that the baby ones are a year-round phenomenon and give such a simple dish as beef stew a delicious flavor. Try it when baby carrots are around.

1 tablespoon unsalted butter
1½ lbs baby carrots
1 large onion, thinly sliced
2½ lbs round steak in one piece
½ cup beef stock
½ cup white wine
½ cup fresh coriander, chopped
Salt, freshly ground black pepper

Heat the butter in a frying pan and sauté the carrots and the onion until the onion is transparent. Set aside. Brown the steak on both sides in the butter in a flameproof casserole which will hold it comfortably. Smother it with the carrots and onion. Add the stock, wine, coriander and salt and pepper to taste. Simmer, covered, over very low heat until the steak is tender, about 2 hours.
SERVES 6-8.

PORK STEW FROM PUEBLA
Tinga Poblano de Cerdo

Pork and the exotic smokey flavor of *chipotle* chili seem meant for each other. It makes a very rich tasting stew that is easy enough to cook and good for a dinner party. As *chipotle* is a hot chili be cautious if your guests are unused to *picante* food.

2 tablespoons corn oil or lard
3 lbs boneless pork shoulder, cut into 2 inch pieces
Salt
2 chorizo sausages, skinned and chopped
1 onion, finely chopped

1 clove garlic, chopped

1 lb tomatoes, peeled, seeded and chopped

½ teaspoon dried oregano, crumbled

2 canned *chipotle* chilies, or to taste, chopped

12 small new potatoes, freshly cooked and peeled

1 avocado, peeled, pitted and sliced

Heat the oil or lard in a large, heavy frying pan and brown the pork pieces all over. Transfer to flameproof casserole, pour in enough water barely to cover, season with salt and cook, covered over low heat at a gentle simmer until tender, about 2 hours. Strain off and reserve the stock and leave in the casserole.

In the fat remaining in the frying pan fry the sausages and lift out with a slotted spoon into the casserole. Sauté the onion and garlic until the onion is soft, add the tomatoes, oregano and *chipotles* and cook, stirring for 5 minutes until the mixture is thick and well blended. Add the reserved stock and season to taste with salt. Add the potatoes and cook, uncovered, over very low heat for about 15 minutes. Garnish with the sliced avocado. **SERVES 8.**

PORK CHOPS WITH APPLES
Lomo de Puerco con Manzanas

This recipe, clearly a Mexican adaptation of Normandy Pork Chops with Calvados, probably arrived with Maximilian and Carlota. Many of the old recipes for this dish are so over-seasoned that the flavors cancel each out. In this version, my own, where a certain purity has been restored, it comes out very well. One concession is allowed; add a little chopped, seeded *serrano* or *jalapeño* chili if liked.

2 tablespoons unsalted butter

3 large, tart apples, peeled, cored and coarsely chopped

6 thick pork chops, rib end

Salt, freshly ground black pepper

1 teaspoon Dijon mustard

1 cup dry sherry

¼ cup blanched almonds, finely ground

Butter a flameproof casserole and cover the bottom with the apples. Heat the remaining butter in a frying pan and brown the chops on both sides and arrange them on top of the apples. Add the chilies at this point if using. Season with salt and pepper. Mix the sherry with the mustard until smooth and pour over the chops. Cover and cook in a preheated 350°F oven for 1 hour or until the chops are tender. Check from time to time to see if the dish is drying out as the juiciness of the apples varies greatly. If necessary add a little sherry and chicken stock, half and half.

When the chops are tender, arrange on a heated serving dish and keep warm. Add the almonds to the casserole and cook, stirring from time to time, on top of the stove to heat through, and thicken the sauce slightly. Serve separately. **SERVES 6.**

PORK WITH *POBLANO* CHILIES
Puerco con Rajas

The *poblano* chili is so deep a green it is almost black-green and is the chili used for stuffing. It has a rich flavor and can be hot or not so hot. When ripe and dried it turns into the chile *ancho*, one of the amazing things chilies do in Mexico. It took quite a long time for me to convince myself of the ability of this fruit to metamorphose so completely. This chili when fresh is the one used for *rajas* (strips).

3 lbs boneless shoulder of pork cut into 2-inch pieces

Salt

2 tablespoons corn oil or lard

1 large onion, finely chopped

2 lbs tomatoes, peeled, seeded and chopped

4 *poblano* chilies, peeled, seeded and cut into strips (page 18)

Put the pork pieces into a flameproof casserole, add enough water barely to cover, season with salt, cover and simmer over low heat until the pork is tender, about 2 hours. Drain, reserve the stock and return the pork to the casserole.

Heat the oil or lard in a frying pan and sauté the onion until it is tender. Add the tomatoes and the *poblano* strips and cook, stirring, until the mixture is thick and well blended. Season with salt and pour the mixture over the pork. If necessary add a little of the pork stock. Simmer, uncovered, for 15 minutes or until the sauce has reduced to a heavy consistency. **SERVES 8.**

PORK STEW MICHOACÁN-STYLE WITH *TOTOPOS*
Guiso de Puerco Estilo Michoacán

My mother-in-law gave me the recipe for the *totopos*. Cooks, or rather señoras, have argued that these are not *totopos* which were something different. I don't care. My mother-in-law said this was the correct recipe, and I stick to that. Nice recipe anyway. So is the whole dish.

3 lbs boneless pork shoulder, cut into 2-inch pieces

Salt

2 tablespoons corn oil or lard

2 large onions, finely chopped

2 cloves garlic, chopped

¼ lb tomatoes, peeled, seeded and chopped

4 canned *chipotle* chilies, sliced

8 oz can *nopalitos* (cactus pieces), rinsed and chopped

1 large avocado, peeled, pitted and sliced

Freshly grated Parmesan cheese

Put the pork into a flameproof casserole with 2 cups water and salt, cover and simmer over low heat until tender, about 2 hours.

Heat the oil or lard in a frying pan and sauté the onions and garlic until the onion is tender. Add to the casserole with the tomato, *chipotle* and cactus pieces, season to taste with salt and simmer, uncovered, gently for 15 minutes to blend the flavors and reduce the sauce which should be fairly thin. Serve with avocado, Parmesan and *Totopos* (below). **SERVES 6-8.**

TOTOPOS

2 *ancho* chilies, toasted and soaked

1½ cups *masa harina*

½ cup cooked red kidney beans, mashed

1 teaspoon salt

Lard

Purée the chilies in the food processor. Mix the *masa*, the beans and salt together with the chilies. Make into half size tortillas on the tortilla press (page 36). Heat the lard in a frying pan and fry the tortillas on both sides. Drain on paper towels and keep warm until ready to serve.

LOIN OF PORK, PUEBLA-STYLE
Lomo de Puerco Poblano

I have always used loin of pork in Mexico and it was very good indeed but I have found it too expensive nowadays and use shoulder of pork instead. I find it makes an admirable substitute.

3 *ancho* chilies

3 *mulato* chilies

6 large mint leaves, chopped

1 sprig *epazote*

¼ teaspoon dried oregano, crumbled

¼ teaspoon ground cumin

3 cloves garlic, crushed

1 bay leaf, crushed

¼ teaspoon ground cinnamon

Salt, freshly ground black pepper

2 cups dry red wine

3 lbs boneless shoulder of pork, cut into 2-inch pieces

Toast the chilies lightly in a dry frying pan. Tear off the stems, shake out the seeds and tear into pieces. Put into a bowl with warm water to cover and soak for 30 minutes. Drain and reduce to a purée in a food processor. Mix with all the other ingredients except the pork. Marinade the pork in the mixture for 24 hours in the refrigerator, turning the pieces occasionally. Transfer the pork and marinade to a flameproof casserole, cover and cook over low heat until the pork is tender, about 2 hours. **SERVES 8.**

POT *MOLE* ATLIXO-STYLE
Mole de Olla Estillo Atlixo

This *mole*, from Atlixo in Puebla, is a perfect illustration of what Mexican cooks combined when they put together the foods of the Old and New Worlds. It is in the spirit that gave birth to *churrigueresco*, the architectural style of the 18th century which makes baroque look austere. Not content with the

Spanish chorizo sausage they add *longaniza*, a garlicky pork sausage flavored with rosemary and paprika and best substituted if unavailable with Polish *kielbasa*. Almonds and sesame seeds join peanuts and *pepitas* (native pumpkin seeds). Pueblan cooks had such talent that their lavishly sauced *moles* succeed and so do the churches swamped in elaborate carving and gold leaf.

6 *ancho* or *mulato* chilies

2 tablespoons corn oil or lard

1 chorizo sausage, skinned and chopped

3 *longaniza* or 1 *kielbasa* sausage, skinned and chopped

½ lb lean boneless pork, chopped

3½ lbs chicken, cut into serving pieces

1 onion, chopped

1 clove garlic, chopped

¼ lb tomatoes, peeled, seeded and chopped

2 tablespoons sesame seeds

1 tablespoon blanched almonds, chopped

1 tablespoon peanuts

2 tablespoons *pepitas*, hulled pumpkin seeds

1 teaspoon dried oregano, crumbled

Salt, freshly ground black pepper

2 cups chicken stock

Toast the chilies lightly on both sides in a dry frying pan. Pull off the stems, shake out the seeds and tear into pieces. Put into a bowl with hot water to cover and stand for 30 minutes.

Heat the oil or lard in a frying pan and sauté the sausages, then the pork and finally the chicken pieces until they are golden and transfer to a flame-proof casserole.

In the food processor combine the prepared chilies, onion, garlic, tomato, sesame seeds, nuts and oregano and blend until smooth. In the fat remaining in the frying pan cook the mixture for 5 minutes, stirring. Stir in the stock. Season to taste with salt and pepper. Pour over the meats in the casserole, cover and simmer gently over low heat for about 1 hour, or until the chicken is tender. **SERVES 8.**

VEAL WITH CAPERS
Ternera con Alcaparras

After haunting the chili sellers in the markets and buying chilies fresh, dried and canned, in my innocence I thought I knew something about them. I'm still learning and find that tracking down the *chile largo* of this recipe close to baffling. I think it is the one known as banana or Hungarian wax, or large or guero or, in Oaxaca as *Chile de Onza*. It is pale yellow, about 4 inches, tapering and medium hot. The description is more useful than the name. And to think I once believed it was simply called *chile largo* because my cook came from a region where that was what it was called. I think in Yucatán it is also called *xcatik*. If not available use any medium-hot chili, such as *jalapeño*.

2 lbs veal for stew, cut into 1-inch pieces

Salt

2 onions, chopped

1 clove garlic, chopped

4 oz canned Spanish capers

3 canned *largo* chilies, chopped

1 lb tomatoes, peeled, seeded and chopped

Freshly ground black pepper

2 tablespoons corn oil or lard

Put the veal into a flameproof casserole, cover with salted water, bring to a simmer and cook over low heat, covered until tender about 2 hours. Skim regularly to remove any scum that rises to the surface. Strain, reserve the stock, return the veal to the casserole and set aside.

Combine in a food processor the onions, garlic, all but 1 tablespoon of the capers, chilies and the tomatoes and process to a smooth purée. Heat the oil or lard in a frying pan, pour in the mixture and cook, stirring, over moderate heat for about 3 minutes. Add enough of the veal stock to bring the sauce to medium thick consistency and season with salt and pepper. Pour the sauce over the cooked veal and cook over low heat just long enough to heat through and blend the flavors. Arrange in a warm serving dish and garnish with remaining capers. **SERVES 6.**

VEAL IN PRUNE SAUCE
Ternera en Salsa de Ciruelas Pasas

This colonial dish clearly owes everything to France, probably to Napoleon III's ill-fated invasion of Mexico. The tomatoes are the only New World ingredient. I think the French were the only invaders of Mexico that are really liked. The Aztec lady cooks were gourmets which might explain it. Food is a great maker of friendship.

1½ cups large pitted prunes, chopped

1 cup dry red wine

4 tablespoons unsalted butter

6 veal cutlets

2 onions, finely chopped

1 clove garlic, chopped

1 lb tomatoes, peeled, seeded and chopped

Salt, freshly ground black pepper

¼ teaspoon freshly ground nutmeg

Put the prunes into a bowl, pour the wine over them and let them stand for at least 2 hours before using. Heat the butter in a frying pan and sauté the veal cutlets until lightly golden on both sides. Transfer them to a flameproof casserole. In the butter remaining in the pan sauté the onion until it is tender, add the garlic, tomatoes, salt and pepper to taste and the nutmeg. Pour the mixture over the veal, cover and cook over low heat until the meat is tender, about 1½ to 2 hours. Add the prunes and wine and continue to cook, uncovered, for 15 minutes to blend the flavors and slightly thicken the sauce. **SERVES 6.**

VEAL STEW
Mole de Olla para Ternera

This is one of those exuberant dishes the Mexican cook so delights in creating and all too often fails to record.

2 lbs boneless veal for stew, cut into 1-inch pieces

6 small new potatoes

1 cup peas, if frozen thoroughly thawed

1 lb cut green beans

2 onions, chopped

1 clove garlic, chopped

½ cup fresh coriander, chopped

6 *serrano* or 3 *jalapeño* chilies, seeded and chopped

½ lb Mexican green tomatoes (*tomatillos*), fresh or canned

2 tablespoons corn oil or lard

Salt, freshly ground black pepper

Put the veal into a flameproof casserole with salted water just to cover, bring to a gentle simmer, cover and cook until the veal is tender, about 1½ hours. Skim from time to time to remove any scum that rises to the surface. Strain and reserve the stock. Rinse out the casserole and return the veal to it. Cook the potatoes, peas and beans separately in boiling salted water. Do not overcook. Drain thoroughly and add to the veal. Peel the potatoes or not according to taste.

In a food processor combine the onions, garlic, coriander, chilies and *tomatillos* and process to a purée. Heat the oil or lard in a frying pan, add the mixture and cook, over moderate heat, stirring, for 5 minutes. Stir in the reserved stock to thin the sauce which should be fairly thin. Season with salt and pepper and pour over the veal and vegetables in the casserole. Cook, uncovered, over low heat for 15 minutes, or just long enough to heat through. Do not let it come to the boil. **SERVES 6.**

VEAL IN GREEN SAUCE
Ternera en Salsa Verde

Mexican veal which could just as accurately be called baby beef lends itself extremely well to these ingredients, the *tomatillos* and *jalapeños* for flavor and the romaine lettuce for color, the almonds for thickening the sauce.

2 lbs boneless veal for stew, cut into 1-inch pieces

1 large onion, chopped

2 *jalapeño* chilies, seeded and chopped

½ cup fresh coriander, chopped

¼ cup slivered almonds

6 outside leaves romaine lettuce, chopped

½ lb Mexican green tomatoes (*tomatillos*), fresh or canned

4 tablespoons unsalted butter

Salt, freshly ground black pepper

Put the veal into a flameproof casserole and cover it with salted water. Bring to a simmer and remove any scum that rises to the surface. Cook, uncovered, over low heat until tender, about 1½ hours. Drain, reserve the stock and return the veal to the casserole.

In a food processor combine the onion, garlic, chilies, coriander, almonds, the romaine lettuce and *tomatillos* and process to a purée. Heat the butter in a frying pan, pour in the mixture and cook over gentle heat, stirring, for 5 minutes. Thin the sauce with enough of the reserved stock to bring it to medium consistency. Season with salt and pepper, pour it over the veal and cook, uncovered, long enough to heat it through, but do not let it come to the boil. plainly cooked white rice is very good with this. **SERVES 6.**

VEAL IN PECAN SAUCE
Ternera en Nogada

The Aztecs took to the almond and the walnut when they were introduced by the Spanish conquerors. Here, however, the colonial cooks used their own native pecan to thicken and flavor the introduced veal.

2 lbs veal for stew, cut into 1-inch pieces

2 onions, chopped

1 clove garlic, chopped

½ teaspoon dried thyme, crumbled

¼ teaspoon dried oregano, crumbled

2 cups chicken stock

2 tablespoons unsalted butter

½ cup pecans, finely ground

Salt, freshly ground black pepper

1 cup sour cream

Put the veal into a flameproof casserole with half the onions, the garlic, thyme, oregano and stock. Bring to simmer, skim off any scum that rises to the surface and cook, covered until the veal is tender, about 1½ hours. Drain and return the veal to the casserole. Strain and reserve the stock.

Heat the butter in a frying pan and sauté the rest of the onion until it is tender. Add the ground nuts and sauté for a minute or two. Transfer the mixture to the food processor with about ½ cup of the stock and process until smooth. Pour into a saucepan, add the rest to the stock, season to taste with salt and pepper, heat through then whisk in the sour cream until the sauce is hot and smooth. Pour over the veal and cook just long enough to heat through. **SERVES 6.**

LAMB YUCATÁN-STYLE
Carnero Yucateco

The Mayan Empire was already in decline when the Spanish invaded. It stretched from Guatemala into Mexico and had important cities in Yucatán, now the ruins of Uxmal and Chichén Itzá. It reached as far as Palenque, one of the most beautiful of the Mayan ruins. There are still Mayan areas in Mexico and there is still a great deal of Mayan influence in modern Mexican food. One of the strongest is the use of annatto (*achiote*) which is the seed of the tropical tree *Bixa Orellana*. The seeds are surrounded by an orange-red pulp, which is very hard. When ground they give not only a rich golden color but a subtle delicate flavor. The color can be released by adding the seeds briefly to hot oil which it colors.

2 lbs boneless lamb, cut into 1-inch pieces

1 onion, finely chopped

1 clove garlic, chopped

Sprig *epazote*

¼ lb tomatoes, peeled, seeded and chopped

Salt, freshly ground black pepper

1 cup hulled pumpkin seeds (*pepitas*)

1 tablespoon annatto seeds (*achiote*)

1 tablespoon corn or peanut oil

1 teaspoon lime, or lemon juice

Put the lamb, onion, garlic, *epazote*, tomato, salt and pepper into a flameproof casserole with enough water to cover, bring to a gentle simmer over low heat, cover and cook until the lamb is tender, about 2 hours. In a food processor combine the *pepitas* and the *achiote* and grind as fine as possible. If preferred grind the *pepitas* separately and shake them through a sieve. Grind the *achiote* in a small spice or coffee grinder then combine the two. Heat the oil and add the seeds. Fry them for 3 or 4 minutes taking care not to let them burn. Add them to the cooked lamb, taste for seasoning and simmer, over low heat, uncovered until the sauce is quite thick, about 5 minutes. Add the lime juice and stir. **SERVES 6.**

LEG OF LAMB WITH CHILI
Pierna de Carnero Enchilada

6 *ancho* chilies

3 cloves garlic, slivered

4 lbs leg of lamb

Salt, freshly ground black pepper

1 large onion, chopped

¼ lb tomatoes, peeled, seeded and chopped

Pinch sugar

2 tablespoons corn or peanut oil

2 cups chicken stock

Toast the *anchos* lightly on both sides in a dry frying pan, tear off the stems, shake out the seeds and tear into pieces. Put into a bowl with hot water just to cover and leave to soak for 30 minutes.

Insert the slivers of garlic into the lamb then season the meat all over with salt and pepper. Put it into a casserole into which it will fit comfortably and set aside. In a food processor combine the prepared chilies with the onion, tomato and pinch of sugar and process to a coarse purée. Heat the oil in a frying pan and cook the mixture, stirring, for 5 minutes, stir in the stock and pour it over the lamb. Seal the casserole with aluminum foil and the lid and place in a preheated 350°F oven and cook for about 4 hours, or until the lamb is tender. **SERVES 6-8.**

LAMB STEW
Estofado de Carnero

This recipe demonstrates the main influence on the indigenous Mexican kitchen arising from the conquest. They created the colonial kitchen which persists today only modified by new kitchen tools and improved agricultural methods. From the Arabs who had dominated Spain for several centuries before Spain's conquest of Mexico come the almonds, raisins and lamb, and from Spain comes the sherry and from Mexico the chilies and tomatoes.

3 *ancho* chilies

2 lbs boneless stewing lamb cut into 1-inch pieces

2 cloves garlic, chopped

¼ cup raisins

¼ teaspoon ground cloves

¼ teaspoon ground cinnamon

Salt, freshly ground black pepper

1 cup dry sherry

¼ cup toasted slivered almonds

Toast the *anchos* lightly on both sides in a dry frying pan, tear off the stems and shake out the seeds. Tear the *anchos* into pieces and put them into a bowl with hot water barely to cover and soak for 30 minutes. Drain and transfer to a food processor and blend smooth. Add enough water to bring it to the consistency of thin cream, about 1½ cups. Set aside.

Combine the lamb, tomatoes, garlic, raisins, cloves, cinnamon, and salt and pepper in a flameproof casserole. Pour the reserved chili mixture over the lamb, stir, bring to a simmer over low heat, cover and cook until the lamb is tender, about 2 hours. Five minutes before serving pour in the sherry and at the last minute sprinkle the almonds. Rice is good with this. **SERVES 6-8.**

SONORA-STYLE TRIPE
Menudo Estilo Soñora

This northern Mexican dish, like a pot-au-feu, is both soup and meat. It is famous as a hang-over cure especially at New Year. After a too late night, *Menudo* is served for breakfast and is wonderfully restorative. One is always advised to take plenty of the crumbled dried red chili *pequín* that is customarily served with it. *Menudo* also makes a perfectly respectable lunch or dinner at any time, when no advice on the amount of chili to be taken should be offered.

2 lbs honeycomb tripe

2 pig's feet

Salt

2 cups frozen corn kernels, thoroughly defrosted

1 bunch spring onions, trimmed and chopped, using
  white and green parts

½ cup fresh coriander, chopped

Freshly ground black pepper

18 lime or lemon slices

Dried *pequín* chilies, crumbled

Fresh or dried oregano, chopped

1 Spanish onion (large), finely chopped

Put the tripe and pig's feet in a large, heavy saucepan, cover with salted water, bring to a simmer, cover and cook until the meats are tender, about 3 hours. Tripe is sometimes processed so that it needs little precooking. Nibble a small piece to judge and adjust the cooking time accordingly. The pig's feet will take a long time. Cool in the stock, lift out the tripe and cut into squares or strips. Remove the bones from the pig's feet and cut the meat into pieces. Return the meats to the stock. Add the corn, spring onions, coriander and salt and pepper to the stock and simmer gently for 5 minutes. Serve in deep soup plates, warmed, with the lime slices, oregano, chilies and onion in small bowls on the side. These are added to the soup-stew to suit individual taste. Have plenty of hot tortillas and guacamole. **SERVES 6-8.**

MEAT BALLS
Albondigas

Every region in Mexico has its meat balls. This version is a family one from the north and the family had all sorts of variations for them so that they were never entirely the same. I used to make half-size ones and serve them on cocktail sticks with drinks. Cooks often stuff them with a piece of hard-boiled egg or *pimiento*-stuffed green olive. The meat balls are poached not fried making them deliciously soft in texture.

1 *ancho* chili

1 slice firm white bread

Milk

½ lb finely ground lean beef

½ lb finely ground lamb

½ lb finely ground pork

¼ lb boiled ham, finely chopped

1 large egg, lightly beaten

Salt, freshly ground black pepper

2 tablespoons corn oil or lard

1 onion, finely chopped

2 cloves garlic, crushed

1 lb tomatoes, peeled, seeded and chopped

½ teaspoon dried oregano, crumbled

2 cups meat stock

Toast the *ancho* lightly in a dry frying pan, pull off the stem, shake out the seeds and tear into pieces. Put into a bowl, cover with hot water and soak for 30 minutes.

Soak the bread in milk, squeeze dry. In a large bowl mix together the meat and the bread, season to taste with salt and pepper and thoroughly mix in the egg. Form the mixture into 24 balls each about 1½ inches in diameter and set aside.

Heat the oil or lard in a frying pan and sauté the onion until it is lightly browned. Add the garlic, tomatoes, oregano and prepared *ancho*. Taste for seasoning, cook for a few minutes then stir in the stock. Pour into a large saucepan, bring to a simmer and add the meat balls, bring back to a simmer, cover and poach for 1 hour. Serve in deep bowls with the sauce. **SERVES 6.**

VARIATION:
The meat mixture may be varied using pork, veal and lamb. Some cooks add 2 small zucchini, finely chopped, to the meat and omit the bread, some add cooked rice instead of bread. Cumin and mint are added to the meats as well as oregano. Canned chipotle chilies, can be added to the sauce instead of the ancho.

GRILLED STEAK, TAMPICO-STYLE
Carne Asado a la Tamiqueña

This is one of those rare dishes that became an instant and enduring success, like Caesar salad. It is the creation of José Luis Loredo who came from Tampico to Mexico City in 1939 to open the Tampico Club. There are variations in the accompaniment but it is essentially the same whenever served in the Republic. Among the traditional accompaniments are *Rajas de Chile Poblano* and now that Dr. Michael Michaud is growing them commercially at Sea Spring Farm in Dorset, the dish can be enjoyed without making the long journey to Mexico whenever you want it. The steak most used is fillet opened up into strips but following the advice of my dear friend the late James Andrews Beard, I tried skirt steak with great success. Jim thought highly of skirt steak.

**¾ lb tender thin steak, fillet or skirt cut into 2-inch wide,
    ½-inch thick strips**

Season the steak on both sides with salt and freshly ground pepper and a little lime juice. Have ready the following accompaniments:

Frijoles Refritos (page 159)

Guacamole (page 74)

Rajas de Chile Poblano (page 82)

Salsa Verde (page 80)

2 *enchiladas* **filled with fresh cheese** (page 45)

Hot tortillas (page 26)

To pan fry the steaks heat a cast iron frying pan with a little oil until hot and fry the strips of steak about 2 minutes a side for rare, longer if liked. Serve on heated plates garnished with the *rajas* and surrounded by the other accompaniments. **SERVES 2.**

COLD MEATS FROM POTOSINO
Fiambre Potosino

The central state of San Luis Potosino has a thriving cattle industry and is a big grower of the *agave* (maguey) from which *mezcal*, similar to tequila, is made. The *fiambre*, literally cold meat, is a great favorite for family entertaining on the cattle ranches. On Sundays, for *comida*, tables are set outdoors and friends and relations are invited for what is, in effect, a picnic but also a lavish meal. I remember it, patting out tortillas and cooking them on a charcoal brazier. It was a very grand affair, not the usual less formal family get-together. Accompaniments vary, sometimes tortillas are quartered and fried crisp, sometimes flour tortillas and more usually *tamales blancos, tamales* without any filling are served. Fresh rolls and butter can be served but sometimes César and I felt tortillas ought to be there. It is a matter of taste.

The meats:

2 lbs boneless pork loin

2 veal tongues, about 1 lb each

3½ lbs chicken

3 pig's feet, halved

Salt

Marinade:

2 cups olive oil

⅔ cup wine vinegar

Salt, freshly ground black pepper

2 teaspoons Dijon mustard

½ cup fresh coriander or flat parsley, chopped

1 clove garlic, crushed

1 tablespoon drained, chopped capers

The garnish:

1 lettuce, preferably romaine

1 lb large tomatoes, peeled and sliced

3 large avocados, peeled and sliced

5 canned *chipotle* chilies, stuffed with cottage or similar cheese

Radishes, ripe olives and finely chopped onion

Cook each of the meats separately, covered, in simmering salted water. Allow about 2 hours for the pork and veal tongues, 1 hour for the chicken and 3 hours for the pig's feet. Cook each of the meats in its own stock. When cool enough to handle, slice the pork and the skinned veal tongues, divide the chicken into serving pieces, bone and cut up the pig's feet. Set all aside.

Make the marinade. In a bowl mix together all the ingredients and pour half the marinade over the meats and leave to season for an hour or longer. To serve arrange all meats on a shallow serving dish lined with lettuce leaves. Garnish the dish with the rest of the garnish ingredients and serve the rest of the marinade as a vinaigrette dressing separately. **SERVES 8-10.**

SMOKED TONGUE WITH MEXICAN GREEN TOMATOES
Lengua Ahumada con Tomatillos

César's Texan cousin Carmen gave me this recipe which came, I think, from the then family cook Ermila. I cannot begin to describe the taste except to say that it is rich and delicate at the same time, simple and complex and blissfully easy to cook. Carmen cannot have given me a better gift than this.

1 smoked beef tongue, weighing about 5 lbs

1 onion, stuck with a clove

1 onion, chopped

2 cloves garlic

6 peppercorns

1 bay leaf

2 tablespoons corn oil or lard

18 small new potatoes, freshly cooked and peeled

**3 or more canned *serrano* or *jalapeño* chilies,
according to taste, chopped**

¼ cup fresh coriander, chopped

**1 lb Mexican green tomatoes (*tomatillos*), fresh or
canned, chopped**

Salt, freshly ground black pepper

Put the tongue into a large, heavy saucepan into which it fits comfortably
with enough water to cover and cook, covered at a gentle simmer for 1 hour.
Drain, add fresh cold water, the onion stuck with a clove, 1 whole clove garlic, the peppercorns and bay leaf, cover and simmer for 2 hours or until
tongue is tender. Cool in the stock, lift out and skin and remove any fat and
trim the root end and slice quite quickly. Put into a flameproof casserole and
set aside. Strain and reserve the stock.

Heat the oil or lard in a frying pan and sauté the chopped onion and a
chopped clove of garlic, until the onion is soft. Add them to the casserole. In
the same oil or lard sauté the potatoes and add them to the casserole with the
chilies, coriander and the *tomatillos*. Season to taste with salt and pepper and
add enough of the reserved stock to cover. Cover and simmer over low heat
to blend the flavors and heat everything through. The tomatoes should
disintegrate into the sauce. **SERVES 6-8.**

VARIATION:

*Fresh tongue is more popular in Mexico than smoked and veal tongues are also available. Cook
the tongues in the same way and then steep them in any chosen sauce. They are very good in
Adobo (page 76) or Salsa de Almendra Verde (page 85) or Roja (page 86) or in many of the
sauces in the Salsa section.*

A GAUDY DISH
Angaripola

Angaripolas, apart from cookery, are gaudy ornaments on clothes. The chorizos
plus the saffron and tomatoes give this dish a gaudy color, hence its funny
name.

3 pig's feet, split

1 onion, stuck with a clove

1 carrot, peeled and chopped

2 or 3 sprigs flat parsley

¼ teaspoon thyme

¼ teaspoon oregano

1 bay leaf

Salt, freshly ground black pepper

2 chorizo sausages, skinned and chopped

Corn oil or lard

3½ lbs chicken, cut into serving pieces

2 lbs boneless shoulder of pork, cut into 1-inch pieces

1 large onion, finely chopped

1 lb tomatoes, peeled, seeded and chopped

½ teaspoon saffron threads, ground

6 canned *jalapeño* chilies, cut into strips

2 tablespoons capers

½ cup *pimiento*-stuffed green olives, halved

In a large heavy saucepan simmer the pig's feet in salted water to cover, with the onion stuck with a clove, parlsey, thyme, oregano, bay leaf and pepper until tender, about 3 hours. Cool in the stock, lift out and remove the bones, cut the meat into pieces. Strain the stock and set aside.

Film a frying pan with a little oil or lard and sauté the chorizos. Drain and set aside. In the fat remaining in the pan which will be orange-red from the sausages, lightly sauté the chicken pieces until golden, set aside. Sauté the pork pieces until browned. Drain and set aside. Sauté the onion and garlic until the onion is tender. Drain and set aside. In a flameproof casserole combine chicken, pork, sausages, meat from pig's feet, tomatoes, saffron, 2 cups of the reserved stock, onion and garlic. Bring to a simmer and cook, covered over low heat until the meat and chicken are tender, about 1 hour. Five minutes before serving stir in the *jalapeños*, capers and olives.

SERVES 8-10.

BARBECUE
Barbacoa

Mexican *barbacoa* is entirely different from the charcoal grill barbecue with which we are all familiar. The English word barbeque taken from the Spanish *barbacoa* came into use in 1697. It referred to a rough framework used in America either for sleeping, or for smoking or drying meat over a fire. By 1809 it had come to mean, in the United States, an open-air social entertainment at which animals were roasted whole. Today it means meats, fish, fowl or vegetables cooked over an open fire, basted with barbecue sauce. *Barbacoa* is clearly an example of the earth oven, probably the oldest form of cooking.

There are examples of this all over Latin America. In Yucatán it is the *pib*, in the Andes the *pachamanca* from the Quechua, in Chile the *curanto* which is rather like the New England clambake.

I've never been able to find a Nahuatl word for *barbacoa* which everyone in Mexico uses, so perhaps *barbacoa* is Nahuatl and we have stolen it for our type of barbecue. It is the persistence of the form of cooking that fascinates. The best *barbacoa* is supposed to come from the Valley of Mexico site of Mexico City, the Federal District and the State of Mexico. The two best sources are the town of San Juan Teotihuacán near the pyramids of the Sun and Moon, and the village of Texcoco, which goes back to pre-Columbian days. It is a favorite Sunday *comida* dish for eating out or taking home for picnic eating. The very best I've ever eaten came from César's cousin Humberto on the family ranch which he looked after. We were staying with Humberto and his wife China and I found it hard to understand just how *barbacoa* was made. Their English was little better than my Spanish at the time and Humberto came up with the simplest and best of solutions. He would, he said, make a *barbacoa* for the next day's *comida*, and since this would be a Sunday this idea was applauded. He went off to kill a lamb, I didn't stay around for the slaughter but went off to enjoy a margarita, while Humberto, César and some of the many children the couple had produced helped or hindered in the essential preliminary. The slaughtered lamb was skinned, dressed and cut into sections, backbone, legs, shoulders, ribs and head. Poor little lamb, life is very cruel.

After breakfast the following day which was beautifully clear and not too hot, a hole was dug in the garden, 4 feet deep and 2 feet square and plastered with mud so that the sides would not collapse. The children had collected some light, porous stones and put them on the pit bottom. They were volcanic rocks, plentiful in Mexico. They hold heat very well and don't split. Then we filled the pit with dry wood, set it alight, and let it burn down to smokeless ashes, heating the stones. And we drank beer. And Humberto and César talked politics and China kept an eye on the newest of her children which were collectively referred to as *el tribu*, the tribe. While I made notes and tried not to look useless, *agave* leaves, from the plant that makes pulque and tequila, were collected. They should not really be called leaves but sometimes it is easier to use a wrong term rather than explain about *xerophytic* plants. They were cleaned with a cloth and the fire in the pit was used to toast them on both sides until they were limp, then the pit was lined with the overlapping leaves with the tops laid back on the surface of the ground around the pit, so that it looked like an open flower. They were weighted down with stones while the next step was prepared. Humberto lowered a grate into the pit, on top of the stones and put a large enamelled bowl which China brought. This contained the ingredients for *Consomme de Barbacoa* (Barbecue Consomme).

There was a lot of giggling at my awe stricken appreciation of how much work was involved but there were four men (Humberto, César, Eulogio, the eldest son and Humberto Jr.) and China and two maids, plus me, with a notebook, useless, but admiring. China put an oven rack over the bowl and the pieces of lamb were arranged on it. The lamb was not salted as this toughens the meat, China told me. Next the *agave* (maguey) leaves were folded down over the lamb and then a metal sheet was put on top of this. Wood would have done equally well, then more *agave*, then a *petate* (a palm mat) and the pit was sealed with mud. The heat from the volcanic stones which were heated by the burning wood was now sealed in and we all went off to wait the 4 to 6 hours needed for the feast to cook. The juices from the *agave* and the meat drippings fill the bowl with a delicious soup which is served with the meat, *pot-au-feu* fashion.

We were ready in 4 hours when the pit was opened and an incredible perfume arose. There was something like tequila in it from the *agave*, and from the lamb and the soup vegetables. With it we had *Salsa Borracha* (Drunken Sauce) (page 84), which is made with pulque but if this is not available which is likely even in Mexico, use *salsa verde* (green sauce) (page 80) or any sauce you like. Lots of hot tortillas and guacamole complete the menu and beer or pulque are the traditional drinks. It had been a memorable cookery lesson for me and I now understood how my hunting ancestors from the ancient past had celebrated.

BARBECUE CONSOMME
Consomme de Barbacoa

½ cup rice, soaked for 15 minutes

½ cup raw chick peas (*garbanzos*)

1 cup (about) potatoes, peeled and thinly sliced

2 large carrots, peeled and thinly sliced

1 small cabbage, trimmed and quartered

3 canned *chipotle* chilies, sliced

Sprig of *epazote*

Salt, freshly ground black pepper

Put all the ingredients into the basin in the pit as directed in the main instructions.

BARBECUED SUCKLING PIG, YUCATÁN-STYLE
Cochinita Pibil

The earth oven in the Mayan regions of Mexico was called a *pib*, and earth ovens everywhere were prepared in the same basic way only instead of *agave*, plantain or banana leaves are used to line the pit. Annatto (*achiote*) is the essential spice and the juice of Seville (bitter) oranges are the introduced Old World ingredient. It is extremely popular though a companion dish, *Pollo Pibil* (Barbecued Chicken), easier to do, even more so.

1 suckling pig, weighing about 10 lbs

2 cups Seville (bitter) orange juice or mixture of orange and lime/lemon juice

Salt

½ teaspoon black peppercorns, lightly crushed

¼ teaspoon ground cumin

12 cloves garlic, chopped

1 teaspoon dried oregano, crumbled

1 tablespoon annatto (*achiote*), finely ground

Score the suckling pig all over, in a crisscross pattern, with a sharp knife, or have the butcher do it. Rub thoroughly with orange juice and salt. In the food processor combine the peppercorns, cumin, garlic, oregano and annatto and process until smooth. The seeds of annatto are very hard and a small spice grinder or coffee mill are the best things to use for the preliminary grinding. Add the remaining orange juice and pour the marinade into a bowl. Rub the pig all over with the marinade and refrigerate for 24 hours. Line a large utensil, that will hold the pig comfortably with banana leaves, put in the pig and pour the remaining marinade over it, and cover with more banana leaves.

Put the tub with the prepared pig in the *pib*, cover as for the barbecued lamb, close the *pib* and leave for 3 hours. Remove from the pit and serve, cut into serving pieces with hot tortillas, and a hot Yucatán sauce (*Ixni-Pec*) (page 78).

POULTRY

•

Aves

The number of poultry dishes in Mexico is almost endless. For the most part they derive from the Aztec *mollis* (literally, a sauce made with any of the chilies), though as they are colonial dishes, any of the ingredients introduced by the Spanish are equally present. In Yucatán, known as *La Tierra del Faisan y Venado*, "the land of the pheasant and the deer," there are a great many turkey dishes including the *Pavo en Relleno Blanco*, Turkey with White Stuffing, which so baffled me when I was a newcomer, for the stuffing was not white, as it included ground pork and ground beef, which I thought outrageous ingredients anyway, in any turkey stuffing.

Before the conquest the most popular bird was the turkey which may have been domesticated as early as 200 B.C. There are reports from the earliest days after the arrival of the Spanish, of one of the many markets around the capital Tenochtitlán selling year-round, 8,000 birds every 5 days. Quail, *curassow* (pheasant), dove, muscovy duck and other birds, were also popular, but not as popular as turkey.

With the conquest came the chicken which has become the most popular bird in modern times, partly because it makes the best light stock, the Mexican cook's most popular cooking medium.

My first excitement was the national dish, famed for the bitter chocolate in its sauce, *Mole Poblano* and I learned to make it with such enthusiasm that once in Paris, unable to obtain a turkey in a hurry, I cooked a creditable *Mole Poblano* with a rather splendid rabbit. Our guest was a BBC man who made a broadcast saying he had had chocolate rabbit for Christmas. However, nothing equalled the excitement I felt when I was introduced to the green dishes, the chicken dishes made with *tomatillos* and coriander sauce.

It happened, in my early days, when we were invited to dinner, real *cena* at night, not *comida*, for some work connected with the UN Information Center, which César was head of at that time. Our host was a Welsh gentleman, his wife a Spanish lady, and their daughter, who was my age and passionately interested in Mexican cuisine, which her parents weren't. While UN business was talked the daughter and I went off to the kitchen where she was cooking *Pollo Almendrado Verde*, Green Chicken with Almonds.

I could hardly believe the taste, so subtle and new to me. I had tasted Mexican green tomatoes (*tomatillos*) once before in New York, with smoked beef tongue, and been enchanted with it, but the chicken dish opened a door to a kitchenful of delights. I was given the recipe by that gifted young woman whose name I lost in the years that have passed, and I set about finding more green dishes.

On visits to Oaxaca I met *siete moles*, six of them with chicken, and in Puebla the *tingas*, robust stews with a more European approach to the cooking method, but very Mexican, as a *tinga* must include *chipotle* chili with its exotic flavor.

There is a great diversity in the poultry dishes and I had a most entertaining time finding them, but no time as amusing as an expedition that led to an enduring friendship, and the recipe for *Pollo Frito* from the Jardin de San Marcos, the site of the old agricultural fair held yearly on the grounds of the garden in Aguascalientes, the capital of the small central state of Aguascalientes (literally Hot Waters) named for its mineral springs. It is great farming country, noted for its grains, vegetables and fruit, above all its grapes. There is a yearly *Festival de la Uva* (Grape Festival) and a special event was got up for the diplomatic corps and others that year, with the leading female film star the guest of honor at a *comida*.

The star was late, and we were all gathered in a central hall of the banquet site waiting, frankly, for the *uva* in the form of wine. Suddenly there was a move to herd the women guests into a large side room to seat them, segregated, with Coca-Cola, to talk about babies. I refused to go and was joined by the daughter of the American cultural attaché, still a valued friend, seeking sanctuary from this awful fate. The cultural attaché of an Asian country, who had perfect English, but no Spanish, was swept in with the ladies and had a haunted look when let out later for the *comida*. César rescued him, and he was safe for the rest of the festivity. And we did finally get a taste of the *uva*, sherry, I think, and wine with our food.

The banquet hall was large and we were seated at a horseshoe-shaped table with the guest of honor and notables at the top. The film star continued to be late, but finally arrived. Waiters emerged, each carrying a large tureen full of soup to serve each group of diners. One gentleman, not used to waiting so long for lunch (I think it was well past 4 P.M. by now), maddened by hunger, seized the tureen when it was presented to him, convinced it was all that was to be had, refusing to relinquish it, intending to scoff the lot. The other waiters on the soup round came to their comrade's rescue bravely putting their tureens down on the table where hungry guests could get at them. They wrested the tureen from the starving gentleman, served him a hearty bowlful, and the battle was over. They resumed their own tureens, mercifully intact, and continued on their errands of mercy.

The film star did not take soup or indeed any of the banquet food. She combed her hair, checked her makeup and called for a steak. We weren't important enough to be seated near her and went on with our food, which I am sure was quite splendid, though the excitement has driven it out of my memory. The star finished her steak and left, walking from the place of honor round the huge room to the exit. The gentlemen stood, and she later made an official protest that the ladies remained seated when they should have stood as a mark of respect. With the star gone the waiters went too, seeing no point in further festivity, and, as no more food was to be had, the guests went too.

But the next day we went to the older agricultural fair at the Jardin de San Marcos and I got my recipe for *Pollo Frito* and a *comida* including it. It was worth the journey.

CHICKEN IN MILD RED CHILI SAUCE
Pollo en Salsa de Chile Ancho

It never ceases to amaze me that the dried red *ancho* chili with its mild rich flavor starts life as the dark green *chile poblano*. The *ancho* is the most used chili in Mexico, its unripe, undried version the *poblano* is also popular, especially for stuffing. The *jalapeño* in this recipe is added for those who like a little *picante* touch in the dish.

6 *ancho* chilies

3 tablespoons corn or peanut oil

3½ lbs chicken, cut into serving pieces

2 onions, chopped

2 cloves garlic, chopped

1 lb tomatoes, peeled, seeded and chopped

Sprig *epazote*

2 cups chicken stock

Salt, freshly ground black pepper

1 *jalapeño* chili, seeded and chopped (optional)

Toast the *anchos* in a dry frying pan and when cool enough to handle, pull off the stems and shake out the seeds. Tear the *anchos* in pieces and put them into a bowl with hot water to cover and leave to soak for 30 minutes.

Heat the oil in a frying pan and sauté the chicken pieces until they are golden. Transfer them to a flameproof casserole and set aside. In a food processor combine the *anchos*, onions, garlic, tomatoes, *epazote* and *jalapeño* if using, and process to a purée. Cook in the oil remaining in the frying pan, stirring, for 5 minutes. Stir in the chicken stock, season to taste with salt and pepper and pour over the chicken. Cover and simmer over low heat until the chicken is tender, 45 minutes to 1 hour. Serve with a green salad, radishes and sliced avocado dressed with oil and vinegar. **SERVES 6.**

SMOTHERED CHICKEN
Tapado de Pollo

This a beautifully simple recipe and a luxurious one as well when made with chicken breast fillets. Other chicken parts can be used instead, thighs for example, but they need longer cooking. If using, sauté them in oil briefly then poach them in chicken stock until almost tender and cook as in the recipe. If the dish seems to be drying out during cooking, add a little stock but not enough to make the dish soupy.

6 tablespoons olive oil

6 chicken breast fillets, skinned and boned

1 large onion, finely chopped

2 cloves garlic, finely chopped

¾ lb tomatoes, peeled and sliced

1½ cups baby peas, if frozen, thawed

1 lb small zucchini, trimmed and sliced

2 pears, peeled, cored and sliced

2 slices fresh pineapple, peeled and cut into chunks, or equivalent amount canned in its own juice

2 ripe plantains or 2 large under-ripe bananas, peeled and sliced

Salt, freshly ground black pepper

Heat 4 tablespoons of the oil in a frying pan and sauté the chicken breasts for a minute on each side. Transfer them to a heavy flameproof casserole. Make a layer of half the vegetables and fruit, season with salt and pepper and sprinkle with 1 tablespoon of olive oil. Repeat with the other half of the vegetables and fruit. Cover and cook on top of the stove until all the ingredients are tender. The chicken breasts will take about 6 to 8 minutes. If the dish seems to be drying out pour in a little warm chicken stock. Serve with warm tortillas, guacamole and pickled *jalapeños*. **SERVES 6.**

DUCK IN ORANGE JUICE
Pato en Jugo de Naranja

The Aztecs and Maya-Toltecs had ducks but the colonial kitchen has few recipes. This is a colonial recipe using the native bird and the imported orange. It works very well. Probably the orange used would have been a Seville (bitter) one as the sweet orange was introduced into Europe later than the Seville orange, but either will do in this dish, especially as the Seville has a limited season.

5 lbs young duckling, cut into serving pieces

Flour

Salt and freshly ground black pepper

2 tablespoons corn oil

1 cup fresh orange juice

½ lb tomatoes, peeled, seeded and chopped

1 onion, finely chopped

1 clove garlic, chopped

2 tablespoons toasted sliced almonds

¼ cup seedless raisins

½ cup chopped flat parsley or coriander

1 bay leaf

¼ teaspoon dried thyme

¼ teaspoon dried oregano

¼ cup dry sherry

Prick the duckling pieces with a fork to release the fat. Season flour with salt and pepper and put the duckling in it, shaking to remove the excess. Heat the oil in a large frying pan and brown the duckling in it. Transfer to large, heavy casserole. Add all the ingredients except the sherry, cover and place in a preheated 325°F oven for 1½ hours. Lift the duckling pieces to a warmed serving platter and keep warm.

Skim the excess fat from the sauce in the casserole and reserve. Stir in the sherry. In a small bowl mix 1 tablespoon of flour with a little of the reserved duck fat and add it to the casserole bit by bit, over low heat, stirring constantly until smooth. Cook for a few minutes longer, still stirring. Pour a little of the sauce over the duckling and serve the rest separately. **SERVES 6.**

CHICKEN WITH *CHIPOTLE* CHILI
Pollo con Chipotle

Chipotle is another example of the mysterious change that comes over chilies when they ripen and are dried. In this case the ripe *jalapeño* is also smoked. It is very hot and has an exotic flavor. It is popularly used in *adobo* or *escabeche* sauces. Use as few or as many chilies as your personal taste dictates.

3 tablespoons corn or peanut oil

3½ lbs chicken, cut into serving pieces

1 large onion, finely chopped

1 clove garlic, chopped

1 lb tomatoes, peeled, seeded and chopped

1 sprig *epazote*

1 or more canned *chipotle* **chilies**

Salt

Heat the oil in a frying pan and sauté the chicken pieces until they are golden on both sides. Transfer them to a flameproof casserole. In the oil remaining in the frying pan, sauté the onion and garlic until the onion is tender. Add to the chicken with the tomatoes, *epazote* and *chipotles* and pour in enough stock barely to cover. Add salt if necessary. Cover and simmer over low heat until the chicken is tender, about 1 hour. **SERVES 6.**

CHICKEN TABLECLOTH STAINER
Manchamanteles de Pollo

This dish really comes from Guadalajara but can be widely enjoyed in many parts of the Republic, especially in Mexico City. However the Oaxacans say it is one of their own, one of the seven *moles* they cite when claiming to be the Land of the Seven *Moles*. My recipe was the one taught me by Francisca, the fabulous Zapotecan cook I was lucky to have when I was first in Mexico. The Zapotecs were the first culture in Oaxaca so when Francisca said there should be *pasillas* as well as *anchos* in the dish, I agreed though I don't think I ever came across the combination elsewhere. It is hard not to spill some of the sauce on the tablecloth, and it is a lurid red but it washes out.

2 *ancho* chilies

2 *pasilla* chilies

3½ lbs chicken, cut into serving pieces

2 tablespoons corn oil or lard

3 chorizo sausages, skinned and chopped

1 ripe plantain, peeled and sliced, or 1 large firm banana, peeled and sliced

2 thick slices fresh pineapple, peeled and cubed

1 large onion, chopped

2 cloves garlic, chopped

2 tablespoons flaked blanched almonds

¼ teaspoon ground cloves

½ teaspoon ground cinnamon

1 lb tomatoes, peeled, seeded and chopped

2 cups chicken stock

2 tablespoons lime or lemon juice

Toast the chilies lightly in a dry frying pan, lift out and pull off the stems and shake out the seeds. Tear into pieces and put into a bowl with warm water and soak for 30 minutes. Heat the oil or lard in a large, heavy frying pan and sauté the chicken pieces until lightly brown. Lift out and drain on paper towels, add to the casserole. Reserve the fat in the pan. Arrange the fruits in the casserole over the chicken. In a food processor combine the onion, garlic, almonds, cloves, cinnamon, tomatoes and chilies and process to a coarse purée. Heat the oil remaining in the frying pan and add the purée, cook, stirring for 5 minutes. Stir in the stock and pour the mixture into the casserole. Cover and cook over very low heat until the chicken is tender, about 1 hour. Just before serving stir in the lime or lemon juice. **SERVES 6.**

GREEN CHICKEN
Pollo Verde

There are probably as many versions of *Pollo Verde* in Mexico as there are cooks. In many ways this is the one I like best because it is so delicate and the flavor so subtle.

1 cup fresh coriander leaves

1 large onion, chopped

1 clove garlic, chopped

10 oz can Mexican green tomatoes (*tomatillos*), drained or ½ lb fresh

Salt

Chicken stock

3½ lbs chicken, cut into serving pieces

Combine the coriander, onion, garlic and the green tomatoes in a food processor. If using canned *tomatillos*, add the liquid from the can, if fresh an equivalent amount of chicken stock. Reduce to a fairly coarse purée. It should have some texture. Put the chicken pieces into a large, heavy flame-proof casserole and pour the purée over. Season with salt if necessary. Cover and cook over very low heat until the chicken is tender, about 1 hour. Check from time to time if any more liquid is needed. If so, add a little chicken stock. The sauce should not be thin. **SERVES 6.**

ANOTHER GREEN CHICKEN
Otro Pollo Verde

My cook, Enriqueta, gave me this version which we worked out and cooked together. I lost her to marriage and a family which she limited to two, one boy, one girl. She was a very special person and we kept in touch for years whenever César and I were in Mexico. The romaine lettuce gives the sauce a fine green color and thickens it too.

3½ lbs chicken, cut into serving pieces

1 cup chicken stock

1 cup dry white wine

Heart of 1 romaine lettuce, chopped

½ cup chopped coriander leaves

½ cup chopped flat leafed parsley

4 canned *jalapeño* chilies, seeded, rinsed and chopped

1 small white onion, chopped

**10 oz can Mexican green tomatoes (*tomatillos*),
    or ½ lb fresh**

3 tablespoons corn oil

Salt

Combine the chicken pieces in a flameproof casserole with the stock and wine, bring to a simmer, cover and cook over low heat until the chicken is tender, 45 minutes to 1 hour. Set aside. In a food processor combine the lettuce, coriander, parsley, chilies, onion and green tomatoes, and reduce to a purée. If necessary add some of the liquid from the chicken. Heat the corn oil in a frying pan and cook the purée, which should be heavy, for 3 or 4 minutes, stirring from time to time. Add to the chicken, stirring to mix and heat it very gently without letting it come to a boil which would alter the color of the sauce. **SERVES 6.**

GREEN CHICKEN WITH ALMONDS
Pollo Almendrado Verde

The version of this which I was so generously given had both dry sherry and orange juice in the poaching liquid. I've never been able to make up my mind if I like them and I sometimes add them and sometimes just have an extra cup of chicken stock when cooking the dish. I've marked them optional and the cook can decide. This sort of choice is typical of the Mexican kitchen.

2 tablespoons olive oil

2 tablespoons butter

3½ lbs chicken, cut into serving pieces

1 large onion, finely chopped

1 clove garlic, chopped

**2 cups light chicken stock or 1 cup
    of chicken stock and ½ cup each dry sherry and
    orange juice**

Salt, freshly ground black pepper

1 cup finely ground, blanched almonds

10 oz can Mexican green tomatoes (*tomatillos*), or ½ lb fresh

½ cup chopped fresh coriander

Heat the oil and butter in large, heavy frying pan and sauté the chicken pieces until they are lightly golden on both sides. Transfer them to a flameproof casserole. Sauté the onion and garlic in the fat left in the pan until the onion is soft. Transfer them to the casserole with the chicken stock and sherry and orange juice if using, salt and pepper to taste and simmer, covered, over very low heat until the chicken is tender. In a food processor combine the ground almonds, drained green tomatoes and coriander and reduce to a purée. Stir into the chicken and cook, uncovered, for 5 minutes. The sauce should be slightly thicker than heavy cream. If it needs thinning either use a little of the liquid from the canned green tomatoes, or some chicken stock. **SERVES 6.**

FRIED CHICKEN IN THE STYLE OF ST. MARKS GARDEN
Pollo Frito del Jardin del San Marcos

This is the fried chicken one buys from stalls in the grounds of the Jardin del San Marcos, the site of the traditional agricultural fair that is held there.

3½ lbs chicken, cut into serving pieces

2 cups light chicken stock

1 lb tomatoes, peeled, seeded and chopped

1 onion, finely chopped

1 clove garlic, crushed

¼ teaspoon dried oregano, crumbled

Salt, freshly ground black peppercorns

Pinch of salt

1 teaspoon lime or lemon juice

¼ cup olive oil

1 tablespoon unsalted butter

1 lb medium potatoes, cooked, peeled and sliced

3 chorizo sausages, peeled and sliced

Canned *serrano* chilies

Lettuce

Put the chicken pieces into a large saucepan or casserole, pour in the stock, bring to a simmer, cover and cook over low heat for 45 minutes to an hour or until tender. Lift out of the stock and set aside. Add the tomatoes, onion, garlic, cinnamon, cloves, oregano, pepper and sugar and simmer, uncovered, until reduced to a fairly thick sauce. Season with salt, if necessary, and stir in the lemon juice.

Heat the oil and butter in a large, heavy frying pan. Dip the chicken pieces in the sauce and cook for 3 or 4 minutes on each side in the hot fat. Arrange on a hot serving dish and keep warm. Cook the potato slices and chorizos in the same way in the remaining fat and arrange them with the chicken. Warm the remaining sauce and pour it over the chicken. Serve with a bowl of undressed lettuce and dish of *serranos* on the side. **SERVES 6.**

TINGAS

The *tingas* come from Puebla and may be main courses or made into *tostadas*, used as filling for *quesadillas* or bread rolls for snacks. They may be made with chicken or pork and the only essential is that they include *chipotle* chilies in the ingredients. *Tinga* comes from the Aztec and is believed to be a dish that is not at all aristocratic, vulgar and disorderly in fact. Naming of foods is an odd business. There was no frying as we know it in the Aztec or Maya cuisines and in the *tingas* both the indigenous and the introduced cooking methods are used, a good example of the culinary wedding that produced the colonial kitchen. This evolved through the nuns of the religious orders, this originally from the Convent of Santa Rosa, a Dominican order which is also credited with the *Mole Poblano*. The kitchen of the order can still be visited. The kitchen was designed to feed large numbers so like all the convent kitchens, is spacious, the walls hung with earthenware cookpots and casseroles, jugs, all manner of cooking equipment, the charcoal ovens decorated with multicolored tiles, altogether a busy and efficient workplace. My kitchen, the outside one, in Bangkok, had a charcoal burning stove, decorated with tiles, not unlike the colonial Mexican ones. I found that one could cook almost anything in it. In fact one day my cook, a young Thai boy, Tongdee Pholomai, and I made a creditable loaf of bread with the aid of an oven made from a kerosene tin, set on the charcoal stove. Cooking is a very friendly art.

CHICKEN STEW FROM PUEBLA
Tinga Poblano de Pollo

3½ lbs chicken, cut into serving pieces

2 cups light chicken stock

2 tablespoons corn oil or lard

3 chorizo sausages, skinned and chopped

1 onion, chopped

1 clove garlic, chopped

2 tablespoons flat parsley sprigs, chopped

2 tablespoons coriander leaves, chopped

1 lb tomatoes, peeled, seeded and chopped

2 canned *chipotle* chilies, chopped

Salt, freshly ground black pepper

Pinch of sugar

1 avocado, peeled and sliced lengthwise

Put the chicken pieces into a casserole or saucepan, pour in the stock, bring to a simmer, cover and cook until the chicken is tender, 45 minutes to 1 hour. Drain and reserve the stock. Skin and bone the chicken and cut into 1 inch pieces, approximately. Return to the casserole, cover to keep warm. Heat the oil or lard in a large frying pan and fry the chorizos until browned. Lift out and set aside. In the remaining fat fry the onion and garlic until the onion is golden brown. Add the parsley, coriander, tomatoes, chilies, salt, pepper, and a pinch of sugar. Cook for 10 minutes then add the reserved sausage and chicken and cook, stirring occasionally until the mixture is thick and has lost some moisture. It should be thicker than heavy cream, moist but not runny. Serve garnished with avocado slices. **SERVES 6.**

VARIATION:

Tinga Poblano de Cerdo *(Pork Stew from Puebla) uses boneless shoulder or loin of pork in place of chicken.*

CHICKEN WITH PRUNES
Pollo con Ciruelas

This is a colonial dish with echoes of French cooking perhaps coming into the kitchen through Napoleon III's ill-fated adventure in Mexico with Maximilian and Carlota, though it could be earlier. Once pitted prunes became

261

available so did the dish to us. I had and have my lazinesses and getting the pits out of prunes is one of them.

½ lb pitted prunes

2 teaspoons corn oil

1 tablespoon butter

3½ lbs chicken, cut into serving pieces

1 onion, finely chopped

1 clove garlic, chopped

½ teaspoon *chile pequín* (dried red chili) crumbled, or 1 or 2 fresh *serrano* chilies, seeded and chopped

1 lb tomatoes, peeled, seeded and chopped

1 cup chicken stock

Salt, freshly ground black pepper

½ cup dry sherry (optional)

Steep the prunes in enough hot water barely to cover and set aside. Heat the oil and butter in a large frying pan and sauté the chicken pieces until golden brown on both sides. Transfer them to a flameproof casserole. In the fat remaining in the pan sauté the onion, garlic and chilies and add them together with the tomatoes to the casserole. Drain the prunes and chop them coarsely. Add them to the casserole with the stock. Season to taste with salt and pepper, cover and simmer until the chicken is tender, 45 minutes to an hour. If using the sherry add it five minutes before serving. **SERVES 6.**

TWO CULTURES CHICKEN
Pollo Mestizo

I was messing about in the kitchen while César and our good friend Jorge Casteñada talked serious business about the United Nations and the world in general. Jorge was with the Mexican Foreign Office and rose to Foreign Minister but at that time was with the United Nations delegation and I was happy half listening, half cooking. I was putting together a chicken dish from remembered instructions and when dinner was ready confessed I didn't know what it was called. Jorge said it was one of his mother's favorites and he didn't know either so why don't we christen it? That's how it got its name as, like so many Mexicans it is half Mexican, half Spanish, *mestizo* in fact.

2 tablespoons olive oil

1 tablespoon butter

3½ lbs chicken, cut into serving pieces

1 cup dry white wine

1 cup pineapple juice

Bay leaf

Salt, freshly ground black pepper

½ lb tomatoes, peeled, seeded and chopped

1 onion, chopped

2 cloves garlic, chopped

8 oz can Spanish *pimientos morrónes*, chopped with juice
or 2 sweet red peppers peeled, seeded and chopped

2 chorizo sausages, skinned and chopped

2 tablespoons capers, drained

12 small new potatoes, freshly cooked and peeled

3 *jalapeño* chilies

Heat the oil and butter in a large, heavy frying pan and sauté the chicken pieces until lightly golden on both sides. Transfer to a flameproof casserole and add the wine, pineapple juice, bay leaf and salt and pepper to taste. Cover and simmer until the chicken is almost tender, about 45 minutes. In a food processor combine the tomatoes, onion, garlic, *pimientos* and juice, or chopped red peppers and process to a smooth purée. Sauté the chorizos in the fat remaining in the frying pan, drain on paper towels and add to the casserole. Pour the purée in the frying pan and cook, stirring, in the remaining fat for 5 minutes. Add to the casserole with the capers and potatoes. Rinse the *jalapeños*, deseed and cut into strips, and add to the casserole. Taste for seasoning and simmer over low heat to heat through and finish cooking the chicken, about 15 minutes. **SERVES 6.**

CHICKEN IN RED PUMPKIN SEED SAUCE
Pipián Colorado de Pepitas

6 *ancho* chilies

3½ lbs chicken, cut into serving pieces

2 cups chicken stock

1 cup hulled pumpkin seeds (*pepitas*)

1 large onion, chopped

1 or 2 cloves garlic, chopped

1 sprig *epazote*

1 lb tomatoes, peeled, seeded and chopped

2 tablespoons corn oil or lard

Salt, pinch of sugar

In a dry frying pan toast the *anchos* lightly. When they are cool enough to handle pull off the stems and shake out the seeds. Tear them in pieces and put them into a bowl covered with warm water and let stand for 20 minutes.

Put the chicken into a large flameproof casserole, pour in the stock, cover and simmer over low heat until the chicken is almost tender, about 45 minutes. Drain, reserve the stock, return the chicken to the casserole and keep warm. Grind the *pepitas* in a food processor or nut grinder as finely as possible then shake through a sieve. Set aside. Combine the prepared *anchos*, onion, garlic, *epazote* and the tomatoes in a food processor and reduce to a purée.

Heat the oil or lard in a heavy frying pan and pour in the mixture with the *pepitas* and cook, stirring, over low heat for 5 minutes stirring constantly. Stir in enough of the reserved stock to bring the mixture to medium thick consistency. Season to taste with salt and the pinch of sugar. Pour the sauce over the chicken and cook over very low heat until the chicken is tender, about 15 minutes. Serve with a plain white rice, or *Arroz Amarillo* (Yellow Rice) (page 139) or *Arroz Gualdo* (Gold Rice) (page 140). **SERVES 6.**

CHICKEN IN GREEN PUMPKIN SEED SAUCE
Pipián Verde de Pepitas

Cortés commented on the sauces thickened with Mexican pumpkin seeds at the Conquest and Fray Sahagún sampled sauces from the big *ollas* (pots) in the main marketplace of Tenochtitlán, capital of Mexico and now the site of modern Mexico City. The Maya to the south had been using the pumpkin seeds (*pepitas*) long before that. The *pipiánes* are dishes of great antiquity and I was quite awed when I set out to learn about them. César knew all about their historical background and I seemed to move through the centuries as I used modern electrical equipment to achieve the dishes enjoyed by Aztecs, Mayas and their Spanish conquerors. They are as popular today as they were in the remote past. They are widely available in health food shops and supermarkets.

3½ lbs chicken, cut into serving pieces

2 cups chicken stock

1 cup hulled pumpkin seeds (*pepitas*)

6 *serrano* chilies, seeded and chopped

½ lb Mexican green tomatoes (*tomatillos*), canned or fresh

1 large onion, chopped

1 clove garlic, chopped

½ cup chopped fresh coriander

2 tablespoons corn oil or lard

Salt

Put the chicken pieces into a heavy flameproof casserole, add the stock, cover and simmer over low heat until almost tender, about 45 minutes. Drain, reserve the stock and keep the chicken warm. Grind the pumpkin seeds in a food processor or nut grinder and shake through a sieve. Combine the *serranos*, *tomatillos*, onion, garlic and coriander in a food processor and process to a purée.

Heat the oil or lard in a large, heavy frying pan and cook the mixture, together with the ground *pepitas*, over low heat for 2 or 3 minutes, stirring constantly. Add enough of the reserved chicken stock to bring the sauce to medium thick consistency. In a casserole combine the chicken and sauce, cover and cook over very low heat until the chicken is tender, about 15 minutes. Serve with hot white rice. **SERVES 6.**

CHICKEN IN GREEN SESAME SEED SAUCE
Pipián Verde de Ajonjoli

> 3½ lbs chicken, cut into serving pieces
>
> 2 cups chicken stock
>
> 1 cup sesame seeds
>
> 1 large onion, chopped
>
> 1 clove garlic, chopped
>
> ½ cup chopped fresh coriander
>
> 1 lb *tomatillos*, canned and drained, or fresh
>
> 6 *serrano* chilies, seeded and chopped
>
> 2 tablespoons corn oil or lard
>
> Salt

Put the chicken pieces in a heavy flameproof casserole, pour in the stock, cover and poach until the chicken is nearly tender, about 45 minutes. Drain, reserve the stock, and keep the chicken warm in the casserole. Toast the sesame seeds for a minute or two in the frying pan, then pulverize in a food processor or nut grinder. Set aside. In the food processor combine the onion, garlic, coriander, *tomatillos*, *serranos* and process to a coarse purée.

Heat the oil or lard in a heavy frying pan, add the purée and the sesame seeds and cook, stirring for 2 or 3 minutes. Add enough of the reserved stock to bring the sauce to medium thick consistency. Taste for seasoning and add salt if necessary. Pour the sauce over the chicken in the casserole and cook over low heat for 15 minutes longer or until the chicken is tender and the flavors blended. Serve with Arroz Amarillo (Yellow Rice) (page 139) or plain white rice. **SERVES 6.**

CHICKEN IN RED SESAME SAUCE
Pipián Rojo de Ajonjoli

Apart from having chicken as the poultry this dish has probably changed little in the centuries since Fray Sahagún sampled a version of it from one of the earthenware *ollas* where it was simmering away in the main marketplace of the Aztec capital. From his writings one gathers he found it good indeed. The *pipián* recipes illustrate the Mexican cook's delight in playing variations on a kitchen theme. There are the red and green *pipiánes* with pumpkin seeds or with sesame seeds. The recipes may look similar to the casual eye, but the finished dishes have a vastly different taste.

6 *ancho* **chilies**

3½ lbs chicken cut into serving pieces

2 cups chicken stock

1 cup sesame seeds

1 large onion, chopped

1 or 2 cloves garlic, chopped

1 sprig *epazote*

1 lb tomatoes, peeled, seeded and chopped

¼ teaspoon ground cloves

¼ teaspoon ground cinnamon

2 tablespoons corn oil or lard

Salt, pinch of sugar

Toast the *anchos* lightly in a dry frying pan. When they are cool enough to handle pull off the stems, shake out the seeds and tear the *anchos* to pieces. Put them into a bowl with warm water to cover and let them soak for 20 minutes.

Put the chicken into a large flameproof casserole, pour in the stock, cover and simmer over low heat until the chicken is almost tender, about 45 minutes. Drain, reserve the stock and return the chicken to the casserole to keep warm. Pulverize the sesame seeds in a food processor or nut grinder and set aside. Combine the *anchos*, onion, garlic, *epazote*, tomatoes, cloves and cinnamon in the food processor and blend to a coarse purée.

Heat the oil or lard in a large, heavy frying pan, add the sesame seeds and toast them, stirring over a moderate heat for a minute or two, then add the purée and continue to cook, stirring, for 5 minutes. Pour enough of the reserve stock to bring to medium thick consistency, season with salt if necessary and the pinch of sugar. Pour the sauce over the chicken in the casserole and cook over low heat for 15 minutes, or until the chicken is tender and the flavors blended. Serve with plain white rice. **SERVES 6.**

TURKEY IN CHILI AND CHOCOLATE SAUCE PUEBLA-STYLE
Mole Poblano de Guajolote

This is the most famous of all the *moles* and is the great national festival dish, appropriate for any grand occasion, and for family festivities like engagements, weddings, baptisms, birthdays, anniversaries or for family Sunday *comida*, or indeed just whenever one feels like it. It is a very ancient dish dating back before the Conquest.

Emperor Moctezuma had it served at the banquet he gave to the Spanish conqueror Hernán Cortés and it goes a long way to explaining Mexican cuisine. *Molli*, in Nahuatl, which became *mole* (pronounced molay) in Spanish, means a sauce, not sauces served with things but things cooked in sauces, an admirable cooking method in high altitudes where liquids boil at a lower temperature than at sea level. It has changed in detail over the centuries but it and all the other *moles* have retained their fundamental characteristics. One change for the better was the arrival of the blender and later the food processor. This was a three-day affair when chilies, spices and so on had to be ground on a *metate*, a sloping triangular piece of volcanic rock on three legs, two in the front and one at the back, with the *metlapil*, the grinding stone or pestle, terribly hard work. My first cook said my kitchen was ill equipped because I had only one blender. With two blenders *mole poblano* became a one-day cooking affair and with the advent of the food processor even easier.

Legend has it that Sor Andrea of the Convent of Santa Rosa invented this most famous of *moles* in the 17th century to honor Bishop Fernandes de Santa Cruz and the viceroy of New Spain, Don Tomas Antonio de la Cerda y Aragon on the viceroy's visit to Puebla, invented, out of her head... this I do not believe but it is passionately believed by most of Puebla and much of Mexico. I have my own theory which I believe to be probable and logical but which in Mexico caused pursed lips and raised eyebrows. I can't prove it but then who can prove that Sor Andrea put together all those alien foods so felicitously? I think it probable that when the aristocratic native Indian girls at the convent heard that the guests were a viceroy and a bishop and were to be entertained with the best food possible, they equated them with their own high priest and the emperor, certainly with royalty. They gave Sor Andrea what is clearly a royal recipe. They would not have mentioned it earlier since among the Aztecs chocolate was forbidden to women and was reserved for royalty, the military nobility, the higher ranks of the clergy and top merchants. The good nuns are to be thanked for saving the dish from possible oblivion in the dark days, for the old regime, that followed the Conquest. They must also be credited with introducing their own refinements, cloves and cinnamon, though they might have done better with the original herbs and spices. And frying the turkey pieces, an innovation since frying did not exist in the Aztec-Maya cuisines. We will never know the truth of the matter but who cares when the existing dish is so very good?

There is another legend that strains credulity. Fray Pascual was in charge of his convent's kitchens when the visiting viceroy, Don Juan de Palafox y Mendoza came to dine. He tidied up the kitchen making a neat pile of spices and herbs and presumably chilies when an errant wind blew them into the *cazuelas*, earthernware pots, of simmering turkey and changed them into *mole*.

Oaxaca claims to be home of seven *moles*, one of them is *Manchamanteles* (Tablecloth Stainer) and the famous *Mole Negro* (Black Mole) uses *chilhuacle* chilies, native to Oaxaca. The state claims to grow sixty chili varieties that grow nowhere else, but there are chilies near enough in flavor to use as substitutes. The six *moles*, one red, one black, green, yellow, *Manchamanteles*, and the sixth *mole* called *Chichilo*. I became an *afficionada* of *mole verde* before I had even visited Oaxaca and have been so since. It is a favorite all over the Republic especially in Guadalajara though Oaxaca claims it as its own.

TURKEY *MOLE* PUEBLA-STYLE
Mole Poblano de Guajolote

6 *ancho* chilies

4 *pasilla* chilies

4 *mulato* chilies

1 8-lb turkey, cut into serving pieces

2 oz lard

2 onions, chopped

4 cloves garlic, chopped

½ teaspoon anise

2 tablespoons sesame seeds

2 tablespoons chopped coriander sprigs

1 stale tortilla or 1 slice white bread toast, cut up

1 lb tomatoes, peeled, seeded and chopped

1 cup flaked, blanched almonds

½ cup seedless raisins

½ teaspoon ground cloves

½ teaspoon ground cinnamon

½ teaspoon ground coriander seeds

½ teaspoon black peppercorns, ground
1½ oz Mexican chocolate or unsweetened chocolate
Salt

Toast the chilies in a dry frying pan, tear off the stems and shake out the seeds. Tear them into pieces and put into a bowl with hot water to cover and soak for 30 minutes. Put the turkey pieces into a large, heavy pan, cover with cold, salted water and simmer, covered for 1 hour. Drain, reserving the stock. Pat the turkey pieces dry with paper towels. Heat the lard in a large frying pan and sauté the turkey pieces, a few at a time, until lightly browned on both sides. Transfer to a large flameproof casserole, reserving the lard.

In a food processor combine the onions, garlic, half of the sesame seeds, the fresh coriander, the tortilla or toast, the tomatoes, the almonds, raisins, cloves, cinnamon, coriander seeds and peppercorns and chilies and process to a coarse purée. If necessary do this in batches. Heat the lard remaining in the frying pan, adding 1 tablespoon if necessary and cook the purée, stirring, for 5 minutes. Add 2 cups of the reserved turkey broth, the chocolate broken into pieces, and salt if necessary. Cook, stirring, over very low heat until the chocolate has melted. The sauce should be quite thick. Pour the sauce over the turkey pieces in the casserole and cook over the lowest possible heat for 30 minutes. Just before serving sprinkle with the remaining sesame seeds. Serve with blind *tamales* or with hot tortillas, and guacamole. **SERVES 8-10.**

NOTE:
Some cooks, especially in Oaxaca, like to fry the chilies in lard before putting them to soak. The sauce should be thick enough to coat the back of a spoon. Add a little more turkey stock if it is too thick. The sauce will be abundant and any left over should be kept for use with other dishes.

VARIATION:
Efrain Huerta and his wife Thelma, both poets and family friends, gave me a great deal of information about the cooking of Puebla. I was immensely grateful and have used the insights given me to good effect, I hope. This one changes Mole Poblano *considerably though it seems such a small addition. Add 4 canned* chipotle *chilies to the food processor with the other ingredients to be processed to a purée. They flavor and heat. They make a subtle change and I have often wondered if this variation is really from Puebla or from Oaxaca or whenever. They also said it was a good idea to add some* epazote, *that essentially Aztec-Maya herb. These are both foreign flavors in this cuisine of Old and New Worlds, this mixed marriage.*

TURKEY *MOLE* PUEBLA-STYLE WITH TWO CHILIES
Mole Poblano de Dos Chiles

I've always had a suspicion that this *mole* is not actually from Puebla but that the cook who gave the recipe and cooked it with me thought calling it Puebla-style enhanced its value. It doesn't really matter. It is made just as often with chicken.

6 *mulato* chilies

6 *pasilla* chilies

1 8-lb turkey, cut into serving pieces

1 lb boneless pork cut into 1 inch pieces

3 tablespoons lard or corn oil

1 cup flaked, blanched almonds

½ cup peanuts

1 tortilla or slice of toast, coarsely chopped

2 tablespoons sesame seeds

4 tablespoons ground cloves

½ teaspoon ground cinnamon

½ teaspoon anise

1 lb tomatoes peeled, seeded and chopped

1 oz Mexican or unsweetened chocolate, broken into pieces

Salt

Toast the chilies lightly in a dry frying pan. When cool enough to handle pull off the stems and shake out the seeds. Tear chilies into pieces and put into a bowl with hot water to cover. Leave to soak for 30 minutes. Put the turkey and pork pieces into a large heavy saucepan with water to cover. Cover and simmer for 1 hour. Drain, reserving the stock. Dry the turkey and pork with kitchen towels. Heat the oil or lard in a large, heavy frying pan and sauté the turkey and pork, a few pieces at a time so as not to crowd the pan, until browned on both sides. Transfer them to a large flameproof casserole. In a food processor combine the almonds, peanuts, tortilla, half the sesame seeds, cloves, cinnamon, anise, tomatoes and the prepared chilies and process to a coarse purée.

Heat the oil or lard remaining in the frying pan and cook the purée for 5 minutes stirring constantly. Add 2 cups of the reserved stock, the chocolate, and salt to taste and simmer, stirring until the chocolate has melted. Pour over

271

the turkey and pork, cook over very low heat covered for 1 hour, taking care not to let it burn. The sauce should be medium thick. If necessary add a little more stock. Just before serving sprinkle with the remaining sesame seeds. If liked toast the sesame in a dry frying pan for about a minute. Serve with blind *tamales*, or tortillas, or plain white rice and guacamole. **SERVES 8 TO 10.**

CHICKEN IN GREEN CHILI SAUCE
Pollo en Mole Verde

8 *poblano* chilies

3½ lbs chicken, cut into serving pieces

2 cups chicken stock

1 cup hulled pumpkin seeds (*pepitas*)

½ cup flaked walnuts

½ cup almonds

1 large onion, chopped

1 clove garlic, chopped

12 oz *tomatillos* (Mexican green tomatoes), chopped

½ cup chopped fresh coriander

Salt

2 tablespoons lard or corn oil

Toast the *poblanos*, impaled on a kitchen fork, over a gas burner until they are charred. Put them into a brown paper or plastic bag for 20 minutes then take out and rinse off the charred papery skin. Slit them open and remove the seeds and chop the *poblano* coarsely.

Put the chicken pieces into a flameproof casserole, pour in the chicken stock, cover and simmer until the chicken is almost tender, about 45 minutes. Drain, reserve the stock, return the chicken to the casserole and keep it warm. In a nut grinder or food processor pulverize the *pepitas* as finely as possible and shake through a sieve. Set aside.

In a food processor combine the walnuts, almonds, onion, garlic, *tomatillos*, coriander and prepared *poblanos* and process to a coarse purée. Add the *pepitas*. Heat the lard or oil in a large heavy frying pan and pour in the purée. Cook stirring, for about 3 minutes, thin to medium sauce consistency with the reserved chicken stock and pour over the chicken. Cover and cook over very low heat until the chicken is tender, about 15 minutes. Do not let the sauce boil. Season with salt if necessary. Serve with plain white rice. **SERVES 6.**

CHICKEN WITH RICE
Arroz con Pollo

This is quintessentially a Spanish dish and is found all over Latin America, each version different in some way and each different from the original. It is a perennial favorite.

½ **cup olive oil**

3½ **lbs chicken, cut into serving pieces**

Salt, freshly ground black pepper

2 **medium onions, thinly sliced**

1 **clove garlic, chopped**

1½ **lbs tomatoes, peeled and sliced**

2 **or more canned** *serrano* **chilies, chopped**

½ **teaspoon ground cumin**

¼ **teaspoon ground saffron**

4 **cups chicken stock**

2 **cups rice, preferably short-grain**

2 **Spanish canned** *pimientos morrónes*, **cut into strips, or 2** *pimientos*
  (sweet red peppers) peeled, seeded and cut into strips

Heat the oil in a large frying pan. Season the chicken pieces with salt and pepper and sauté in the oil until golden and transfer to a flameproof casserole, ideally one of earthenware. In the oil remaining in the frying pan sauté the onions and garlic and add them to the chicken, with tomatoes, *serranos*, cumin, saffron and stock. Cover, bring to a gentle simmer and cook for 30 minutes.

In the oil, adding a little more if necessary, sauté the rice, stirring from time to time, until it has absorbed all the oil, taking care not to let it burn. Add the rice to the chicken, cover and continue to simmer until the chicken is tender and the rice is cooked and quite dry—about 30 minutes. Garnish with the *pimiento* strips. **SERVES 6.**

DRUNKEN CHICKEN
Pollo Borracho

Any recipe with any alcohol in it is called *borracho* in Mexican cookbooks. There is a certain optimism expressed, so little alcohol for such a large result. Wine only arrived after the Conquest and its effects in the pot were exaggerated if appreciated.

2 tablespoons corn or peanut oil

2 teaspoons butter

3½ lbs chicken, cut into serving pieces

¼ lb cooked ham, coarsely chopped

1 cup seedless raisins

¼ teaspoon ground cloves

¼ teaspoon ground cinnamon

¼ teaspoon ground coriander seed

¼ teaspoon ground cumin

2 cloves garlic, chopped

2 cups dry white wine

Salt, freshly ground black pepper

½ cup toasted, slivered almonds

12 *pimiento* stuffed green olives, halved

1 tablespoon capers, drained

Heat the oil and butter in a heavy casserole and sauté the chicken pieces until golden on both sides. Add the ham, raisins, all the spices, garlic, white wine, and salt and pepper to taste. Cover and simmer gently over low heat, until the chicken is tender, about 1 hour. Add the almonds, olives and capers and heat through, uncovered, for about 5 minutes. Serve with rice. **SERVES 6.**

PHEASANT IN GREEN PUMPKIN SEED SAUCE FROM YUCATÁN
Faisan en Pipián Verde de Yucatán

I first had this when, on a trip to Mérida, we visited a restaurant-cum-night-club called El Faison y Venado named for Yucatán the land of the pheasant and deer. At intervals the waiters abandoned their ordinary duties and assuming costumes performed dances that were said to illustrate their states' history, deer dance and so on. It is unkind to say they were comic, but they were. The food however was superb. Choose young pheasant and have a pheasant per person.

2 young pheasants, weighing about 2 lbs each
Salt, freshly ground black pepper
2 tablespoons corn oil
1 tablespoon annatto
1 cup hulled pumpkin seeds (*pepitas*)
1 onion, chopped
2 cloves garlic, chopped
2 sprigs *epazote*
8 oz Mexican green tomatoes (*tomatillos*), either fresh or canned
2 cups chicken stock

Split the pheasant in half lengthwise. Pat dry with paper towels and season with salt and pepper. In a large casserole heat the butter and oil and sauté the pheasant halves on both sides. Pour in enough of the chicken stock to cover and simmer, covered until the pheasants are tender, about an hour. The time will vary with the age of the birds.

In a grinder or food processor pulverize the *pepitas* and shake them through a sieve. Grind the annatto. Set aside. Combine the onion, garlic, *epazote* and *tomatillos* in a food processor and blend until smooth. Put the mixture in a saucepan with the *pepitas* and annatto and pour in the stock from the pheasants. Cook over low heat at a gentle simmer, stirring from time to time until the mixture has thickened. Pour it over the pheasants and cook for 5 to 10 minutes to heat the pheasants through and blend the flavors. **SERVES 4.**

VARIATION:
To make Faisan en Pipián Rojo, *substitute 10 oz red tomatoes, peeled and chopped for the* tomatillos *and purée 1* ancho *or* mulato *chili, prepared in the usual way with the onion, garlic and tomatoes as in the* pipián verde.

PIGEONS IN SHERRY
Pichones en Salsa de Vino Jerez

Pigeons were a favorite of César's and they were very good in Mexico. The Spanish influence is very strong here with only New World tomatoes changing the dish from its original.

6 young pigeons, ready dressed

2 tablespoons butter

1 large onion, finely chopped

1 clove garlic, chopped

1 lb tomatoes, peeled, seeded and chopped

Salt, freshly ground black pepper

1½ cups dry white wine

½ cup toasted, slivered almonds

¼ lb boiled ham, coarsely chopped

½ cup dry sherry

Split the pigeons lengthwise, leaving them each in one piece. Heat the butter in a frying pan and sauté the pigeons until lightly browned on both sides. Arrange the birds overlapping in a large, flameproof casserole. In the butter remaining in the frying pan sauté the onion and garlic until soft. Add the tomatoes and cook until the mixture is thick and well blended. Season with salt and pepper and pour in the wine. Stir to mix and pour over the pigeons. Cover and bring to simmer. Cook until the pigeons are tender, about 45 minutes. In a food processor combine the ham and almonds and blend until smooth. Add to the casserole with the sherry and cook for 5 minutes longer. Serve with plain white rice and young green peas. **SERVES 6.**

CHICKENS IN THE KITCHEN GARDEN
Pollos en Huerto

This very old recipe is the one from which the simpler *Tapado de Pollo*, is derived. It is a good example of the exuberance of the Aztec reaction to new things, and reminds one of the ornate altars in the church at Tepotzotlan, so overdone in decoration that somehow it works, as does this dish. The cook may vary the ingredients, adding corn, lima beans, or other fresh garden vegetables.

4 lbs chicken cut into serving pieces

Salt, freshly ground black pepper

4 tablespoons corn oil or lard

2 onions, sliced

2 cloves garlic, chopped

1 lb tomatoes, peeled, seeded and chopped

1 bay leaf

3-4 sprigs fresh coriander, or flat-leaved parsley

1 teaspoon annatto seeds, ground

¼ teaspoon ground cloves

¼ teaspoon ground cinnamon

¼ lb young carrots, peeled and sliced

¼ lb sweet potatoes, peeled and thickly sliced

¼ lb white potatoes, peeled and thickly sliced

2 cups dry white wine, about

¼ lb young zucchini, trimmed and sliced

1 cup young green peas

¼ lb cut green beans

1 large firm banana, peeled and sliced or 1 ripe plantain, peeled and sliced

2 tart apples, peeled, cored and cut into chunks

2 peaches peeled, pitted and sliced

2 pears peeled, cored and sliced

2 quinces cored, peeled and sliced (optional)

4 slices fresh pineapple, cut into chunks

6 large ripe olives

¼ cup seedless raisins

3 or more canned *jalapeño* chilies, deseeded if liked and cut into strips

Season the chicken pieces with salt and pepper. Heat the oil or lard in a frying pan and sauté the chicken pieces until golden on both sides. Transfer to a large flameproof casserole. In the fat remaining in the frying pan sauté onions and garlic until the onions are soft and add to the casserole with the tomatoes, bay leaf, coriander or parsley, annatto, cloves, cinnamon, carrots, both kinds of potatoes, and the wine. Cover and simmer gently for 30 minutes. Add the other ingredients, and continue cooking over low heat for 30 minutes longer, or until the chicken is tender when all the vegetables should be cooked. **SERVES 6-8.** *Frozen vegetables should be thawed and drained and cooked according to package instructions.*

CHICKEN IN *ADOBO*
Pollo en Adobo

Adobo in Spanish means a pickle sauce, but in Mexico means a very thick chili sauce which almost always contains vinegar. *Adobo* varies from recipe to recipe, from cook to cook.

6 *ancho* chilies or *guajillo* chilies for a hotter dish

4 tablespoons corn oil or lard

3½ lbs chicken, cut into serving pieces

1 large onion, chopped

1 clove garlic, chopped

¼ teaspoon ground cloves

¼ teaspoon ground cinnamon

½ teaspoon ground coriander seed

½ lb tomatoes, peeled, seeded and chopped

Salt, freshly ground black pepper

1 teaspoon sugar

2 tablespoons mild vinegar (white or cider)

2 cups chicken stock

Toast the chilies lightly in a dry frying pan. Lift out and pull away the stems and shake out the seeds. Tear into pieces and put into a small bowl with hot water barely to cover, soak for 30 minutes.

In a large frying pan heat the oil or lard and sauté the chicken pieces until golden on both sides. Transfer to a large flameproof casserole. In a food processor combine the onion, garlic, cloves, cinnamon, coriander, salt, pepper and sugar and the vinegar and process to a coarse purée. In the fat remaining in the frying pan cook the mixture for 5 minutes, over gentle heat, stirring constantly. Add the stock and pour over the chicken, cover and cook over low heat for 1 hour. Remove the casserole lid for the last 15 minutes of cooking to reduce the sauce which should be very thick. Serve with lettuce, olives, capers, sliced radishes, sliced avocado and a bowl of pickled *serrano* or *jalapeño* chilies. **SERVES 6.**

STUFFED TURKEY
Pavo Relleno

In Mexico a small lady turkey called a *pipila* would be used for this. Small and tender, it is also believed to have a more delicate flavor. Since the Aztec domesticated the turkey, male and female, I felt I was in no position to argue.

1 8-lb turkey, ready to cook

For the stuffing:

2 tablespoons lard or corn oil

1 onion, finely chopped

1 clove garlic, chopped

2 lbs ground pork

1 large, firm banana or 1 ripe plantain, peeled and sliced

1 tart green apple, peeled, cored and chopped

3 tablespoons seedless raisins

¼ cup toasted, slivered almonds

1 or 2 *jalapeño* chilies, seeded and chopped

½ lb tomatoes, peeled, seeded and chopped

Salt, freshly ground black pepper

Butter

Flour

Chicken stock

Dry white wine

Heat the lard or oil in a large frying pan and sauté the onion and garlic until the onion is soft. Add the pork and sauté it until it is lightly browned, stirring constantly. Add the banana, apple, raisins, almonds and chilies. Drain any excess fat then add the tomatoes. Add salt and pepper to taste. Cook for a few more minutes. Cool the mixture before stuffing the turkey. Place the stuffed turkey, breast side up, on a rack in a roasting pan, and cover the bird with two layers of cheesecloth soaked in butter. Roast in a preheated 325°F oven for 2 to 2½ hours, or until the turkey is cooked, basting several times right through the cheesecloth with pan drippings or melted butter. Make a gravy with the pan drippings, just enough plain flour to thicken slightly, and a mixture half stock and half wine. Season to taste with salt and pepper.
SERVES 6-8.

CHICKEN WITH CHESTNUTS
Pollo con Castanas

This is a colonial dish and reflects Spanish longing for the foods of its home kitchen. There is nothing from the New World here, no chilies, no tomatoes. I remember in my early days in Mexico getting a craving for quiche lorraine and Irish stew. Homesickness takes one in odd ways. César yearned for *chilaquiles*.

1 tablespoon sesame seeds

2 tablespoons olive oil

2 tablespoons butter

4 lbs chicken cut into serving pieces

Salt, freshly ground black pepper

2 large onions, finely chopped

1½ cups chicken stock

½ cup dry sherry

2 tablespoons lemon or lime juice

¼ lb boiled ham, coarsely chopped

¾ lb peeled and cooked chestnuts, about

½ cup slivered almonds, finely ground

Toast the sesame seeds in a dry frying pan for about two minutes. Set aside. Heat the oil and butter in a large heavy frying pan. Season the chicken pieces with salt and pepper and sauté in the fat until golden on both sides. Transfer to a flameproof casserole. In the fat remaining in the pan sauté the onions until transparent and add to the casserole with the stock, sherry, lemon or lime juice. Cover and simmer over low heat for 1 hour or until the chicken is tender. Add the ham. In a food processor combine the chestnuts with a little stock from the chicken if necessary and process until smooth. Stir into the casserole with the almonds and cook 5 minutes longer. Sprinkle with sesame seeds just before serving. Serve with rice. **SERVES 6.**

CHICKEN WITH MUSHROOMS
Pollo con Hongos

We never seemed to be in the right place at the right time of year for mushrooms though the part of the Ortiz family that lived in Queretaro were keen eaters of mushrooms of various kinds. Of course we ate *huitlacoche* (corn fungus) whenever it was around but the other mushrooms, in a number of shapes, sizes and colors eluded me. There was so much to learn, especially when it came to the family of the cultivated *capsicums*. I comfort myself with the thought that I couldn't cook with these fungi anyway. I have experimented with available mushrooms like oyster, fresh shiitake, morels and so on instead of the fresh mushrooms available in farmers' markets and supermarkets.

3 *ancho* chilies

2 tablespoons corn oil

2 tablespoons butter

3½ lbs chicken, cut into serving pieces

1 lb mushrooms with stems, sliced

1 onion, chopped

1 clove garlic, chopped

½ lb tomatoes, peeled, seeded and chopped

2 sprigs of *epazote*

Salt, freshly ground black pepper

Pinch of sugar

1 cup chicken stock

½ cup heavy cream

Toast the *anchos* lightly in a dry frying pan. Tear off the stems and shake out the seeds. Tear the *anchos* in pieces and put them into a small bowl with warm water to cover and soak for 30 minutes.

Heat the oil and butter in a large frying pan and sauté the chicken pieces until they are golden on both sides. Transfer them to a flameproof casserole. In the fat remaining in the pan sauté the mushrooms and add them to the chicken. Reserve the fat. In a food processor combine the onion, garlic, tomatoes, *epazote* and *anchos* and process to a coarse purée. Heat the fat remaining in the frying pan, add the purée and cook for 5 minutes over low heat, stirring constantly. Season to taste with salt, pepper and sugar and stir in the chicken stock. Pour the mixture over the chicken and cook, over low heat, until the chicken is tender, about 1 hour. Just before serving stir in the cream and cook long enough to heat through without letting the sauce boil. **SERVES 6.**

RABBIT CREOLE-STYLE
Conejo a la Criolla

There are many rabbit-like animals in Latin America, as well as rabbits, which seem to be almost universal. There are many ways of cooking them in Spain and this is clearly a colonial recipe with a Mexican cook collaborating with the Spanish kitchen, to flavorful results especially for rabbit lovers.

2 tablespoons corn oil

2 tablespoons butter

4-lb rabbit, cut into serving pieces, or rabbit joints

1 large onion, finely chopped

1 clove garlic, chopped

½ cup chopped flat parsley leaves, or fresh coriander

1 canned *jalapeño* chili, cut into strips

1 lb tomatoes, peeled, seeded and chopped

1 cup strong beef stock

1 cup dry sherry

Salt, freshly ground black pepper

2 tablespoons lemon juice

¼ cup hazelnuts, finely ground

Heat the oil and butter in a heavy casserole and sauté the rabbit pieces until they are browned on both sides. Lift out and set the rabbit aside. Cook the onion, garlic and parsley in the remaining fat until the onion is soft. Add the chili, tomatoes, stock and sherry. Season the rabbit with salt and pepper and return it to the casserole. Cover and cook at a gentle simmer until the rabbit is tender, about 2½ to 3 hours though the time will vary. Add the ground hazelnuts and simmer for 5 minutes longer. **SERVES 6.**

DESSERTS AND PUDDINGS

•

Postres

The pre-Columbian Mexican kitchen had no desserts or puddings as we know them. Lacking milk, cream, butter, eggs, flour and sugar it was not possible to make cakes or any of the things that are commonplace as far as we are concerned. Without cattle there was no gelatine so no jellies or anything jellied. However there was a wealth of fruit; the strawberry from Chile, the pineapple from Brazil, guavas, pawpaws (*papayas*), the anonas, cactus fruits, tamarillos, and a great many others, some of which have not yet migrated even now. They were not entirely bereft, as Emperor Moctezuma and his subjects enjoyed *tamales* stuffed with strawberries and sweetened with honey.

It was the Spanish nuns, especially in Puebla, who created the desserts for which colonial Mexico is now famous. They were influenced by the sugar-rich desserts brought to Spain and Portugal by the cooks of the Middle East, the Moorish invaders. It is interesting that the Spanish nuns practically ignored chocolate and vanilla, local ingredients, for the cinnamon and cloves they had brought with them. Chocolate, sometimes flavored with vanilla and sweetened with honey, was taken as a drink after meals. It was forbidden to women and was restricted to kings, priests, nobles and the top ranks of the merchant class. The nuns would not have been inclined to experiment with this very foreign drink to create their kind of desserts.

With the adoption of Christianity the special foods for religious holidays changed and, of course, so did those to celebrate national holidays. Christmas was where I met my Waterloo. Not only was it the Christmas of Europe but the Christmas of southern Europe, modified by Mexico. No Christmas day presents and a tree, and a late midday meal with traditional foods, it was a different routine including a denunciation by the local bishop warning against the adoption of such heathen practices as Christmas trees. That bishop would have denounced the Yule log had it been around but it wasn't. What upset me most was having to open presents on Christmas Eve because I could see no use for Christmas Day if that happened. I don't think César and I ever quite sorted that one out. I did, however, find the *Posadas* (Inns) fun once I had sorted them out. It was because of my curiosity about *Ensalada de Noche Buena* (Christmas Eve Salad) which is traditionally eaten on Christmas Eve, when a supper usually including *Pavo Relleno* (Stuffed Turkey) or *Mole Poblano* (Turkey *Mole* in Puebla Style) is served and gifts are exchanged following the custom of France and other Latin countries. The supper served after midnight mass, is the culmination of a series of parties called the *Posadas* which begin on December 16. They commemorate the search by *Los Santos Peregrinos*, the Holy Pilgrims Mary and Joseph, for room at an inn in Bethlehem for the birth of the infant, Jesus. Plaster images of Mary and Joseph are carried at the head of a procession of host and guests around the garden and through the house. Or around the apartment. Each person carries a lighted candle, a litany is sung, and through special hymns there is a reenactment of the request for shelter, the repeated refusals, and finally the offer of the manger.

Sometimes an ambitious household will have a real donkey with some small girl and boy of the family dressed to represent Mary and Joseph. We attended one such ambitious *Posada* and it was, predictably, a disaster. The guests all came late, and poor tired little Mary kept lurching off the donkey, three parts asleep, while Joseph, worn out with the excitement of the party, whimpered alongside her. The donkey was very young too, and not house-broken, and the long hours of waiting took their toll. After the religious ceremony which lasted about half an hour, came the breaking of the *piñata*, a big clay *olla* (pot), covered with cardboard cut to represent an animal, a boat, a flower, a clown all brilliantly decorated with cut up tissue papers as the fancy of the maker dictates. The *olla* is filled with fruits, candies and small, unbreakable gifts. It is strung on a rope, usually in the patio, and often from a tree and the children, blindfolded, take turns one by one to break the swinging *piñata* by hitting it with a stick, while the others manipulate the rope to move it out of reach. Eventually a lucky thwack broke the *olla* and the contents spilled out with all the children scrambling for them while, mercifully, we got drinks, alcoholic and soft. As well as drinks there were great plates of fruit and candies and typical holiday foods like *buñuelos* (fritters).

After the Christmas Eve party there is pause until the *Día de los Reyes* (Kings' Day, Twelfth Night) January 6, which marks the end of the Christmas season and is celebrated with *Rosca de Reyes* (Kings' Day Ring) and gifts for the children.

There is a curious festival held in Oaxaca on Christmas Eve called *Noche de Rabano* (Radish Night). Large radishes are in season at this time of year, and they are cut into fancy shapes, much as one makes radish roses, and used to decorate stalls and restaurants around the plaza. Oaxaca is a great pottery center famous for its green glaze and black pottery and all year the vendors save up imperfect dishes. On Radish Night one eats *buñuelos* served on them then breaks them. I remember how, by midnight the square was full of smashed crockery. I never did manage to find out more about the ceremony but then Oaxaca is full of ancient mysteries and I expect this goes back to celebrating the end of the year.

Another Oaxacan festival I remember with particular pleasure is the *Guelaguetza* held in July, a homage to the God of Corn, *Centeotl* when everyone prayed for a good harvest. It was also called Monday of the Hill (*Lunes del Cerro*). We were invited by a lady that the UN Information Center was involved with. It is a time of general festivity with Zapotec, Mextec, Mixe and other Indians arriving in the city to stage their distinctive dances, dressed in their special costumes, magnificently colorful and varied. I wish I had known more about Oaxaca at the time but I was dazzled by the brilliance of it all, the weather, the costumes, the dances by men in great feathered head-dresses and then finding I was some sort of guest of honor and was to receive gifts. They judged the size of the handmade sandals by what they thought appropriate for a tall, slim, blue-eyed blond. I gave them to the artist husband of my husband's Texan cousin who was visiting. They were big even for him. But I kept the carved wood tray with its vividly colored flowers and still have it, the colors undimmed by time. *Buñuelos* are also eaten at this festivity, served in pottery bowls that are thrown, after the *buñuelos* are eaten, at the cathedral wall. You are supposed to make a wish when you perform the ritual. I didn't. I took my bowl, black pottery, home with me and, like the tray, still have it.

BRIDE'S COOKIES
Pastelitos de Boda

This recipe for Bride's cookies (the best known of all the *polvorones*, Mexican sugar cookies) was given me by my friend Adriana Keathley Glaze, the dancer and actress. It comes from her mother, the late Angelica Martinez Keathley. I prefer it to any other *polvorones* I have tried. The cookies are as easy to make as they are delicious. If pecans are not available use another nut such as walnut, almond, brazil nut, cashews or peanuts.

1 cup plain flour
½ cup confectioners' sugar
1 cup unsalted butter, softened at room temperature
Pinch salt
1 cup pecans, finely chopped
1 teaspoon vanilla extract

Sift the flour, sugar and nuts together into a large bowl. Stir in the vanilla then work in the butter with the fingertips until it forms into a ball. Shape the dough into 36 patties, put on a baking sheet and cook in a preheated 350°F oven for 30 minutes, or until the cookies are delicately brown. Lift off the baking sheet, cool slightly on wire racks then dust thickly with confectioners' sugar. Vary the size of the cookies to larger or smaller as you wish.

VARIATIONS:

Polvorones de Canela *(Cinnamon Cookies). Follow the recipe above replacing the pecans with ¼ cup flour and 1 teaspoon ground cinnamon. While still warm from the oven, roll in a mixture of 2 cups confectioners' sugar and 2 teaspoons ground cinnamon sifted together. Cook, then roll a second time.*

***For plain* Polvorones** *(Sugar Cookies) leave out the pecans and add ½ cup flour. Make as above.*

FRITTERS
Buñuelos

This is the family recipe for *buñuelos* and though it has no hole in the center and is somewhat smaller it is closer to the fritters of Oaxaca than others I have enjoyed. Whatever form they take they are fundamentally the same, but I draw the line at the suggestion that in the north *buñuelos* are just flour tortillas, cut into pieces, fried, dusted with sugar and cinnamon and dunked in sugar syrup. It is possible that might taste alright but I don't think they can be called *buñuelos*. I'll stick with the variations that I discovered in travelling around the Republic.

1 teaspoon salt

1 teaspoon baking powder

2 tablespoons granulated sugar

4 cups all-purpose flour

2 large eggs, beaten

1 cup milk

¼ cup unsalted butter, melted

Oil for frying

Sugar and cinnamon or sugar and cloves for dusting fritters

In a large bowl sift together the salt, baking powder, sugar and flour. Whisk the milk into the beaten eggs and gradually beat in the flour mixture, then stir in the melted butter. Turn the dough onto a lightly floured board and knead gently until the dough is smooth and elastic, then let it rest, covered with a cloth for an hour.

Divide the rested dough into 24 balls then roll them out on a floured surface into circles 4 inch or 6 inch according to taste. Fry in a deep fryer in oil heated to 375°F until delicately browned on both sides, about 2 minutes. Drain on paper towels, dust with cinnamon or cloves mixed with sugar and serve as a cookie or serve as a dessert doused with syrup used for *Capirotada* (page 295). **MAKES 24 *BUÑUELOS*.**

VARIATION:

A friend in Cuernavaca, south of Mexico City, gave this recipe though I find it popular in Veracruz and other places. Make the basic recipe in the same way and divide the dough into 24 balls. Flatten the balls into circles ½ inch thick then poke a hole in the center. The handle of a wooden spoon is good for this. Fry the fritters in a frying pan with 2 inch hot oil or in a deep fryer.

For Oaxaca buñuelos *flavor the mixture with ½ teaspoon ground anise and sprinkle the fried* buñuelos *while still hot with cinnamon sugar. If liked roll out to 8 inch or even larger circles.*

KINGS' DAY RING
Rosca de Reyes

January 6, Twelfth Night, Epiphany, Kings' Day, *Día de los Reyes*, the date on which the Three Kings came to visit the Infant Jesus with their gifts, is a traditional gift-giving holiday in Mexico. It is also traditional to serve the *Rosca de Reyes*, which has a tiny china doll, representing the infant, baked in it. Although in many countries it is simply considered good luck to get the piece of the cake with the doll in it, it is sometimes believed that, if a girl gets it, she will be married within a year. Mexico, however, has a further refinement. Whoever gets the doll is obliged to give a party on February 2, Candlemass Day, regarded as the special day of godparents. It is the day on which Mary and Joseph presented Christ at the temple where Simeon claimed him as God's true light, and candles are taken to church to be blessed. Friends from Oaxaca told me they were kept on the family altar and when there was a special need for help from God one was lighted and a prayer said. There are no very exciting foods traditional to the day but there is an *agua fresca*, a special drink which is half drink, half salad. I was never very enamored of it and César resolutely turned his back on it.

2½ teaspoons active dry yeast or 1 cake compressed yeast

1 teaspoon sugar

¼ cup lukewarm water

2½ cups granulated sugar

½ teaspoon salt

2 large eggs, well beaten

4 large egg yolks

½ cup unsalted butter, softened at room temperature

Grated rind of 1 lemon or lime

1½ cups mixed, chopped candied fruits and peels

1 small china doll

Melted butter

1 cup confectioners' sugar, sifted

2 tablespoons light cream

Maraschino cherries, halved

Sprinkle the yeast and the sugar over the lukewarm water in a small bowl to prove until frothy, about 5-10 minutes.

In a large bowl sift half the flour with the salt and sugar. Beat in the eggs, egg yolks, butter, grated lemon rind, yeast and water, until well blended. Dust 1 cup of the fruits with flour and combine with the mixture. Add the remaining flour and mix to a soft but not sticky dough. Add a little more flour if necessary. Turn out onto a lightly floured board and knead until the dough is smooth and satiny, about 5 minutes. Shape into a ring, tucking the china doll into the dough. Put on a greased baking tray, cover loosely with a cloth, and leave in a warm, draft-free place to rise until double in bulk, 2 hours or more.

Brush the risen ring with melted butter and put into a preheated 350°F oven and bake for 30 minutes. Remove from the oven, and cool. Mix the sugar and cream and spread over the ring. Decorate with the remaining fruits and peels and with the halved maraschino cherries.

CANDELMASS DAY DRINK
Agua Fresca para la Candelaria

8 cups water

1½ cups granulated sugar

2 beets, cooked, peeled and finely chopped

½ cup roasted, unsalted, peeled peanuts, finely ground

½ cup blanched almonds, finely ground

½ cup seedless raisins

1 cup pitted prunes, finely chopped

1 small romaine lettuce, finely shredded

1 *jicama*, weighing about 1 lb, peeled and finely chopped, or if not
    available 2 large cooking apples, peeled, cored and finely chopped

Combine the water and sugar into a large glass or china jug, stir and leave until the sugar has dissolved, stirring from time to time. Add all the other ingredients, stir and refrigerate for at least 2 hours. Serve, unstrained in small bowls, or strained in tumblers. **SERVES 8.**

BREAD OF THE DEAD
Pan de Muerto

In Mexico November 2, All Souls' Day, is not a day of sorrow though it is a day when Mexicans visit their family graves as a mark of love and respect. They take with them a special round coffee cake, *Pan de Muerto* (Bread of the Dead) which is decorated with baked pieces of dough in the form of alternating teardrops and bones, and bunches of *zempazuchitl* flowers, a bright orange marigold. The visit to the grave is like a picnic with the dead symbolically participating. Candy skulls are sold, and while you wait, your name is written on them in a contrasting color. One is supposed to nibble cheerfully away at one's own inevitable future. I confess that I was too much upset on my first November 2 to appreciate being given a skull with my name on it. I felt perhaps I was being urged on my way. Apart from that, everything was gay and brilliant, from blue sky and yellow sun to the orange marigolds and bright skirts, shirts and *rebozos* worn by members of the family parties lovingly tending graves in the family plot. Other mourning days are for weeping. All Souls' Day is a fiesta.

César's work took us to Morelia, capital of Michoacán, one All Souls' Day, and I had the great privilege of seeing something of the ceremonies in the region. They are very close to the spirit of the past which links people to the continuity of life, the dead not wholly lost to us here.

In Janitzio, the small island in Lake Patzcuaro, Michoacán, the ceremony is extremely elaborate, suggesting rites belonging to the pre-Christian faith of the region. Two days ahead of time the men of the village go duck hunting, using the traditional harpoon instead of guns. The women make *tamales* filled with duck meat cooked with chili sauce. They take these on All Souls' Eve to the cemetery, along with huge bunches of marigolds and a candle for each family member who has died. The women and older children keep an all-night vigil at the graves while the men keep vigil at home. The following day the family has a feast of *tamales* served with *atole*, coffee, *pulque*, beer, tequila, and *Pan de Muerto*. They believe the dead have feasted symbolically on the *tamales*, absorbing their spiritual essence.

5 teaspoons active dry yeast

1 teaspoon sugar

½ cup lukewarm water

4 cups all-purpose flour, sifted

1 teaspoon salt

½ cup sugar

1 cup butter, melted

6 large eggs, lightly beaten

1 tablespoon orange blossom water

2 tablespoons anise water

Grated rind 1 small orange

In a bowl prove the yeast with the sugar in the lukewarm water until foamy, 5-10 minutes. Add enough flour to make a light dough. Turn onto a lightly floured board and knead briefly. Shape into a ball, and put into a warm draft free place, lightly covered, until doubled in bulk, about 1 hour.

To make anise water: simmer 1 teaspoon anise seeds in 3 tablespoons water for 2 or 3 minutes. Cool and strain.

Sift the remaining flour with the salt and sugar in a bowl and work in the cooled melted butter, the eggs, the orange blossom water, anise water and grated orange rind. Turn the dough out onto a lightly floured board and knead until smooth and elastic. Add the sponge—the risen dough—and knead again until satiny. Cover with a cloth and let the dough rest in a warm, draft-free place for about 1½ hours until it has doubled in bulk. Shape into 2 round loaves, setting aside enough dough for the decorations. Put the loaves on a greased baking sheet and decorate with a cross made of pieces of dough, alternately shaped like bones and teardrops. Roll two small pieces of dough into knobs and attach them to the center of each loaf. Cover the decorated loaves and stand in a warm place until doubled in bulk.

Bake the loaves in a preheated 375°F oven for about 30 minutes, or until done. When cool, frost the loaves and sprinkle with colored sugar crystals.

To make the frosting add sifted icing sugar to ¼ cup boiling water or milk until it is of spreading consistency. **SERVES ABOUT 12.**

ALMOND PUDDING
Almendrado

This is a truly elegant dessert or pudding. It is not difficult to make and has the added advantage of being able to be made ahead of time which is a great bonus if you are having it for a party. It looks pretty, tastes wonderful and is a good example of how much the ancient Aztecs took to the almond when the Spanish introduced it. It was the delicacy of almonds that appealed then and still does appeal to Mexican cooks.

1 tablespoon unflavored gelatin

¼ cup cold water

1 cup boiling water

6 large egg whites, stiffly beaten

1 cup granulated sugar

½ teaspoon almond extract

1¼ cups toasted slivered almonds

Sprinkle the gelatin over the bowl of cold water to soften. Add the boiling water and stir until the gelatin is dissolved. Add the sugar and stir until it's dissolved. Stir in the almond extract. Chill the mixture until it begins to thicken then beat until frothy. Fold in the egg whites gently but thoroughly. Have ready a mold rinsed out in cold water. Pour in a layer of the mixture. Top with a layer of almonds, repeat until all the mixture is used, ending with a layer of almonds. Chill until firm.

This looks very attractive unmolded. Finish with a layer of the gelatine mixture and save enough almonds to sprinkle on top.

Custard Sauce:

2 cups whole milk

6 large egg yolks

¼ cup granulated sugar

Pinch of salt

½ teaspoon vanilla extract

½ cup heavy cream

Heat the milk in the top of a boiler until a film shines on top. It should not boil. In a bowl beat the egg yolks with the sugar and salt until they are light and lemon colored and form a ribbon when the whisk is lifted. Beat them very gradually into the warm milk. Set the double boiler over boiling water and continue to cook the mixture stirring constantly until it is thick enough to coat the spoon. Remove the sauce from the heat, cool and stir in the vanilla extract. Beat the cream until it is stiff and fold it into the cooled custard. Serve with the *Almendrado*. **SERVES 6.**

FRITTERS
Sopaipillas

These fritters, which look like little fat pillows, are good served with soup, guacamole or any other dip. They will stay puffed, if refrigerated, and can be reheated in the oven. As a dessert, with syrup or simply sprinkled with sugar and ground cinnamon, they are very good. They are fun to make though I have doubts each time I make them as to whether they will puff even though they always do.

2 cups all-purpose flour

2 teaspoons baking powder

1 teaspoon salt

2 tablespoons butter or other shortening

½ cup cold water

Oil for frying

In a large bowl sift the flour, baking powder and salt together. Work in the shortening with your fingertips or a pastry blender until the mixture resembles a coarse meal. Work in the water gradually to make a pastrylike dough. Turn this out onto a lightly floured board and knead until smooth. On a floured board roll out as thin as possible and cut into 2 inch to 3 inch squares. In a deep fryer or frying pan with oil to a depth of 2 inches, heated to 375°F, fry the *Sopaipillas* one at a time which will puff up as they brown. As one side puffs, turn to puff and lighty brown the other side. Drain on paper towels. **MAKES 20 TO 30 ACCORDING TO SIZE.**

CARAMEL CUSTARD
Flan

Whatever it is called, *Crème Renversée au Caramel*, Caramel Custard, or Flan, as in Spain and Mexico, it has an astonishing and enduring popularity. It is without doubt Mexico's favorite dessert made in a large caramelized mold, or in individual caramelized custard cups. Most cookbooks and cooks in their instructions for making caramel give instructions for heating sugar with a little water. I find this unnecessary if a properly heavy small saucepan is used. I just put sugar into the saucepan and melt it on moderate or low heat to caramel.

To caramelize the mold: In a small heavy saucepan heat ½ cup granulated sugar over moderate heat, stirring from time to time with a wooden spoon until the sugar melts and turns a rich, golden brown. Have ready a large mold or 6 custard cups, warmed by standing in hot water. Pour the caramel into the mold (or custard cups) turning it in all directions so that the caramel covers the bottom and sides. As soon as it stops running, turn the mold upside down on a plate. Caramelize the custard cups in the same way.

To make the Flan:
4 cups whole milk
½ cup granulated sugar
8 large eggs, lightly beaten
1 teaspoon vanilla extract
Pinch of salt

Heat the milk until a film shines on top, remove from the heat and cool. In a bowl beat the sugar into the eggs, add the milk, vanilla and salt and mix well. Strain the mixture into the prepared mold or custard cups. Put the mold into a baking tin filled with hot water that reaches half the depth of the mold or the custard cups and bake in a preheated 350°F oven for 1 hour, or until a knife inserted into the center of the custard comes out clean. The water in the baking tin should not boil. Take out the custard and let it cool then chill in the refrigerator. To unmold run a wet knife between the custard and the mold then put a serving plate upside down over the mold and invert it quickly. Flans are served at room temperature. If they are chilled too long in the refrigerator the caramel will harden, so if there is any doubt stand the mold in warm water for a few minutes before unmolding it. It should slide out easily with caramel runny not turned into toffee. **SERVES 6.**

VARIATIONS:

Flans can be varied in a number of ways, using the basic recipe.

For coconut flan: Add 1 cup fresh grated coconut to the egg mixture.

For almond flan: Add 1 cup ground, blanched almonds.

For chocolate flan: Add 2 tablespoons of cocoa powder and 2 tablespoons dark rum.

To change the flavor of the flan substitute ½ teaspoon ground cinnamon and ¼ teaspoon grated lemon rind for the vanilla.

BREAD PUDDING
Capirotada

When Elizabeth Borton fell in love with Luis Treviño she went, after her marriage, to live in Monterrey and she wrote the bestseller (one of her many important books) called *My Heart Lies South*. I read it in New York when I was working for the United Nations as the writer of the Film and Photo section. Later, after I met my husband, César Ortiz Tinoco, I found that his family and the Treviño family were old friends. Later still, we and Elizabeth and Luis both had houses in Cuernavaca. It was an enduring friendship and Elizabeth, like me, was devoted to César's grandmother, Doña Carmelita. This *Capirotada* recipe was given me by the grandmother and approved by Elizabeth who helped me in many ways both when we were in Mexico City and Cuernavaca. It is still the best *Capirotada* I've had and though the Lenten fast has long been abolished when this was a specialty for Lent, it is still a lovely way to use up stale bread.

1 lb *piloncillo*, or brown sugar

4 cups water

2-inch piece stick cinnamon

1 whole clove

Unsalted butter

6 slices white bread, toasted and cubed

3 cooking apples, peeled, cored and sliced

1 cup seedless raisins

1 cup chopped, blanched almonds

1 cup mild Cheddar, or similar cheese, cubed

In a saucepan combine the sugar, water, cinnamon and clove and bring to a simmer. Cook, uncovered, until the mixture has reduced to a light syrup, remove the cinnamon stick and clove and set the syrup aside.

Butter an ovenproof casserole large enough to hold all the ingredients and make a layer of bread cubes followed by a layer of apple, raisins, almonds and cheese. Repeat until all the ingredients are used. Pour the syrup over all, and bake in a preheated 350°F oven for 30 minutes. Serve hot.
SERVES 6.

SHELLS
Conchas

This is a popular sweet bread for breakfast or *merienda* (supper). Spain excels at sweet breads and Mexico has inherited the concept. They are slightly changed from the originals as are all migratory foods.

2½ teaspoons active dry yeast

½ cup lukewarm water

1 teaspoon salt

½ cup granulated sugar

½ cup whole milk

1 large egg, well beaten

3½ cups all-purpose flour

2 tablespoons shortening, melted and cooled

For the topping:

4 tablespoon unsalted butter

½ cup granulated sugar

½ teaspoon salt

1 teaspoon ground cinnamon

1 large egg

½ cup all-purpose flour, sifted

In a small bowl prove the yeast with 1 teaspoon of the sugar and the lukewarm water until frothy, 5-10 minutes. In a saucepan heat the milk until a film shines on top, cool then combine with the yeast mixture. Stir in the egg and pour into a large bowl. Gradually whisk in 1½ cups of the flour then add the melted shortening and whisk in the rest of the flour. Cover, and stand in a warm draft-free place, until double in bulk, about 1 hour. Turn onto a lightly floured board, divide into 12 equal pieces and form into round, flat buns. Spread the topping on the buns. With a small sharp knife draw a lattice pattern across the buns. Put the buns on a greased baking sheet, cover and stand in a warm place to rise again until double in bulk, about an hour. Bake in a preheated 400°F oven for 15 to 20 minutes.

To make the topping: In a bowl cream the butter and sugar together until light and fluffy. Mix in the salt and cinnamon, then the egg and finally the flour. Stir until the ingredients are thoroughly blended.

SWEET ROLLS
Molletes

These sweet breads, truly delectable at breakfast, are one of Mexico's happiest inheritances from Spain which excels in them. I used to make them sometimes but mostly you seek out a good *panaderia* (bakery) and buy your *pan dulce* (sweet bread) there. The variety is endless and they enliven the breakfast coffee as a slice of toast cannot.

2½ teaspoons active dry yeast
½ cup lukewarm water
1 teaspoon sugar
1 teaspoon anise seed
1 teaspoon salt
½ cup granulated sugar
1 cup whole milk
2 tablespoons shortening, melted and cooled
1 large egg, beaten
3½ cups all-purpose flour, sifted
Melted butter
Brown sugar, sifted

In a small bowl prove the yeast with the sugar and lukewarm water until frothy, 5-10 minutes. Stir in the anise seed, salt and sugar. In a saucepan heat the milk until a film shines on top, remove from the heat and cool. Transfer the yeast mixture to a large bowl and mix in the milk, shortening and egg. Gradually beat in the flour to make a soft dough. Cover and stand in a warm, draft-free place to double in bulk, about 1 hour. Turn out onto a lightly floured board and divide into 24 equal pieces. Form into balls and put onto a greased baking sheet. Cover loosely and stand again in a warm draft-free place to double in bulk again, about 1 hour. When the rolls have risen brush with melted butter, sprinkle with brown sugar and bake in a preheated 400°F oven for 15 minutes.

JUNKET DESSERT FROM ZAMORA
Chongos Zamoranos

Chongos translates into "topknot" and this does describe the appearance of these rolls of curds which are served in a light syrup made from sugar and whey. At one time I thought I would never have *chongos* again when junket disappeared from the market, but it came back again and I hope it will always be with us. I've never had *chongos* that were exactly the same either in restaurants or in the homes of friends. It doesn't matter and is comforting when you make your first lot and wonder if they will emerge true to tradition.

4 cups whole milk

2 large egg yolks, lightly beaten

2 rennet (junket) tablets

1 tablespoon cold water

1 cup light brown or granulated sugar to taste

2-inch piece stick cinnamon, broken into pieces

Heat the milk to lukewarm and pour it into a flameproof dish large enough to hold it comfortably. Stir in the egg yolks. Dissolve the rennet in the water and add it to the milk, stirring as little as possible. Put the dish in a warm place for the milk to set, about 30 minutes. As soon as the milk is firm cut an X with a sharp knife across the entire surface and down to the bottom of the dish. Put the dish over very low heat and as the whey starts to separate out put the sugar and cinnamon pieces in between the pieces of curd.

Leave the dish over the lowest possible heat for about 2 hours when the whey will have formed a syrup with the sugar and each of the pieces of curd will be firm enough to be lifted out with a slotted spatula. It is crucial not to let the milk come to a boil during the two hours it is cooking over low heat. Cut the pieces of curd in half lengthwise then roll each one up starting from the pointed end. Put the rolled up curds into a glass serving dish and pour the syrup over them. Serve at room temperature. **SERVES 4.**

ROYAL EGGS
Huevos Reales

These are egg yolks, beaten until they are very thick then poached until set and soaked in flavored syrup. This is one of the recipes from the nuns, probably from Puebla and reflects the ancestry of the dish, from the Middle East, to Spain, to Mexico. The nuns were lavish with eggs and sugar.

2 tablespoons seedless raisins
½ cup dry sherry
12 egg yolks
1 lb granulated sugar
2-inch piece stick cinnamon
2 tablespoons pine nuts or slivered almonds

Put the raisins into a small bowl with the sherry and leave to soak. In a bowl beat the egg yolks until they form a ribbon when lifted on the whisk. They should be very thick and mousse-like. It will take about 5 minutes beating. Pour them into a greased mold, a flan mold will do very well, and stand them in a larger pan, a *bain marie*, with warm water to come about halfway up the flan mold, covered. Put on the lowest shelf of the oven preheated to 350°F until the eggs are set, about 30 minutes. Remove from the oven and cool, and cut into cubes which should be about ½ inch thick.

Combine the sugar, cinnamon stick and 1 cup water in a saucepan and bring to a boil. Let the mixture simmer for 5 minutes. Stir once or twice. Lift out the cinnamon stick, reduce the heat to low, add the egg cubes and poach them until they are saturated with the syrup. Put into a glass serving dish with the raisins, sherry and nuts. Serve at room temperature.
SERVES 6.

FRIED BATTER CAKES
Churros

These are street food in Spain, eaten at every festival and are also a favorite for breakfast. Mexico has adopted them both as street food and indeed at any time. They are named after the *churro*, a Spanish sheep with long coarse hair. In Mexico they are sold at fairs and markets from small portable cooking stalls called *churrerias* (churro shops) where they go straight to the customer from the frying pan. They should be eaten as soon as possible after they are made. No migrant dish escapes unmodified and here a cut-up lime is added to the cooking oil giving the *churros* a distinctive flavor. The ideal equipment for cooking them is a pastry tube filled with a fluted tube, about ½ inch. The fluted tube is believed to be essential but I have found *churros* very co-operative and I've had great success just pushing the dough through a large funnel. The heat of the oil which should be very hot, 375°F, is the really important factor. All the same fluted *churros* look prettier than plain ones.

Oil for deep frying
1 lime, quartered
½ teaspoon salt
Granulated sugar
2 cups all-purpose flour, sifted
1 large egg, lightly beaten

Heat the oil, preferably in a deep fryer or in a frying pan to a depth of 2 inches and add the lime quarters. Remove from the heat. In a saucepan combine 1 cup cold water, the salt and 1 tablespoon sugar and bring to the boil. Add the flour, all at once, and beat with a wooden spoon until smooth. Remove from the heat and beat in the egg until the mixture is very smooth and satiny. Remove and discard the lime pieces from the oil. Heat the oil to 375°F on a frying thermometer. Force the mixture through a pastry tube or large funnel and fry in long strips until golden. Remove from the oil and drain on paper towels. Cut into 3-inch pieces. Roll in sugar. Eat while still warm. **MAKES ABOUT 20.**

VICEROY'S DESSERT
Postre de Virrey

Grandmother's trifle, passed to my mother, who passed it onto me is, in my opinion, the best trifle ever. When I came across *Postre de Virrey* in Mexico, a very good trifle but not as good as mine, I wondered where the Sisters of Mexico's colonial convents got it from. After all Lady Hamilton is said to have introduced trifle into Italy during her stay there calling it *Zuppa Inglese*. I hope the nuns did not get it from the wicked English pirates infesting the coasts of New Spain as Mexico was then called. I don't think pirates are very fancy cooks given to giving out copies of their favorite recipes. I expect, less prosaically, it is a Spanish recipe modified by migration as the Spanish have a formidable array of desserts, cakes, puddings and pastries.

1 cup granulated sugar

16 egg yolks, lightly beaten

1 cup dry sherry

1 teaspoon vanilla extract

4 large egg whites

Pinch of salt

1 cup heavy cream

1 tablespoon sifted confectioners' sugar

2 tablespoons brandy

1 lb sponge cake, cut into ½-inch slices

Apricot jam

Grated chocolate or toasted slivered almonds

Combine the sugar with ½ cup cold water in a saucepan and cook to thread stage (225°F) on a sugar (candy) thermometer. Remove from the heat and stand the saucepan in cold water to cool.

Put the egg yolks and the cooked syrup in the top of a double boiler over hot, not boiling water and cook, stirring constantly with a wooden spoon until the mixture makes a thick custard. Remove from the heat and cool and stir in half the sherry and the vanilla. Set aside. In a bowl beat the egg whites with a pinch of salt until they stand in firm peaks. In another bowl beat the cream with the confectioners' sugar until stiff and stir in the brandy. Fold the egg whites and custard together gently and set aside. Set the cream aside.

Spread the sponge cake slices with apricot jam and make a layer in a glass serving dish. Sprinkle with some of the remaining sherry, enough to moisten but not saturate it. Top with a layer of the custard then cream and continue to make layers of sponge cake sprinkled with sherry, custard and a layer of the whipped cream. Continue until all the ingredients are used up, finishing with a layer of cream. Grate the chocolate on top or sprinkle with the almonds. Chill in the refrigerator. **SERVES 6-8.**

PINEAPPLE PUDDING
Budin de Piña

Any of the puddings that came from the convents use egg yolks lavishly, a cooking inheritance from their Moorish influences. This is a brilliant use of New World pineapple with Old World ingredients.

12 ladyfingers

Apricot jam

2 cups finely chopped fresh pineapple

½ cup ground almonds

4 large egg yolks, lightly beaten

**½ cup to 1 cup granulated sugar according to the sweetness
   of the pineapple, and personal taste**

½ cup dry sherry

¼ teaspoon ground cinnamon

Sour cream

Toasted slivered almonds

Split the ladyfingers and spread with a thin layer of apricot jam. In a saucepan combine the pineapple, almonds, egg yolks, sugar, half the sherry and the cinnamon and cook, over low heat, stirring constantly with a wooden spoon until the mixture has thickened. Remove from the heat and cool.

In a glass serving dish put half the ladyfingers and sprinkle with half of the remaining sherry. Top with half the pineapple sauce. Add a layer of the rest of the ladyfingers, the rest of the sherry, and the pineapple sauce. Chill, spread with sour cream, and decorate with slivered almonds. **SERVES 6.**

ALMOND SNOW
Flan de Almendra

The almond is the one nut that everybody seems to love and Mexican cooks more than most. This is an easy recipe to make, a pretty, light and elegant dessert.

2 cups whole milk
½ cup granulated sugar
¼ cup almonds, finely ground
4 large egg whites
Pinch of salt
1 tablespoon Kirsch
Butter
Toasted, slivered almonds

In a saucepan bring the milk to the boil with the sugar and ground almonds, and cook over very low heat, stirring from time to time, for 15 minutes. Cool.

In a bowl beat the egg whites with the pinch of salt until they stand in firm peaks. Fold the egg whites into the milk mixture gently but thoroughly. Stir in the kirsch. Butter the top of a double boiler, pour in the mixture and cook, over hot water, until the mixture is firm. Remove from the heat and chill. To serve, unmold onto a serving plate and stick with the slivered almonds.
SERVES 6.

Polvorones *(pages 286-287) are good with this. Choose plain ones as others may conflict with the delicacy of the almonds.*

HAZELNUT CAKE
Pastel de Avellana

This was given me by the wife of one of Tío Miguel's team of employees, young men who were learning how to succeed in business, in a firm manufacturing steel tubes or some such, quite beyond me. I've always loved hazelnuts and was very pleased when the young señora gave me both cake and recipe. I was rather taken aback when Tío Miguel said she should have copied the recipe from a book, not given me her very own family one. The Tío knew a lot of things but not much about writing cookbooks.

½ cup cake flour

1 teaspoon baking powder

½ cup hazelnuts

3 large eggs, separated

⅔ cup granulated sugar

½ cup unsalted butter, clarified

½ teaspoon vanilla extract

Pinch of salt

In a bowl sift together flour and baking powder and set aside. In a nut grinder, or food processor, put the nuts and grind fine. Set aside.

Lightly butter a 9 inch x 1½ inch deep cake tin. Coat with flour, shaking to remove the excess.

In a bowl beat the egg yolks until they are thick and creamy, then gradually beat in the sugar until the mixture forms a ribbon when lifted from the whisk. Stir in about ⅓ cup of water, into the egg yolks, then beat in the ground nuts. Stir the flour mixture into the egg mixture, a little at a time. Stir in the clarified butter taking care not to add any of the milky residue at the bottom of the pan. Add the vanilla.

Beat the egg whites with the pinch of salt until they form firm peaks and whisk ½ into the butter. Fold in the remaining whites gently but thoroughly.

Pour the cake batter into the prepared cake tin and bake in a preheated 350°F oven for 30 to 35 minutes or until a toothpick inserted into the center comes out clean.

Remove the cake from the oven and let it stand in the tin, for 10 minutes, then turn it out onto a cake rack with the top uppermost. Cool for 1 hour then spread with warm apricot glaze.

For apricot glaze push 4 oz jam through a sieve into a saucepan with 2 tablespoons granulated sugar and cook for 2-3 minutes.

VARIATION:

To make pecan cake, substitute pecans for hazelnuts, omit the vanilla and substitute 1 tablespoon lemon juice for the water when beating the egg yolks.

To clarify butter: melt the butter slowly in a heavy, small saucepan, allow the melted butter to stand for a few minutes then pour off the clear, golden liquid, discarding the milky sediment that settles at the bottom of the pan.

RICE PUDDING
Arroz con Leche

Latin America loves rice and that includes rice pudding, a great Mexican favorite. Like rice pudding in Spain and Portugal it is cooked on top of the stove, not in the oven. It is addictive.

½ cup seedless raisins

½ cup dry sherry

½ cup short grain rice

2 inch piece lemon peel

Pinch of salt

4 cups whole milk

1 cup granulated sugar

Ground cinnamon

2 large egg yolks, beaten

Toasted slivered almonds

Put the raisins into a bowl, pour in the sherry and set aside to soak. In a bowl soak the rice in hot water to cover for 15 minutes. Rinse in cold water, drain and put into a saucepan with the lemon peel, pinch of salt and 1 cup water. Bring to the boil, reduce the heat to very low, cover and cook until the water has been absorbed. Remove and discard the lemon peel. Add the milk, sugar and cinnamon to taste and cook, uncovered, over very low heat until all the milk has been absorbed. Stir in the egg yolks and sherry and raisins and cook for a few minutes longer. Turn into a glass serving dish and sprinkle with the almonds. Serve at room temperature. **SERVES 6.**

VARIATION:

For Arroz Almendrado (Almond Rice Pudding) substitute orange peel for the lemon peel and add ½ cup blanched, ground almonds when adding the milk and sugar to the rice. Omit the raisins and sherry.

STUFFED CHO-CHO
Chayote Relleno

Chayote, cho-cho and *christophene* are the Spanish, English and French names for a tropical squash, *Sechium edule,* originally from Mexico, but now grown in tropical regions throughout the world. The skin is rather prickly and there is a large, single edible seed. The taste is delicate, rather like other summer squashes, and the texture is fine and quite crisp. The seed, when cooked, is very nice to nibble on. It was called *chayotli* in Nahuatl, language of the Aztecs.

3 large cho-chos, each weighing about 12 oz
Salt
3 large eggs, well beaten
1 cup seedless raisins
1 cup granulated sugar
1½ teaspoon freshly grated nutmeg
1 cup dry sherry
6 slices Madeira cake or sponge cake, crumbled
Water biscuits (crackers), crumbled
Toasted, slivered almonds

Halve the cho-chos and put into a saucepan with boiling, salted water to cover, cover pan and simmer over moderate heat until the vegetable is tender, about 20 minutes. When cool enough to handle, take out the seed and scrape the flesh into a bowl, leaving the shells intact. Set them aside.

Mash the pulp with the eggs, raisins, sugar, nutmeg, sherry, and cake, mixing well. If the mixture seems too liquid, stir in enough water biscuit crumbs to thicken it slightly. Put the mixture into the cho-cho shells, sprinkle with the almonds and put into a greased baking dish. Bake in a preheated 350°F oven until golden, about 15-20 minutes. Serve warm.
SERVES 6.

FRUIT PASTES
Ates

Long before I visited Morelia, the capital of Michoacán, I was introduced to *guayabate*, guava paste, eaten with cream cheese and water biscuits (crackers) as dessert. Famous among other foods of the *ates* are the fruit pastes known in English as fruit cheese. It was easy to buy and of excellent quality and I didn't bother to learn about other Mexican desserts while guava paste was around. It really is delicious. A native of Brazil, guavas are now grown in most of the subtropical and tropical regions of the world and whenever they are, they perfume the air. They are a most delectable fruit whether transformed into a Michoacán *ate* or not.

GUAVA PASTE
Guayabate

2 lbs ripe guavas, peeled
2 lbs granulated sugar
1 cup cold water
½ cup cold water

Halve the guavas and scoop out the seeds. In a bowl combine the seeds and the cup of water and leave to soak. Put the guavas into a heavy saucepan with the ½ cup of water, cover and cook over low heat until they are soft, about 30 minutes. Strain the water from the seeds (it will be slightly mucilaginous), add it to the cooked guavas. Discard the seeds. Put the guava mixture into a food processor and reduce to a purée, and pour it into a heavy saucepan. Add the sugar, stirring to mix. Cook, stirring with a wooden spoon over very low heat until the mixture is very thick and a little dropped onto an ice cube will set. Remove from the heat and beat with the wooden spoon until it forms a heavy paste, about 10 minutes. Have ready a loaf tin, 9 x 5 inches and about 3 inches deep, lined with wax paper. Turn the paste into the tin and set it aside for 24 hours. If possible turn the paste out onto a wooden board, lined with wax paper, cover lightly with cheesecloth and set in the sun for 2 days, turning from time to time so that all the surfaces are exposed. If this is not practical put into an airing cupboard to thoroughly dry. To store wrap in foil and keep in a cool place. Serve sliced with cream cheese and salt crackers.

In Michoacán the paste is rolled out into strips about ½ inch thick and when thoroughly dry sprinkled with sugar.

For *Membrillate* (Quince Paste) follow the same recipe as for *Guayabate*, soaking the cores of the fruit and using the water.

To make *Ate de Mango* (Mango Paste), choose fruit that is slightly under-ripe, peel, remove the seed and reduce the flesh to a purée. Weigh and combine in a heavy saucepan with an equal weight of sugar.

To make *Ate de Papaya y Pina* (Papaya and Pineapple) peel both fruits, remove and discard the papaya seeds and the core of the pineapple. Reduce equal amounts of the fruit to a purée in the food processor, and combine in a heavy saucepan with an equal weight of sugar. Cook as for *Guayabate* (Guava Paste).

MILK CANDY FROM CELAYA
Cajeta de Celaya

This is also called *Leche Quemada* (Burnt Milk), though the milk is not burned, but cooked to a soft caramel with sugar. This recipe came from the town of Celaya, in the rich farming and mining State of Guanajuato. It is made with half goat's, half cow's milk and is famous for its excellence. It was originally packaged in the little thin-walled wooden boxes called, in Spanish, *cajetas*. The first *Cajeta* I had was sold in such a box, but it is not really practical as it oozes out and nowadays it is sold in glass jars. Its full name, *Cajeta de Leche Quemada de Celaya* was inevitably shortened to *cajeta*, box, and to this day you buy a box and get a glass jar of milk candy. I don't know where the candy came from originally. It could have been from Celaya using two gifts from the Old World to the New, sugar and milk but the fact is that it is popular all over Latin America, recipes varying only very slightly.

The *Cajeta* can be eaten by itself with a spoon, spread on biscuits, or served over ice cream or any other way you choose. It is not necessary to stand at the stove, stirring constantly, until the milk and sugar changes to a thick caramel, about 1½ hours. Put the pan over very low heat and find some other job to do in the kitchen, and stir the *Cajeta* just from time to time, until the last 5 minutes of cooking when it does need constant attention to keep it smooth not grainy.

At one time there was a fashionable shortcut, outside Mexico, for making the candy. Tins of sweetened condensed milk were put into a large casserole and cold water was poured in to cover them completely. The water was brought to the boil, the pan left uncovered, and the heat reduced to low so that the water barely simmered. After 2½ to 3 hours the condensed milk will have been transformed into *cajeta*. The cans were then lifted out of the pan, set aside to cool, then opened and the candy scooped out. If the water level fell during the cooking, boiling water was added to keep the tins covered.

The candy was chilled before serving and, if liked, a little sweet sherry, Madeira or muscatel was stirred in over low heat just long enough to be absorbed. Alas, something went wrong with this shortcut, and a careless cook ruined the scheme as her tins exploded and no one wished to carry on with it. Since my sister and I once sent a whole pressure cooker of split pea soup up to her kitchen ceiling, curing me of any affection for this form of cooking, I can understand why the traditional way of making *cajeta* survived.

4 cups whole milk

**4 cups goat's milk if possible or
   use 8 cups whole milk**

3 cups granulated sugar

¼ teaspoon baking soda

Small piece stick cinnamon

Combine the whole milk in a heavy saucepan with the sugar and cook over low heat, stirring from time to time until the mixture turns golden. Stir the baking soda into the goat's milk, or remaining milk if only cow's milk is available, in a heavy saucepan, add the cinnamon and bring to the boil. Don't let it boil over. Simmer for 2-3 minutes then remove and discard the cinnamon. Add the hot milk to the caramel mixture in the other saucepan very gradually, stirring to mix. When the two lots of milk and the sugar are thoroughly mixed put over very low heat and cook, stirring from time to time until the mixture is thick. As the mixture begins to thicken stir constantly, that is in the last 5 minutes or so of cooking. Cool slightly and pour into a glass serving bowl, or into a jar, and chill. **MAKES ABOUT 4 CUPS.**

VARIATIONS:

For Cajeta Envinada *(Milk Candy with Wine) follow the instructions in the main recipe using all cow's milk and omitting the cinnamon. When it is thick and almost cooked stir in 1 cup of sweet sherry, Madeira or muscatel and continue cooking, stirring, until the wine has been absorbed.*

For Cajeta de Almendra Envinada *(Milk Candy with Almonds and Wine) follow the main recipe but pulverize ¼ cup blanched almonds and add them to the milk, using all cow's milk and the baking soda. Omit the cinnamon and bring to the boil. The add to the caramel mixture. When almost cooked stir in the wine as above.*

TURNOVERS
Empanadas

Wheat was introduced into Mexico by Spain, and these turnovers are, of course, Spanish in origin. They enjoy a special place in the cuisines of Latin America and may be small, medium or large, stuffed with meat, poultry, fish, shellfish or sweet things like candied fruits, jam or fruit. I have eaten versions of them all over Latin America from Mexico to Chile and Argentina. The larger sizes are good for a light lunch, the small ones are fine to accompany drinks, the sweet ones for dessert.

2 cups all-purpose flour

½ teaspoon salt

1 teaspoon baking powder

½ cup shortening

½ cup ice water

Oil for deep-fat frying

Sift the flour, salt and baking powder into a bowl. Cut the fat into small pieces and rub into the flour with the fingertips to form a coarse meal. With a fork mix enough water to make a fairly stiff dough. Gather the dough into a ball. Roll out on a lightly floured board to about ⅛ inch thickness and cut with a cookie cutter into 12 (4-inch) or 24 (2-inch) circles. Put 2 tablespoons or for the smaller *empanadas* 1 tablespoon of the chosen filling in the middle of each, wet the edges of the pastry with water, fold over and press the edges firmly together. Deep fry in hot oil until golden brown, or bake in a preheated oven 450°F for 15 minutes.

Fillings:

A favorite Mexican savory filling consists of cold boiled potatoes, diced, fried in butter with a little chopped onion, and moistened with a little *Salsa Ranchera* (page 77). Any leftover meat or fish with a little onion, cheese, hard-boiled egg, chopped, or green olives, moistened with sauce, is fine. *Picadillo* and *Picadillo de la Costa* (pages 221-222) are both excellent fillings. Leftover *Adobo* or *Mole* are also good, indeed any of the *Antojito* fillings may be used. This is a cuisine that invites the creative use of leftovers. Candied fruits, chopped, jams, grated coconut mixed with raisins, crushed pineapple and chopped almonds, and fruit preserves make delicious sweet *empanadas*.

PUMPKIN WITH BROWN SUGAR
Calabaza Enmielada

A pumpkin weighing 3 lbs is ideal for a dish to serve 6. There are so many kinds of pumpkin to choose from, that the best advice is to go looking in markets until you find the kind you want. Avoid those with very dark orange-red flesh for those with lighter flesh. The dessert is rather heavy and is often served at breakfast or for *merienda* (supper) in families where there are children and the family has eaten a hearty *comida*, the daytime main meal.

1 pumpkin weighing 3 lbs, about
1 lb *piloncillo* (local brown sugar) or dark brown sugar

Wipe the pumpkin with a damp cloth and cut it into 6 wedges. Scrape out the seeds and any strings. Choose a saucepan large enough to hold the pumpkin, skin side down with the wedges fitting closely together, and pour in ½ cup cold water. Add the pumpkin pieces and pack into the hollow of each wedge 1½ cups of the sugar, dividing it evenly. Cover and cook over very low heat until the pumpkin is tender when pierced with the point of a small, sharp knife. Check from time to time to see that the water has not evaporated. Combine the remaining sugar in a small saucepan with ¼ cup water, cook to make a syrup. Serve as a sauce with the pumpkin. The brown sugar will have melted and soaked into the pumpkin wedges. Serve in a shallow bowl with the sauce and a glass of cold milk on the side. The milk makes a perfect accompaniment.
SERVES 6.

PANCAKES WITH MILK CANDY AND PECANS
Crepas con Cajeta

I can remember when Mexico City señoras developed a passion for crêpes, French-style pancakes. No fashionable *cena* (dinner) was without them and they did fit into the cuisine very well. Stuffed with *huitlachoche* (corn fungus) for a first course they were very good indeed. I was particularly taken with *crepas* for this dessert. Any crêpe recipe will do, so long as the pancake is really thin and light. In addition *crepas* are very versatile, you can stuff them with almost anything, including leftovers.

1 cup each milk and water

3 large eggs, lightly beaten

¼ teaspoon salt

2 cups all-purpose flour, sifted

3 tablespoons unsalted butter, melted and cooled

In a food processor combine the milk, water, eggs, salt, the flour and the butter and process until smooth. Scrape into a bowl and refrigerate for 2 hours. The batter should have the consistency of light cream.

Make the *crepas* in a 6 inch iron or a non-stick frying pan and film it lightly with oil. Set the pan over moderate heat and when hot pour in 3-4 tablespoons of the batter (have a cup or ladle that will hold this amount), tilt the pan in all directions for the batter to cover the whole pan surface. Cook for about 60 seconds, turn and cook for about 30 seconds to a minute. Lift out onto a plate. Make the remaining *crepas* in the same way, filming the pan with oil for each pancake. Stack them, one on top of the other, and cover with plastic wrap until ready to use. **MAKES 12 *CREPAS*.**

For the filling:

½ recipe *Cajeta de Celaya* (Milk Candy from Celaya) (page 308)

1 cup chopped pecans

Butter

Fill the *crepas* with 1 tablespoon of the *cajeta* and fold them over. Transfer them to a buttered baking dish, overlapping slightly. In a small frying pan with a little butter toast the pecans until they are lightly browned. Preheat the oven to 325°F. Cover the *crepas* with foil and cook in the oven just long enough to warm them through, about 10 minutes. Have ready any leftover *cajeta* and drizzle it over the *crepas* and sprinkle with the nuts. Serve warm. **SERVES 6.**

COCONUT DESSERT
Cocada

Coconuts are readily available all over Mexico and this creamy coconut pudding, in slightly differing forms, is too. I love making it especially if I don't have to grate the coconut myself, or rather pare off the brown skin. It can be made with dried coconut, but fresh is immensely better.

1 cup granulated sugar

1 cup fresh coconut, grated fairly fine

4 cups milk

¼ cup milk

4 large eggs

1 teaspoon vanilla extract

½ cup dry or sweet sherry, according to taste

Whipped cream

Toasted slivered almonds

Butter

Put the sugar and 1 cup cold water into a saucepan and bring to a boil over moderate heat. Stir in the coconut and cook over very low heat until all the syrup has been absorbed, stirring from time to time. Pour in the milk and continue to cook, stirring frequently, over moderate heat until the mixture has the consistency of custard. In a bowl beat the eggs with the ¼ cup milk and the vanilla. Whisk 4 tablespoons of the hot coconut mixture into the eggs, 1 tablespoon at a time combining well, then turn the egg mixture into the rest of the coconut custard, add the sherry and cook over a low heat stirring constantly with a wooden spoon, until the mixture has thickened into a heavy custard. Cool slightly and pour into a glass serving dish and refrigerate. Just before serving spread with whipped cream and sprinkle with the almonds. If preferred omit the cream, dot with butter and run under the grill for a minute or so to caramelize. **SERVES 6.**

SWEET *TAMALES*
Tamales de Dulce

Emperor Moctezuma liked *tamales* stuffed with strawberries sweetened with honey and perhaps flavored with a little vanilla. The strawberry, the kind from which our strawberries have been cultivated, originated in Chile and had obviously found their way north very early. We have the birds to thank for this. Thank the bee for the honey, and the Emperor had a splendid dessert. Sweet *tamales* can be stuffed with all manner of pleasant things. Here are a few of them.

Make *tamal* dough as in the recipe for plain *tamales* (page 65) adding ½ cup to 1 cup granulated sugar, according to taste, to 2 cups *masa harina*. Prepare the corn husks and spread the dough on them. Make a mixture of seedless raisins, slivered almonds and chopped citron and put 1 tablespoon in the center of each *tamal*. Roll up and steam in the usual way, according to the basic recipe.

Tamales de Dulce can also be filled with mixtures of chopped candied fruits, such as pineapple, apricots, cherries, peaches or with preserves. The cook's imagination is the only determining factor, which is one of the nicest things about Mexican cooking; it invites invention. This was a philosophy I found useful in the early days of my time in Mexico as it covered up my mistakes. "I was just experimenting" is a useful cry.

MISCELLANEOUS

THICK CREAM
Crema Espesa

Cream in Mexico is more like French *crème fraîche*, slightly sourer than our own heavy cream. Sour cream is an adequate substitute but heavy cream is so good and so like Mexican cream in thickness that it is worth going to a little trouble and using it to make *Crema Espesa*. Use it whenever cream is called for in a recipe. It is delicious with *enchiladas*, *chilaquiles* and other dishes. Buttermilk is the ideal ingredient for turning heavy cream into *Crema Espesa* or even for converting light cream. If it is not available use lemon juice instead.

1 cup heavy cream
2 tablespoons buttermilk

Have the cream and buttermilk come to room temperature in a warm kitchen then mix them together in a bowl, cover with a clean cloth and stand in a warm draft-free place until it thickens anywhere from 6-12 hours, according to the warmth of the kitchen and the cultures in the buttermilk. Refrigerate and use as needed. **MAKES 1 CUP.**

If using lemon juice combine the cream and the lemon juice in a bowl, 1 tablespoon juice to 2 cups heavy cream, and letting it stand in a warm place for about half an hour.

If a lighter cream is needed either make the *Crema Espesa* with light cream or dilute the heavier cream with a little milk.

DRINKS

•

Bebidas

TEQUILA AND *PULQUE*

Tequila is the best known of all the Mexican drinks but it did not exist until the Spanish invented it, neither Aztecs nor Mayas had invented distilling. That was introduced by the conquerors who had acquired it from their conquerors, the Arabs. The Aztecs made *pulque*, which is the fermented sap of *maguey*, the *agave* or century plant. It is large and beautiful with stiff thick leaves set with sharp spines. The leaves grow up to 10 feet long. Though it is called the century plant, it flowers every 10-15 years after which it dies. When the flower bud reached the size of a big cabbage it was cut out leaving a cavity that filled with a sweet sap which was collected in gourds and fermented into *pulque*, a beer-like drink with a fairly low alcohol content and a high vitamin one. It is "cured" with various fruits such as pineapple or strawberries to give it a more attractive flavor and help to disguise its sour and acrid odor that comes from the fermenting yeast it contains. However it is very popular still and there are numerous *pulquerias* (bars) selling it and rejoicing in names like "My Love," "The End of the World," "My Second Wife." The drinkers are mostly men and I well remember when some old friends took César off to drink *pulque* which he had not done since his student days, and not often then, preferring Mexico's excellent beer. He stank of *pulque* for days, one of the drawbacks of the drink, and I had to keep from getting up-wind of him for my own protection.

Legend has it that when pressure from the Nahuatl tribes in the north drove the Toltecs out of Tula, their capital in the present-day state of Hidalgo, starting them on their long migrations to the west and south, a woman invented the "wine of the earth." She punched holes in the *maguey* plant, (probably *Agave atrovirens*), drew off the sap and fermented it, making *pulque*. Other women joined her in this noble work, and then they gave a party for the elders, both men and women. Four cups were served to each person, but the leader of one of the tribes, a man called Cuexteco, drank a fifth cup against all advice, became drunk, and took off all his clothes. When sobered up and covered with shame, he fled with all his people to the coastal region known as the Huasteca, on the Gulf of Mexico. To this day the inhabitants of this region are said to be hard-drinking people.

The technique for making tequila is very different. After distilling was introduced it was made from the blue *agave*, or *tequilana*, which grows principally in the state of Jalisco, acquiring its name from the small town there. Another similar drink, *mezcal*, made from a different *agave* from the Oaxaca region, and also in northern Mexico, has a slightly stronger flavor. There is a common misunderstanding that these drinks are made from cactus. *Agaves* are succulents belonging to the *Amaryllindaceae*. The cacti, also succulents, are in a group of their own.

The *agave* flowers when it has reached maturity, sending up a single flower stalk which can reach 40 feet high and has thousands of lovely white flowers, but to produce tequila the plant is uprooted and the leaves cut off. At the base is a huge pineapple-like *cabeza* (head) which is processed for the sugary juice which can be fermented then distilled into the spirit tequila, and aged in wood. Most tequila is white but long-aged tequilas called *anejos* are amber-colored and smooth enough to be taken neat. The classic way to drink tequila is the one adopted by the *charros*, gentlemen riders who wear colorful cowboy costumes and enormous sombreros and take part in rodeos on Sundays and holidays. If my memory is accurate I saw *charros* at the Cabello Bayo, a restaurant on the outskirts of Mexico City serving all manner of *antojitos*. Uncle Miguel took us there one Sunday but as he failed to book a table and as it was crowded we got almost nothing to eat but I think I saw a *charro* down a tequila. He was on horseback but the horse did not seem to mind. The *charro* first put a little salt in the space between the base of the thumb and forefinger of his left hand. He held a halved lime in the same hand and held a glass of tequila in the right hand. He licked some salt, swallowed some tequila and sucked the lime. Tequila is still taken in this way but without *charro* costume or horse.

Though there are some special tequila cocktails for the most part all that is needed is to substitute white tequila for vodka or gin in standard cocktail recipes.

THE TEQUILA DRINKS
Margarita

Of all the tequila cocktails this is the most famous. In Mexico it can be bought, ready-made, in bottles needing only to be poured out and ice added. Restaurants sell it by the jugful and it is one of the few drinks that has as much appeal outside its native habitat as in it. There are so many drinks that only taste right in their homelands—many of the rum drinks, for example, but a margarita is as good in London as in New York or almost anywhere else.

½ shell of a lime

Salt

½ cup white tequila

1 tablespoon Triple Sec or Cointreau

1 tablespoon lime juice

3 or 4 ice cubes

Rub the rim of a cocktail glass with the lime rind and spin it in salt to frost it. In a bar glass combine the rest of the ingredients and stir until they are thoroughly chilled. Strain into the prepared glass. **SERVES 1.**

APERITIF FROM LAKE CHAPALA
Aperitivo Chapala

I acquired this recipe when we were staying in the Chapala region when I was quite besotted by the newness of everything. I had already travelled a lot, living in other countries, because of my father's work but nothing was so foreign and exciting as Mexico, the ancient past, the old but not so ancient colonial period, and modern, still exotic, Mexico. This is the aperitif exactly as I had it.

1 cup strained, fresh orange juice

3 tablespoons grenadine syrup

1 teaspoon cayenne pepper or ground hot red *pequín* chili

Salt to taste

Tequila accompaniment

In a bar glass mix the ingredients thoroughly and chill. Serve in liqueur glasses as chasers to tequila or as an aperitif before luncheon or dinner. Delicious with the tiny fried fish called *charilitos fritos*. These are available in many specialty markets and in markets where Indian foods are sold where small fried fish, probably a different species but tasting much the same, are served with curries. I've had them with Thai food.

SANGRITA

Sangrita from Jalisco was originally made with pomegranate juice that is hard to get and it is usually made with Seville orange juice which may be equally hard to get. So a mixture of orange and lime juice is used.

1 lb tomatoes, peeled, seeded and chopped

1 cup fresh orange juice, strained

½ cup lime juice

1 small white onion, chopped

1 teaspoon sugar

Salt

3 *serrano* chilies, seeded and chopped or ½ teaspoon *pequín* chili or cayenne

Tequila

Combine all the ingredients, except the tequila in a food processor and blend until smooth. Pour into a jug and chill thoroughly and serve in ½ cup glasses with ½ cup shot glasses of tequila. Drink by sipping alternately. **SERVES 6.**

TEQUILA SUNRISE

Though it isn't as popular as the Margarita, the Tequila Sunrise is enjoyed by people who are not great tequila fans. Tequila has a different taste but it mixes well and here the grenadine and crème de cassis combine to give it a very beguiling flavor as well as an attractive look.

2 tablespoons lime juice

Rind of ½ lime

¼ cup white tequila

1 teaspoon grenadine syrup

½ teaspoon crème de cassis

Club soda (sparkling water)

Ice cubes

Put the lime juice and rind of the lime into a 8-inch highball (tall) glass with the other ingredients except the club soda and ice cubes. Pour in the sparkling water to fill the glass ½ full, stir to mix, add 3 or 4 ice cubes and serve. **SERVES 1.**

BLOODY MARIA

This is Mexico's version of the Bloody Mary, a cocktail whose origin is claimed by New York bartenders. It can be made in its classic form with vodka, or with gin, Pernod, or tequila.

¼ cup white tequila

½ cup tomato juice

1 tablespoon lemon juice

Dash Worcestershire sauce

Dash Tabasco

Salt, freshly ground black pepper to taste

3 or 4 ice cubes

Put all the ingredients into a cocktail shaker and shake well. Strain in an old-fashioned glass with 1 or 2 ice cubes. **SERVES 1.**

VARIATION:

We were in Acapulco when César's cousin Humberto turned up and gave me this recipe for a Vampiro. *It has become very popular.*

1¼ cups tomato juice

½ cup orange juice

2 tablespoons lime juice

1½ tablespoons very finely chopped onion

½ teaspoon Worcestershire sauce

Salt, cayenne pepper to taste

1 cup white tequila

Ice cubes

Put all the ingredients except the tequila and ice cubes into a food processor and process to a very smooth purée. Pour into a jug and chill in the refrigerator for at least 4 hours. To serve pour ¼ cup tequila into each of 4 old-fashioned glasses and top with the chilled tomato mixture. Stir to mix and add ice cubes if liked. **SERVES 4.**

ISABELLA

This is obviously derived from the Screwdriver and though there is some confusion as to whether the original was made with vodka or gin, and whether it was shaken or stirred, the tequila version is here to stay.

¼ cup white tequila
½ cup freshly squeezed orange juice
3 or 4 ice cubes

Combine the tequila and orange juice and pour into an old-fashioned glass. Add ice cubes and stir. **SERVES 1.**

COCO LOCO

This translates as Crazy Coconut and I first met it in Acapulco, on the beach when we were approached by a young man with a pile of green coconuts, straw and tequila. César was familiar with it as he had been coming to Acapulco since his student days. Long before it became an international resort, Acapulco was a great favorite with the Mexicans and still is. I was used to coconut water from the Caribbean but this was something else. The young man sliced the top off the coconut with a machete, poured in some tequila and handed it to me with a straw. If the water is very abundant you get more tequila added after you have tasted the drink for strength. Sometimes you can scoop out soft cream from the shell when the coconut is beginning to form. It was all very good but the best I had was in Mazatlán on the coast of Sinaloa where there were also magnificent oysters, as well as the Pacific Ocean, a beautiful beach, blue skies and sunshine. The amount of tequila for each coconut is ¼ cup.

THE RUM DRINKS AND OTHERS

Sugar cane was introduced very early into the New World and as a result Mexico produces many excellent rums. Though not as popular as tequila, rum does feature in a number of very good drinks. Rum and Coconut Water is just *Coco Loco* made with rum instead of tequila. As Mexico has an extensive coastline there are lots of coconut palms and hence lots of green coconuts waiting only to have their tops lopped off and some rum poured into the coconut water. I think of it as a Caribbean drink which is where I first met it, but whenever it first saw the light of day, a Mexican beach or a Caribbean island, one thing is sure, where there are coconut palms and rum the two will get together.

As well as drinks like *Rompope* (Cooked Eggnog) there are a number of rum cocktails which are quite original. They use honey, papaya juice and pineapple juice. There are also a number of alcoholic drinks made with the coffee-flavored liqueur Kahlúa and there is even a pineapple beer, *Tepache*.

Mexico also has a very large number of non-alcoholic drinks, some very ancient in origin. There are corn drinks, the *atoles*, made from *masa harina*, variously flavored and mixed with milk and water in different proportions. *Atole* can also be made from grains other than maize. It is a popular drink for *merienda* and goes very well with *tamales*. Fray Sahagún described *atolli* back in the 1550's when there was no milk and the drink was flavored strongly with herbs like *epazote* and with chilies. There is a Oaxacan *atole*, *champurrado* flavored with chocolate that I mistakenly thought must be colonial as chocolate was forbidden to women, I was wrong as it is an ancient drink. Other flavoring for the *atoles* are crushed fruit like pineapple, strawberry, raspberry, blackberry or guavas. Though they are still popular in Mexico they are not the sort of gruel-like drink to appeal to others.

There is another category of non-alcoholic drinks called *Aguas Frescas* (Fresh Waters, literally) and the best known of which is probably *Agua de Jamaica* (Jamaica Flower Water). This is made from *Hibiscus Sabdariffa*, a tropical plant grown for the fleshy red sepals of its flowers. It is called rosella, sorrel, and *flor de Jamaica*, and Jamaica flowers. It makes a beautiful deep pink drink with a light, pleasant flavor. It is immensely popular in the Caribbean where it gets together with rum, especially at Christmas time. Another drink is tamarind water and of course there is *Limonada* (Limeade).

MANZANILLO COCKTAIL
Coctel Manzanillo

Papayas from the state of Colima on Mexico's Pacific coast, are a beautiful deep reddish-orange color, not the pallid yellow of many. The juice made from them is sweet and full of flavor and wonderful by itself or in drinks. This cocktail comes from Manzanillo, the beach resort that makes Colima worth a trip.

¼ cup light rum
¼ cup papaya (pawpaw) juice
½ teaspoon grenadine syrup
Crushed ice

In a cocktail shaker combine all the ingredients and shake vigorously. Strain into a chilled cocktail glass. The drink is sometimes served, stirred not shaken, in an old-fashioned glass over 3 or 4 ice cubes. **SERVES 1.**

ACAPULCO COOLER

¼ cup light rum
2 tablespoons lime juice
Pineapple juice
Ice cubes

Fill a tall glass with ice cubes and pour in the rum and lime juice. Fill up the glass with pineapple juice. Stir. **SERVES 1.**

MÉRIDA

2 tablespoons honey
2 tablespoons lime juice
¼ cup light rum
Club soda (sparkling water)
Ice cubes

In a bar glass mix together the honey, lime juice and rum and pour over 3 or 4 ice cubes in an old-fashioned glass. Add a splash of club soda if liked. **SERVES 1.**

EGGNOG
Rompope

This is best described as a cooked eggnog. It keeps indefinitely if refrigerated. At one time almost everyone made their own *rompope* but fewer do so now as it is sold ready-made. I think it is fun to make and the flavor can be varied by adding 2 tablespoons finely ground almonds when adding the egg yolks. They add a delicate flavor and help thicken the mixture. Cinnamon can be added but I prefer vanilla. Versions of the eggnog are popular throughout the Caribbean.

4 cups whole milk

1 cup granulated sugar

1 vanilla bean

12 large egg yolks

2 cups light rum

In a heavy saucepan combine the milk, sugar and vanilla bean and bring to a simmer. Cook, over very low heat, stirring constantly for 15 minutes. Cool to room temperature, stirring from time to time to prevent a skin from forming. Remove the vanilla bean. Beat the egg yolks until they are very thick and light in color, then gradually beat them into the milk mixture. Return the mixture to the heat and cook over the lowest possible heat, stirring, until the mixture coats a spoon. Cool. Add the rum, bottle, cork tightly and refrigerate for a day or two. Serve in liqueur glasses either as a liqueur or as an aperitif. The drink can also be served over ice cubes in an old-fashioned glass.

VARIATION:

For Rompope Macho *(He-man* Rompope*) put 2 or 3 ice cubes in a large, stemmed wine glass and pour in 2 tablespoons light rum and ¼ cup* rompope. *Add a splash of club soda (sparkling water) and serve.* **SERVES 1.**

TEA
Te

Mexicans are not tea drinkers, preferring coffee but they do like herb teas of which they have a great many. They set great store by camomile as a hangover cure, indeed for any form of stomach upset associated with food and drink.

Anise - antispasmodic for the stomach

Artichoke - for the liver

Asafetida - for bad temper

Boldo - for the gall bladder

Borage - for fever

Camomile - for the stomach and as an inhalation for colds and bronchitis

Cedar - for the stomach

Clove - for toothache

Corn silk - for the kidneys

Hawthorn-cinnamon - for coughs

Jasmine - for the nerves

Manzanita seed - for the kidneys

Marnital flower - for the heart

Muicle - for anemia

Oak (bark and root) - to strengthen the teeth

Orange leaf - for the nerves

Tlalchichinole - for the kidneys

DORADO COCKTAIL

This is made using honey which was important in pre-Conquest Mexico, especially in the Maya regions. It was used in a local ritualistic drink, *blaché* so it does not surprise one when it turns up in tequila cocktail. The Maya also have a honey liqueur, *xtabentum* which I enjoyed in Yucatán, convinced it was good for me as honey is supposed to be good for one.

¼ cup white tequila

1 tablespoon honey

1½ tablespoons lime juice

Crushed ice

In a cocktail shaker combine all the ingredients and shake well. Strain into a cocktail glass, or serve stirred not shaken over 3-4 ice cubes in an old-fashioned glass. **SERVES 1.**

DRUNKEN PINEAPPLE
Piña Borracha

This makes a delicious liqueur and is worth doing whenever really good, sweet pineapples are around.

**3 cups fresh, very ripe pineapple, very finely chopped
  or grated**
2 cups white tequila

Combine the pineapple and the tequila in a large jar, cover securely and refrigerate for at least 24 hours, strain and drink as a liqueur or serve over ice cubes. The pineapple itself is good with cream.

FOR MY LOVE
Por mi Amante

This is really very good and though the best *Por Mi Amante* is made with strawberries, other fruit can be used following the same recipe and cutting larger fruit like peaches into small chunks after peeling them.

4 cups strawberries
2 cups white tequila

Rinse the strawberries, drain thoroughly and hull. Cut them in half and put into a jar with an air-tight lid. Pour in the tequila which should cover the fruit. If necessary add a little more. Seal the jar and refrigerate for at least 3 weeks. Strain and serve very cold as a liqueur. It is a pretty drink, pink and fragrant.

SUBMARINE
Submarino

This is another of the drinks César's young cousin Humberto introduced us to. Neither of us tried it, wisely I think. It is just a version of an older drink, the Boilermaker, when ¼ cup of Scotch whiskey is poured into a 1 cup of beer and drunk without stirring. I think this should be called a Torpedo and the good advice followed never to drink more than two.

Pour a well chilled bottle of any good Mexican beer (they are small bottles) into a well chilled tankard and pour ¼ cup white tequila into the center. Do not stir and serve at once. **SERVES 1.**

MILK *ATOLE*
Atole de Leche

This is the basic *atole* as it is made nowadays using milk.

½ cup *masa harina*

3 cups water

2-inch piece stick cinnamon or a vanilla bean

1 cup granulated sugar, or to taste

3 cups whole milk

Put the *masa harina* into a large saucepan and gradually stir in the water. Add the cinnamon or vanilla, bring to a simmer over low heat and cook, stirring constantly, until the liquid has thickened. Remove from the heat and add the sugar and milk, stirring to mix thoroughly. Return to low heat and cook until the sugar has dissolved. Remove the cinnamon or vanilla bean and serve warm, in cups. **SERVES 8-10.**

VARIATION:

This basic atole *can be varied by using 2 cups water to 4 cups whole milk, or for a richer version, 2 cups water to 3 cups whole milk and 1 cup cream.*

***For* Atole de Almendra *(Almond* Atole*)* *add ½ cup ground almonds with the sugar. When the atole has thickened, remove from the heat and add 3 well-beaten large egg yolks. Return the pan to low heat and cook, stirring constantly, until the gruel is heated through. Do not let it come to a boil.*

***For the fruit* atoles**, *Atole de Fresa, Frambuesa, Zazamora (Atole of Strawberry, Raspberry, Blackberry): To make the fruit atoles add 1 cup of the crushed fruit when adding the sugar. For a pineapple atole add the same amount of crushed fruit but drain* *it as it is very juicy. For a prune* atole *reduce the amount of soaked, pitted and puréed prunes to 1 cup.*

For **Champurrado (Chocolate Atole)** *from Oaxaca, replace the granulated sugar of the basic recipe with brown sugar and add 75g/3oz Mexican chocolate, chopped or grated. Bring the mixture to a simmer beating with a* molinillo *as in Mexican chocolate, or beat with a wire whisk until the sugar and chocolate are dissolved and the mixture is frothy. Serve in cups.*

CHÍA

Father Sahagún mentions *chía* (*Aslvia hispanica*) back in the early days of the Conquest and today it is used in Mexico to make a refreshing drink. The small black seeds are steeped in water and the water flavored. I have an earthenware figure, that is rough textured and tall and hollow. It is for growing *chía* seed into a green garment that can be eaten as salad. The figure is soaked in water then plastered with the *chía* which grows into a green plant a little like mustard and cress.

1 cup *chía* seed

12 cups water

Sugar to taste

Lime or lemon juice to taste, strained

Combine the *chía* and water in a large jug and stand long enough for the seeds to swell up and become gelatinous, a short time only is needed. Add the sugar and lime or lemon juice. Don't strain. Chill before drinking. The *chía* adds a subtle fragrance. **SERVES 12.**

POT COFFEE
Cafe de Olla

I have a hazy memory of sitting in the family car with César, his mother and aunt and Tío Miguel on a cold dark night on a cold dark hillside, and being immensely cheered by a mug of *cafe de olla*. I know I was there because we were allowed to keep our earthenware mugs and I still have mine. It was a cultural event and I think it was a sound and light performance at the pyramids to the Sun and Moon. Tío Miguel was a very cultured man and through him we got to a good many events we might have missed. The coffee is served after meals in the handleless pots in which it is traditionally made, however it can be made in larger quantities in an enamel coffee pot and poured into individual cups. The best coffee is grown in the south, in the hilly regions of Chiapas. It is always dark roasted.

4 cups water

**½ cup *piloncillo* (Mexican brown sugar) or
use dark brown sugar**

2-inch piece stick cinnamon

4 whole cloves

4 tablespoons regular grind, dark roasted coffee

Heat the water, sugar, cinnamon and cloves in a saucepan or heatproof coffee pot over low heat, stirring until the sugar has dissolved. Add the coffee, bring to the boil and simmer for a minute or two. Stir, cover and set in a warm place on the stove, but off the heat, for the grounds to settle. Pour into cups.
SERVES 4.

COFFEE WITH MILK
Cafe con Leche

This is the favored way of drinking coffee for breakfast, not as an after-dinner coffee, when black coffee is preferred. It is a very good drink.

Make coffee about four times stronger than usual, that is about 4 tablespoons coffee to 1 cup water. To serve, dilute the coffee with hot milk according to taste, half and half is usual.

MELON SEED OR ALMOND DRINK
Horchata

This is one of the *aguas frescas* for which Oaxaca is famous. I have had the light, refreshing drink there made from melon seed but found almonds more practical when making it at home.

½ cup almonds, very finely ground

1 cup granulated sugar

2 or 3 strips lime zest (rind) about 2 inches long and ½-inch wide

6¼ cups water

Combine all the ingredients in a large jug and stand for at least 4 hours. Strain through a damp cloth, squeezing hard to extract all the milk from the almonds and the flavor from the lime zest. Serve in glasses with 3-4 ice cubes. **SERVES 6.**

TAMARIND WATER
Agua de Tamarindo

This drink is made from the pulp in the seed pods of a very handsome tropical tree *Tamarindus indica*. The pulp is acid but also has an attractive flavor. Much used in Indian food it can sometimes be bought prepared in shops selling Indian spices.

1 cup ripe tamarind pods

12 cups cold water

Sugar to taste

Remove the outside covering from the pods and put the pods in a large jug with enough water to cover. Let them soak for about 4 hours, or until the pulp has softened. Strain through a fine sieve and discard the seeds. Add the remaining water, sweeten to taste, chill and serve in tall glasses with ice cubes if liked. **SERVES ABOUT 12.**

SANGRÍA

This is the famous Spanish wine drink which Mexico has adapted and altered to its own taste. César had his own version and it was extremely popular at summer parties. There are lots of Sangría recipes from Spain, from California and from places where there is sun and red wine. I find I like César's best. It has stood the taste of time.

CÉSAR ORTIZ'S SANGRÍA

2 cups fresh orange juice

1 cup lime or lemon juice

Superfire sugar to taste

1 bottle Spanish red wine, preferably from the south

Ice cubes

Combine the fruit juices and sugar together and stir until the sugar has dissolved. Pour into a large glass pitcher, add the wine and stir to mix. Refrigerate until ready to serve. Put 2 or three ice cubes into each 1 cup-goblet and fill with sangria. **MAKES ABOUT 10 SERVINGS.**

PINEAPPLE BEER
Tepache

A family cook told me this was used in place of stock in some colonial dishes but I never managed to find any though the *criada* said to use half the amount of sugar if I planned to use the beer in cooking. It makes a pleasant drink.

1 large fresh pineapple

8 cloves

3 inch cinnamon stick

4 cups brown sugar

2 cups pearl barley

Chop the pineapple, unpeeled and put into a food processor and reduce to a coarse purée. Place in a large crock, preferably earthenware with 5½ pints water, the cloves and the cinnamon, cover and stand for 2 days.

Cook the barley in 1 large, heavy saucepan with 4 cups water until the grains burst. Add the sugar and stir. Add the mixture to the pineapple mixture, cover and stand for another 2 days by which time it will have fermented. Line a large sieve with a double layer of dampened cheesecloth or a large linen napkin and set it over a large bowl. Strain the pineapple mixture, twice if necessary. Pour into bottles. Serve in tall glasses with ice cubes. **MAKES ABOUT 12 CUPS.**

POPO Y IXTA

This after-dinner drink is named after the two volcanos that overlook Mexico City. When I was first married I learned to say their names properly and enjoyed the view of them from our bedroom window. César had once climbed Popo and he knew all about the role that they had played in the past and the legends of how they got their names, how Popo had fallen in love with Ixta when they were human and so on. When Elizabeth David was writing her book on the role of ice in cookery she asked César to give her something on the role of ice and snow in pre-Conquest Mexico and he translated a piece from Fr. Bernadhino de Sahagún's great work on Aztec-Maya Mexico in a chapter on frost, snow and hail in agriculture. So when I see Popocatepetl and Ixccihuatl, my head is filled with images and memories though I confess I have only once tasted the liqueur.

Fill a liqueur glass ½ full of Kahlúa and add tequila to fill it up, or add equal quantities of Kahlúa and tequila to the glass. Smog, which could turn out to be a temporary aberration on the part of the human race, has ruined the view of Popo and Ixta but my memory of them is very clear and beautiful.

BULLFIGHTER'S KAHLÚA
Kahlúa Toreador

Mexicans are keener on soccer than on bullfighting though the bullfight still exists. This recipe was given me by Philip S. Brown, a great authority on both food and drink. His is, alas, no longer with us but his expertise lingers on. By putting the ingredients into parts rather than exact measurements he skillfully leaves it up to the drinker to decide how strong he/she wants the drink to be using a large or small egg white according to how large/small the drink is.

1 part Kahlúa
2 parts brandy
1 egg white

Combine the ingredients in a cocktail shaker with crushed ice and shake vigorously, or blend in a blender with the ice. Strain into a chilled cocktail glass. **SERVES 1.**

BLACK RUSSIAN

This is another of Philip Brown's drinks.

1 part Kahlúa
2 parts vodka
3 or 4 ice cubes

Pour the Kahlúa and vodka over the ice cubes in an old-fashioned glass and stir. Or stir with ice cubes until well chilled and strain into a chilled cocktail glass. **SERVES 1.**

CHOCOLATE
Chocolatl

Among the great gifts ancient Mexico gave the world chocolate ranks very high, almost at the top. We owe it to the Olmecs, the first civilization, who found the tree (*Theobroma cacao*), Food of the Gods, growing in the lowland forests of southern Veracruz and Tabasco about 3,000 years ago. This civilization, apart from its genius in making chocolate from the seed pods of the *cacao* tree, is characterized by the enormous basalt heads, portraits of their kings, that dot the landscape. They declined, as civilizations do, and chocolate became an important drink to the Maya who mixed in all manner of herbs, spices (like *achiote*), and chilies. After the decline of the Maya, came the Aztecs who not only drank chocolate but used the beans as currency. Modern Mexico sells its chocolate for drinks already sweetened and mixed with ground almonds and cinnamon. Emperor Moctezuma, at the time of the Conquest, took his chocolate sweetened with honey and flavored with vanilla and served in a cup made of gold. The name chocolate comes from two Nahuatl words *xoco*, bitter and *atl*, water. *Chocolatl* is a variation of the name.

In Aztec Mexico it was a royal drink, forbidden to women and taken only by the Emperor, the upper ranks of the military, the merchant nobility and the upper ranks of the clergy. It puzzles me that *Champurrado*, chocolate *atole*, was available to everyone. Though there was no milk or sugar, drinking chocolate is made in almost the same way now as it was thousands of years ago. They made it foamy by pouring the drink from one vessel to another, the Spanish introduced the little carved *molinillo* beater that is twirled between the palms of the hands, and we have whisks and all manner of things to achieve the same result.

Chocolate was not always taken hot and I made some cold chocolate more or less the way the Aztecs would have done. Use 1½ oz unsweetened chocolate, broken up into 1 cup cold water, add honey and vanilla to taste and beat until the chocolate has dissolved and the drink is foamy. I did this using a *molinillo* but the blender makes the job easier. It makes a stimulating and refreshing drink. The foam on chocolate was esteemed much more highly then than now and I have always meant to whip up a batch of chocolate foam to find out why but I have never got around to it.

The history of chocolate is infinitely fascinating and I shall never forget the sight of those enormous basalt heads of the Olmec kings just sitting in the landscape when César took me to see the beginning of chocolate and the beginning of civilization in his country. His knowledge was deep and comprehensive.

I have always been amazed that the chocolate we drink today is so little changed from the first chocolate that was enjoyed all those thousands of years ago. One thing has changed. Worshippers in colonial Mexico were so crazy on chocolate that the church had to threaten to excommunicate them if they persisted in taking cups of chocolate into Mass with them on Sundays.

To make chocolate use Mexican chocolate and ideally make the drink in an earthenware pot.

Pour 2 cups water or a mixture of milk and water into the pot and drop in 3 oz Mexican chocolate broken into bits. Bring to a simmer and stir until the chocolate has dissolved. Simmer for a minute or two. Off the heat beat until it is foamy. Serve in cups. **SERVES 2.**

MAIL ORDER SOURCES FOR MEXICAN FOOD

Adriana's Caravan
Brooklyn, NY
tel. 1-800-316-0820

John Mako
Horticultural Enterprises
13660 Heartside Place
Dallas, Texas 75234

Kitchen
218 Eighth Avenue
New York, NY 10011
tel. (212) 243-4433

BIBLIOGRAPHY

Dr. Jean Andrews, *The Domesticated Capsicums*, University of Texas Press, Austin, 1990.

Rick Bayless with **Deann Groen Bayless**, *Authentic Mexican: Regional Cooking from the Heart of Mexico*, William Morrow and Company Inc., New York, 1987.

Diccionario de la Cocina - Nuevo cocinero Mexicano en forma de diccionario, Libreria de Ch. Bouret, Paris, 1888.

Maria A. de Carbia, *Mexico en la Cocina de Marichu*, Editorial Epoca, Mexico, 1969.

Sophie D. Coe, *America's First Cuisines*, University of Texas Press, Austin, 1994.

Sophie D. Coe and **Michael D. Coe**, *The True History of Chocolate*, Thames and Hudson, London, 1996.

Richard Condon and **Wendy Bennett**, *The Mexican Stove*, Doubleday & Company Inc., New York, 1973.

Hernán Cortés, *Dispatches of Cortés from the New World*, Grosset and Dunlap, New York, 1962.

Alfred W. Crosby Jr., *The Columbian Exchange: Biological and Cultural Consequences of 1492*, Greenwood Press, Westport, Connecticut, 1972.

Betty Fussell, *The Story of Corn*, Alfred A. Knopf, New York, 1992.

Dr. Alex D. Hawkes, *A World of Vegetable Cooking*, Simon and Schuster, New York, 1968.

Diana Southwood Kennedy, *The Cuisines of Mexico*, Harper & Row, New York, 1972.

Zarela Martinez, *Food From My Heart*, Macmillan, New York, 1995.

Salazar Monroy, *La tipica cocina poblana y sus guisos de sus religiosas*, Puebla, 1945.

Journals and other Documents on the Life and Voyages of Christopher Columbus, translated and edited by Samuel Eliot Morison, The Heritage Press, New York, 1963.

Lourdes Nichols, *Mexican Cookery*.

(Cuales son) las hierbas y especias que Marichu en su cocina?
Editorial Novarod, Mexico, 1959.

Salvador Novo, *Cocina Mexican o historia gastronimica de la ciudad de Mexico*, Editorial Porrua, Mexico, 1973.

Octavio Paz, *The Labyrinth of Solitude*, Grove Press, New York, 1961.

Bernal Diaz del Castillo, *The Conquest of New Spain*, Penguin Books, New York, NY, 1963.

La Cocina Poblana, Puebla Editorial, Puebla, 1939.

Fray Bernadhino Sahagún, *General History of the Things of New Spain*, The School of American Research, 1953.

Elizabeth Schneider, *Uncommon Fruits and Vegetables, A Commonsense Guide*, Harper & Row, New York, 1986.

Raymond Sokolov, *Why We Eat What We Eat*, Summit Books, New York, 1991.

Jacques Soustelle, *Daily Life of the Aztecs on the Eve of the Spanish Conquest*, Stanford University Press, Stanford, California, 1961.

Sturtevant's *Edible Plants of the World* edited by U. P. Hendrick, Dover Publications Inc., New York, 1972.

Josephina Velazquez de Leon, editorial Velazques de Leon, Mexico D.F. Mexico. All her books on the regional kitchens of Mexico.